Dreamwork

Around
the World
and Across Time

"Over the millennia dreams have been assigned different meanings by different people in different cultures. *Dreamwork* provides its readers an opportunity to sample them all, from indigenous shamans to famed storytellers to contemporary psychotherapists. The scope of this book is incredible, and anyone who reads it emerges with a changed perspective and a deeper appreciation of these nightly gifts."

Stanley Krippner, Ph.D., co-author, *Extraordinary Dreams*

"*Dreamwork: Around the World and Across Time* is a tremendous contribution to the soul of humanity. After working as a therapist doing dream work for many years, Leland Shields has done the 'work' and given us this amazing gift of insight into the dream. My sincere appreciation to him, and to the dreamtime that continues to dream itself and the unfolding of Creation in each moment."

Eduardo Duran, Ph.D., author, *Buddha in Redface*

"*Dreamwork* presents a vast selection of perspectives on dreams from psychotherapists, philosophers, novelists, poets, and native traditions. The author's commentary to each of these offers us a path inward to appreciating our own mysterious dreams as well as to developing an understanding of ourselves that transcends our ordinary waking consciousness."

Mitchell D. Ginsberg, Ph.D., author, *The Inner Palace: Mirrors of Psychospirituality in Divine and Sacred Wisdom-Traditions*

"*Dreamwork* is an exciting entrée to a flyby across time, continents and cultures, inviting dreamers to alight anywhere in this amazing anthology of writings to find inspiration and insights for pursuing their own dreamwork practices. Compiled by our guide, a practicing psychotherapist, this treasury of dream fact and fiction from famous personages of various times and perspectives provides brilliant illumination into everyone's nightly journeys into the Dreamtime."

Rita Dwyer, International Association for the Study of Dreams, Past President and Executive Officer

Dreamwork

Around the World and Across Time

AN ANTHOLOGY

Leland E. Shields, MS, MA

BLUE DOLPHIN PUBLISHING

Published by Blue Dolphin Publishing, Inc.
P.O. Box 8, Nevada City, CA 95959
Orders: 1-800-643-0765
Web: www.bluedolphinpublishing.com

ISBN: 978-1-57733-171-1 (softcover)
ISBN: 978-1-57733-190-2 (hardcover)

Library of Congress Cataloging-in-Publication Data

Shields, Leland E., 1954-
    Dreamwork around the world and across time : an anthology / Leland
E. Shields.
        p. cm.
    Includes bibliographical references and index.
    ISBN 978-1-57733-171-1 (pbk. : alk. paper) —
ISBN 978-1-57733-190-2 (hardcover : alk. paper) 1. Dreams. I. Title.

BF1078.S52188 2008
154.6'3—dc22

                                        2008010323

Printed in the United States of America

5   4   3   2   1

TABLE OF CONTENTS

DEFINITIONS OF "DREAM"

Looking at English, Latin, Hebrew, and Chinese definitions for "dream" offers historical reflections connecting dreams and the psyche.

English

> **Dream:** (noun) **1.** A series of images, ideas, emotions, and sensations occurring involuntarily in the mind during certain stages of sleep. **2.** A daydream; a reverie. **3.** A state of abstraction; a trance. **4.** A wild fancy or hope. **5.** A condition or achievement that is longed for; an aspiration: *a dream of owning their own business.* **6.** One that is exceptionally gratifying, excellent, or beautiful: *Our new car runs like a dream.*
>
> The American Heritage® Dictionary of the English Language, Fourth Edition. (Houghton Mifflin Company, 2000). http://www.bartleby.com/61/54/D0385400.html

The English etymology of "dream" has been related to the Old Saxon "drom," meaning deception, illusion, and phantom, Old Norse, "draugr," meaning to lie, and Middle English, "drem," meaning joy and jubilation. There is apparently no consensus on which of these diverse accounts is the accurate derivation of "dream." The ambiguity befits dream interpretation.

Latin

> **Somnio:** *v.* dream; dream of or see in a dream.
> **Somnium:** *n.* dream, vision, fantasy.
> **Alucinor:** to wander in mind, dream, or talk idly.

Also relevant, the original root of "symbol" (Latin: sym-ballein), means "drawing together," while the root meaning of "diabolic" is "pulling apart" (Latin: dia-ballein).

Hebrew

מולח (Chalom): The same verb used commonly to mean "to dream," also means "to be healthy," and "to be strong."

Chinese

夢 : To dream, or a dream.

Mèng, the character meaning faulty or skewed eyesight, is included in many of the Chinese characters for "dream." It is composed of two pictographs, one for eye and the other for rubbing an eye. Another description of the same character describes its lower half as a crescent moon, indicating night.

做夢 :To have a dream.

The first character means "to make" or, "to act as." It includes pictographs for a person, something passed through ten generations, and a hand holding a divining rod. Here it is linked with mèng.

夢見 : To see in a dream or dream about.

Mèng appears once again with the pictograph for an eye above a standing person ("to see").

夢想 : To dream of.

Here mèng appears with a character meaning, "to think," "to ponder," or, "to hope." This character includes pictographs for forest, eye and heart.

Based on material from http://zhongwen.com/ and G.D. Wilder & J.H. Ingram, *Analysis of Chinese Characters*, (New York: Dover Publications, Inc., 1974), pp. 7-8, pp. 32-33, p. 158, and p. 197.

INTRODUCTION

C. G. JUNG SAID, "A dream is nothing but a lucky idea that comes to us from the all-unifying world of the psyche."* It is not necessary that we accept his statement on faith, or even understand it. Instead we can all look to our own experience of dreams. We know when our understanding of a dream hits home; we can feel it. When we pay attention to our dreams, we open windows to unfiltered parts of ourselves. By allowing the dreams to penetrate our waking consciousness we enable parts of ourselves to stitch back together; we begin to feel a little more whole. Although people throughout the world and across time have been fascinated by dreams, their ways of understanding them vary as widely as do the cultures of the dreamers.

In this book I have brought together a variety of perspectives on dreams so that you, the dreamer, can discover what is helpful to you. Some selections are specifically about dreams; others are about how symbols can be helpful in understanding dreams. How did the founders of psychoanalysis suggest we work with dreams? What have contemporary psychologists contributed to the study of dreams? Does scientific sleep research provide helpful information? What insights do indigenous peoples offer for understanding nightmares? In what way have spiritual traditions addressed dreams? We can learn from all the ways that people before us have used and understood dreams. Mine them all for answers to your own questions.

It is not my intent to present a balanced sample; rather, the selections that follow are those that have moved me or been helpful to my clients. Because of my affinity for Jung's ideas, there are a considerable number of

---

*From Carl Jung's essay "The Meaning of Psychology for Modern Man," in *Civilization in Transition*, trans. R. F. C. Hull.

selections from him and those psychologists and thinkers who have been inspired by him. Myth, religion, philosophy, and literature have always explored dreams and the psyche, and I have included selections from these as well. Provocative writings on dreams are everywhere—so much the better for us all.

The Table of Contents can direct you to general topics and authors of interest. The book's first four sections contain selections from the pioneers of psychotherapy, then samples from ongoing developments in psychotherapy, the science of sleep and dreaming, and historical philosophers. These sources tend generally (but not exclusively) to rely on observation, theory, and logical inference as the basis for dream work. The last three sections—with selections from indigenous peoples, myth and religion, and writers and artists—tend generally (but not exclusively) to rely on intuitive understanding of dreams and dream work. Throughout, the individual selections are broken into "bite size" pieces so you can get a taste from an author and try it out for a night's dreams without getting more than you can digest at one time.

Choose an area of interest and read until you find an approach that strikes you. How would you apply it to a dream that you remember? Or, if you have trouble remembering dreams, look up "remembering dreams" in the Index for some ideas about how to recall dreams when you awake. Some selections give insight into the nature of dreams or dreaming, rather than serving as aids to interpretation. Even these, if you find them interesting, will inspire your dreams and dream work in experiential ways.

I have used many of these selections and quotations as catalysts for work in dream groups. As we turn dreams over in new ways the group's vitality and creativity heightens. Some perspectives, such as noting the dramatic flow of the dream, will almost surely help you (see "The stages of a dream," by Marie-Louise von Franz, p. 25); others may stand out for a time and be forgotten. When you find something that stands out, you may want to delve deeper into the original source or author. Those that do not strike you today may be the key to a dream tomorrow.

You will find few answers in these pages about the specific meaning of your dreams. Instead, you will find much about the process of dream work, different approaches or points of view, and ways to formulate questions that can lead to the discovery of dream meaning. It is certainly possible and worthwhile to work alone with your dreams, but be aware of one common pitfall: when each of us looks at our own dreams, it is easy to bring the preconceptions of the waking mind to our interpretations. For example, if I am embarrassed by my weight in waking life, I may be horrified and self-critical when seeing a dream image of my body, even though my loved ones in the dream seem unconcerned about this characteristic. To avoid this kind of misreading, approach the dream with an open mind, asking what new image your psyche offers (Gendlin on bias control, p. 72). Particularly when starting out, it's also helpful to share your dream work with someone you trust, someone who can share their own questions, body-reactions, emotions, and associations. Trust the questions, your own and others', to lead you to connect with the dream. And of course, if working with your dreams doesn't lead toward health and healing, or gets you in trouble, back off and find someone you trust or a professional counselor to help.

I believe you can trust your dreams. Our unconscious offers us dreams as messages that relate to our lives right now. Accept the dream as a gift given by your Self to yourself.

NOTE TO READER:

At the opening of each section of the book, I comment (in italics) on the selections to follow. I also comment (again in italics) before and after some selections. To the extent that you and I are similar, the comments may resonate with you. In the ways that we are different, you may find your own insightful ways into the reading.

By providing direct quotations from original sources I give you access to the authors' voices and styles as well as their ideas, even when they include vocabulary that we now find to be insensitive to gender or race.

Footnotes from the original sources are numbered continuously for each selection; for distinction, my footnoted clarifications to excerpts are within brackets, italicized, and designated by symbols (* and †).

PIONEERS OF PSYCHOTHERAPY

In 1900, Sigmund Freud published The Interpretation of Dreams, *postulating that dreams express the content of the unconscious mind of the dreamer. Through dreams, he presumed, we each gain access to the hidden and mysterious parts of ourselves that are key to our most primary feelings and reactions. C. G. Jung, Alfred Adler, and others followed, adding their own insights about dreams, how we might work with them, and what dreams can teach us. In this section you will find some of the pioneers of Western psychology describing their understanding of dreams and how to interpret them. You will find more writings from Jung than from others; I've found his work particularly helpful to my clients and myself.*

Sigmund Freud

The Viennese neurologist and founder of psychoanalysis, Sigmund Freud pioneered the use of dreams in Western psychology.

PSYCHIC PREPARATION

The next two selections are from Freud's seminal work, The Interpretation of Dreams.

IN THE COURSE OF THESE PSYCHOANALYTIC STUDIES, I happened upon the question of dream-interpretation. My patients, after I had pledged them to inform me of all the ideas and thoughts which occurred to them in connection with a given theme, related their dreams, and thus taught me that a dream may be interpolated in the psychic concatenation, which may be followed backwards from a pathological idea into the patient's memory. The next step was to treat the dream itself as a symptom, and to apply to it the method of interpretation which had been worked out for such symptoms.

For this a certain psychic preparation on the part of the patient is necessary. A twofold effort is made, to stimulate his attentiveness in respect of his psychic perceptions, and to eliminate the critical spirit in which he is ordinarily in the habit of viewing such thoughts as come to the surface. For the purpose of self-observation with concentrated attention it is advantageous that the patient should take up a restful position and close his eyes; he must be explicitly instructed to renounce all criticism of the thought-formations which he may perceive. He must also be told that the success of the psychoanalysis depends upon his noting and communicating everything that passes through his mind, and that he must not allow himself to suppress one idea because it seems to him unimportant or irrelevant to the subject, or another because it seems nonsensical. He must preserve an absolute impartiality in respect to his ideas; for if he is unsuccessful in finding the desired solution of the dream, the obsessional idea, or the like, it will be because he permits himself to be critical of them.

I have noticed in the course of my psychoanalytical work that the psychological state of a man in an attitude of reflection is entirely different from that of a man who is observing his psychic processes. In reflection there is a greater play of psychic activity than in the most attentive self-observation; this is shown even by the tense attitude and the wrinkled brow of the man in a state of reflection, as opposed to the mimic tranquility of the man observing himself. In both cases there must be concentrated attention, but the reflective man makes use of his critical faculties, with the result that he rejects some of the thoughts which rise into consciousness after he has become aware of them, and abruptly interrupts others, so that he does not follow the lines of thought which they would otherwise open up for him; while in respect of yet other thoughts he is able to behave in such a manner that they do not become conscious at all—that is to say, they are suppressed before they are perceived. In self-observation, on the other hand, he has but one task—that of suppressing criticism; if he succeeds in doing this, an unlimited number of thoughts enter his consciousness which would otherwise have eluded his grasp. With the aid of the material thus obtained—material which is new to the self-observer—it is possible to achieve the interpretation of pathological ideas, and also that of dream-formations. As will be seen, the point is to induce a psychic state which is in some degree analogous, as regards the distribution of psychic energy (mobile attention), to the state of the mind before falling asleep—and also, of course, to the hypnotic state. On falling asleep the "undesired ideas" emerge, owing to the slackening of a certain arbitrary (and, of course, also critical) action, which is allowed to influence the trend of our ideas; we are accustomed to speak of fatigue as the reason of this slackening; the emerging undesired ideas are changed into visual and auditory images. In the condition which it utilized for the analysis of dreams and pathological ideas, this activity is purposely and deliberately renounced, and the psychic energy thus saved (or some part of it) is employed in attentively tracking the undesired thoughts which now come to the surface—thoughts which retain their identity as ideas (in which the condition differs from the state of falling asleep). "Undesired ideas" are thus changed into "desired" ones.

There are many people who do not seem to find it easy to adopt the required attitude toward the apparently "freely rising" ideas, and to renounce the criticism which is otherwise applied to them. The "undesired ideas" habitually evoke the most violent resistance, which seeks to prevent them from coming to the surface. But if we may credit our great poet-philosopher Friedrich Schiller, the essential condition of poetical creation includes a very similar attitude. In a certain passage in his correspondence with Körner (for the tracing of which we are indebted to Otto Rank), Schiller replies in the following words to a friend who complains of his lack of creative power: "The reason for your complaint lies, it seems to me, in the constraint which your intellect imposes upon your imagination. Here I will make an observation, and illustrate it by an allegory. Apparently it is not good—and indeed it hinders the creative work of the mind—if the intellect examines too closely the ideas already pouring in, as it were, at the gates. Regarded in isolation, an idea may be quite insignificant, and venturesome in the extreme, but it may acquire importance from an idea which follows it; perhaps, in a certain collocation with other ideas, which may seem equally absurd, it may be capable of furnishing a very serviceable link. The intellect cannot judge all these ideas unless it can retain them until it has considered them in connection with these other ideas. In the case of a creative mind, it seems to me, the intellect has withdrawn its watchers from the gates, and the ideas rush in pell-mell, and only then does it review and inspect the multitude. You worthy critics, or whatever you may call yourselves, are ashamed or afraid of the momentary and passing madness which is found in all real creators, the longer or shorter duration of which distinguishes the thinking artist from the dreamer. Hence your complaints of unfruitfulness, for you reject too soon and discriminate too severely" (letter of December 1, 1788).

And yet, such a withdrawal of the watchers from the gates of the intellect, as Schiller puts it, such a translation into the condition of uncritical self-observation, is by no means difficult.

Most of my patients accomplish it after my first instructions. I myself can do so very completely, if I assist the process by writing down the ideas that flash through my mind. The quantum of psychic energy by which the critical activity is thus reduced, and by which the intensity of self-observation may be increased, varies considerably according to the subject matter upon which the attention is to be fixed.

ONE IMAGE AT A TIME

THE FIRST STEP IN THE APPLICATION OF THIS PROCEDURE *[of uncritical self-observation]* teaches us that one cannot make the dream as a whole the object of one's attention, but only the individual components of its content. If I ask a patient who is as yet unpracticed: "What occurs to you in connection with this dream? he is unable, as a rule, to fix upon anything in his psychic field of vision. I must first dissect the dream for him; then, in connection with each fragment, he gives me a number of ideas which may be described as the "thoughts behind" this part of the dream. In this first and important condition, then, the method of dream-interpretation which I employ diverges from the popular, historical and legendary method of interpretation by symbolism and approaches more nearly to the second or "cipher method." Like this *[cipher method]*, it is an interpretation in detail, not *en masse* . . . it conceives the dream, from the outset, as something built up, as a conglomerate of psychic formations.

Sigmund Freud, *The Interpretation of Dreams*, trans. A. A. Brill (New York: Gramercy Books, a division of Random House Value Publishing, Inc., 1996), pp. 70-73.

Stephen Mitchell and Margaret Black
AN INTRODUCTION TO FREUD

Here Stephen Mitchell and Margaret Black summarize Freud's conceptualization of the nature of dreams. If you choose to test these beliefs against your own dreams, take a dream and ask yourself, "Are there wishes, desires, or needs represented in this dream that I might be unable to allow or accept?"

AMONG THE ASSOCIATIONS generated by Freud's patients were their dreams. Freud treated dreams like any other associations: they were likely to contain hidden thoughts and links to earlier experiences.

Freud himself was a prolific dreamer. He also had certain troublesome neurotic symptoms. Soon, his most important patient became himself. He immersed himself in the new technique he had created, associating to the elements in his own dream life and communicating his self-discoveries in feverish letters to a physician friend . . . By 1895 Freud felt he had grasped the secret of dream formation.

Dreams are disguised fulfillments of conflictual wishes, Freud became convinced (Freud, 1900). In sleep, the dynamic force (the defenses) that ordinarily keeps forbidden wishes from gaining access to consciousness is weakened, as in a hypnotic trance. If the wish were simply represented directly in the dream, sleep would likely be disrupted. A compromise is struck between the force that propels the wish into consciousness and the force that blocks access to consciousness. The wish may appear in the dream only in a disguised form, an intruder dressed up to look as though he belongs. The true meaning of the dream (the *latent dream thoughts*) undergoes an elaborate process of distortion that results in the dream as experienced (the *manifest content* of the dream). Condensation, displacement, symbolism—all are employed in the dream work to transform the unacceptable latent dream thoughts into acceptable, although apparently meaningless, disconnected images, which are strung together into a story (*secondary elaboration*), to throw the dreamer even further off track.

Stephen Mitchell and Margaret Black
FREUD'S DREAM INTERPRETATION

The following selection by Mitchell and Black summarizes another aspect of Freudian dream theory. Don't let the jargon (or doctrine) distract you from finding ways to connect with your own dreams. Look first for concrete application of Freud's approach to your dream work. Then through the lens of your own experience you will know which theories and concepts are meaningful to you.

THE TECHNIQUE FOR INTERPRETING DREAMS follows from this conception of their formation. Each element of the manifest content of the dream is isolated and associated to. The associations to the various elements lead in different directions, exposing the different memories, thoughts, and feelings that had created them (through condensation, displacement, and symbolization). Eventually the various lines of association coalesce in the nodal latent dream thoughts. Dream interpretation reverses the process of dream formation, tracing the path from the disguised surface to the hidden secrets lying beneath.

Stephen A. Mitchell and Margaret J. Black, *Freud and Beyond*, (New York: Basic Books, 1995), pp. 8-9.

C. G. Jung

Carl Gustav Jung, a Swiss psychiatrist and early follower of Sigmund Freud, added optimism to early psychology. Jung believed our psyches inherently strive for wholeness and connection to the world. Try embracing a dream of yours, whatever it contains, and see if you feel even a little more whole.

DREAMS UNIFY THE SOUL

A DREAM IS NOTHING BUT A LUCKY IDEA that comes to us from the dark, all-unifying world of the psyche. What would be more natural, when we have lost ourselves amid the endless particulars and isolated details of the world's surface, than to knock at the door of dreams and inquire of them the bearings which would bring us closer to the basic facts of human existence?

Here we encounter the obstinate prejudice that dreams are so much froth, they are not real, they lie, they are mere wish-fulfillments. All this is but an excuse not to take dreams seriously, for that would be uncomfortable. Our intellectual hubris of consciousness loves isolation despite all its inconveniences, and for this reason people will do anything rather than admit that dreams are real and speak the truth. There are some saints who had very rude dreams. Where would their saintliness be, the very thing that exalts them above the vulgar rabble, if the obscenity of a dream were a real truth? But it is just the most squalid dreams that emphasize our blood-kinship with the rest of mankind, and most effectively damp down the arrogance born of an atrophy of the instincts. Even if the whole world were to fall to pieces, the unity of the psyche would never be shattered. And the wider and more numerous the fissures on the surface, the more this unity is strengthened in the depths.

C. G. Jung, "The Meaning of Psychology for Modern Man," in *Civilization in Transition*, trans. R. F. C. Hull (New York: Bollingen Foundation, 1964), pp. 145-146.

BRING AN OPEN MIND

Here Jung presents some concrete ways we can work with dreams.
See also a similar passage of Freud's (on p. 3) that emphasizes the
importance of not judging ourselves in the dream-work process. It can
be surprisingly difficult to maintain an open attitude in dream work,
as demonstrated to me by client after client, and in myself when I face
some of my own dreams. Commonly, we are humiliated, flattered,
horrified, or amused by dream events and are predisposed to make
positive or negative interpretations.

ONE SELECTS SOME SPECIALLY STRIKING PORTION of the dream, and
then questions the subject about the associations that attach themselves
to it. He is directed to say frankly whatever comes into his mind concerning
this part of the dream, eliminating as far as possible any criticism.
Criticism is nothing but the censor at work; it is the resistance against the
complex, and it tends to suppress what is of the most importance.

The subject should, therefore, say absolutely everything that comes
into his head without paying any attention to it. This is always difficult at
first .... For it is toward oneself that one has the strongest resistances.

Jung used "complex" to refer to a group of emotionally charged ideas
that arise around a topic that is disturbing to an individual.

C. G. Jung, *Dreams*, ed. Gerhard Adler, trans. R. F. C. Hull (Princeton, New Jersey: Princeton
University Press, 1974), p. 9.

THE SHADOW:
DARK ASPECTS OF THE PERSONALITY

Those parts of ourselves or others that we find most offensive, despicable, or simply incompetent often arise in our dreams to haunt us. Jung refers to the images that carry these disturbing characteristics as "the shadow." The shadow is so unacceptable, or even shameful, we try to hide it from ourselves and others. The more dangerous we perceive the shadow to be to our ego-self and the more we wish to disown it, then the more frightening, unrecognizable, and faceless its image will appear in a dream.

THE SHADOW IS A MORAL PROBLEM that challenges the whole ego-personality, for no one can become conscious of the shadow without considerable moral effort. To become conscious of it involves recognizing the dark aspects of the personality as present and real. This act is the essential condition for any kind of self-knowledge, and it therefore, as a rule meets with considerable resistance. Indeed, self-knowledge as a psychotherapeutic measure frequently requires much painstaking work extending over a long period.

Closer examination of the dark characteristics—that is, the inferiorities constituting the shadow—reveals that they have an *emotional* nature, a kind of autonomy, and accordingly an obsessive or, better, possessive quality. Emotion, incidentally, is not an activity of the individual but something that happens to him. Affects occur usually where adaptation is weakest, and at the same time they reveal the reason for its weakness, namely a certain degree of inferiority and the existence of a lower level of personality. On this lower level with its uncontrolled or scarcely controlled emotions one behaves more or less like a primitive, who is not only the passive victim of his affects but also singularly incapable of moral judgment.

PROJECTIONS

In the following selection, Jung introduces the concept of "projection,"
which he defines as our tendency to see our own fears, feelings, or desires
as residing in another person, thereby allowing us to deny responsibility
and to blame the other for aspects of ourselves that we can't accept.

ALTHOUGH, WITH INSIGHT AND GOOD WILL, the shadow can to some extent be assimilated into the conscious personality, experience shows that there are certain features which offer the most obstinate resistance to moral control and prove almost impossible to influence. These resistances are usually bound up with projections, which are not recognized as such, and their recognition is a moral achievement beyond the ordinary. While some traits peculiar to the shadow can be recognized without too much difficulty as one's own personal qualities, in this case both insight and good will are unavailing because the cause of the emotion appears to lie, beyond all possibility of doubt, in the *other person.* ...

The effect of the projection is to isolate the subject from his environment, since instead of real relation to it there is now an illusory one. Projections change the world into the replica of one's own unknown face.

Here Jung told us to be patient and accepting when frightening and
disparaging (shadow) figures disturb our dreams. Be kind to yourself at
such times. You are attempting something very difficult. You now have
the opportunity to see who shows up in negative roles. If more than one
person or thing scares you in a dream, what do they have in common?
What part of yourself might that be?

C. G. Jung, *Psyche and Symbol*, ed. Violet S. de Laszlo, trans. R. F. C. Hull (Princeton, New Jersey: Princeton University Press, 1991), pp. 8-9.

WHO SPEAKS TO US IN DREAMS?

Here Jung admonishes us to watch our dreams for alternate or even radical solutions to our struggles.

. . . IN EACH OF US there is another whom we do not know. He speaks to us in dreams and tells us how differently he sees us from the way we see ourselves. When, therefore, we find ourselves in a difficult situation to which there is no solution, he can sometimes kindle a light that radically alters our attitude—the very attitude that led us into the difficult situation.

Rather than being discouraged by encountering the same struggles in your dreams as you have while awake, look closely. Did any of the dream characters find a solution? How can you manifest that solution in your waking life?

C. G. Jung, "The Meaning of Psychology for Modern Man," in *Civilization in Transition*, trans. R. F. C. Hull (New York: Bollingen Foundation, 1964), p. 153.

BALANCE THE PSYCHE

. . . CONSTANT OBSERVATION pays the unconscious a tribute that more or less guarantees its co-operation. The unconscious as we know can never be "done with" once and for all. It is, in fact, one of the most important tasks of psychic hygiene to pay continual attention to the symptomatology of unconscious contents and processes, for the good reason that the conscious mind is always in danger of becoming one-sided, of keeping to well-worn paths and getting stuck in blind alleys. The complementary and compensating function of the unconscious ensures that these dangers, which are especially great in neurosis, can in some measure be avoided. It is only under ideal conditions, when life is still simple and unconscious enough to follow the serpentine path of instinct without hesitation or misgiving, that the compensation works with entire success. The more civilized, the more conscious and complicated a man is, the less he is able to follow his instincts. His complicated living conditions and the influence of his environment are so strong that they drown the quiet voice of nature. Opinions, beliefs, theories, and collective tendencies appear in its stead and back up all the aberrations of the conscious mind. Deliberate attention should then be given to the unconscious so that the compensation can set to work. Hence it is especially important to picture the archetypes of the unconscious not as a rushing phantasmagoria of fugitive images but as constant, autonomous factors, which indeed they are.

C. G. Jung, *Psyche and Symbol*, ed. Violet S. de Laszlo, trans. R. F. C. Hull (Princeton, New Jersey: Princeton University Press, 1991), pp. 20-21.

THE CAVE OF REGENERATION

THE CAVE IS THE PLACE OF REBIRTH, that secret cavity in which one is shut up in order to be incubated and renewed. The Koran says of it: "You might have seen the rising sun decline to the right of their cavern, and as it set, go past them on the left, while they [*the Seven Sleepers*] stayed in the middle. The "middle" is the centre where the jewel reposes, where the incubation or the sacrificial rite or the transformation takes place. . . .

The legend has the following meaning: Anyone who gets into that cave, that is to say into the cave which everyone has in himself, or into the darkness that lies behind consciousness, will find himself involved in an—at first—unconscious process of transformation. By penetrating into the unconscious he makes a connection with his unconscious contents. This may result in momentous change of personality in the positive or negative sense. The transformation is often interpreted as a prolongation of the natural span of life or as an earnest of immortality.

In many dreams, figurative and literal places of transformation appear spontaneously. In one of my client's dreams, she moved from the midst of a disturbing interaction among family members to a retreat in the basement for food and rest.

TRANSFORMATION AND INDIVIDUATION

Individuation is Jung's term for the process by which an individual distinguishes himself or herself from others or the demands of others. Jung used the term to describe the process of by which we learn to accept our selves and express that self in the world. In the selection that follows, Jung distinguishes transformation that occurs due to external circumstances (and which leads to feelings of diminution and enlargement) from transformation that arises from internal balance (individuation).

... THE MOST BEAUTIFUL AND IMPRESSIVE DREAMS often have no lasting or transformative effect on the dreamer. He may be impressed by them, but he does not necessarily see any problem in them. The event then naturally remains "outside," like a ritual action performed by others. These more aesthetic forms of experience must be carefully distinguished from those which indubitably involve a change in one's nature. ...

An example of the alteration of personality in the sense of diminution is furnished by what is known in primitive psychology as "loss of soul". ... occasionally something similar can happen to civilized man . . . The tonus [*muscle tone*] has given way, and this is felt subjectively as listlessness, moroseness, and depression. One no longer has any wish or courage to face the tasks of the day. One feels like lead, because no part of one's body seems willing to move, and this is due to the fact that one no longer has any disposable energy. ...

... the possibility of enlarging [*the personality*] exists, at least during the first half of life. ... We therefore tend to assume that this increase comes *only* from without, thus justifying the prejudice that one becomes a personality by stuffing into oneself as much as possible from outside. But the more assiduously we follow this recipe, and the more stubbornly we believe that all increase has to come from without, the greater becomes our inner poverty. Therefore, if some great idea takes hold of us from outside, we must understand that it takes hold of us only because something in us responds and goes out to meet it. ... Real increase of personality means consciousness of an enlargement that flows from inner sources. ...

... As I have pointed out, in addition to the technical processes of transformation, there are also natural transformations. . . . Nature herself demands a death and a rebirth. . . .

Natural transformation processes announce themselves mainly in dreams. Elsewhere[1] I have presented a series of dream-symbols of the process of individuation. They were dreams which without exception exhibited rebirth symbolism. In this particular case there was a long drawn out process of inner transformation and rebirth into another being. This "other being" is the other person in ourselves—that larger and greater personality maturing within us, whom we have already met as the inner friend of the soul. That is why we take comfort whenever we find the friend and companion depicted in ritual. . . .

> *Dreams over time often reflect the process of transformation. A client of mine dreamed of swimming in the ocean and playing with a baby. Until I mentioned it, she hadn't realized that over the years of our sessions she had related numerous dreams that contained bodies of water, yet this was the first in which she was in the water. I felt heartened by this development which reflected a new and intimate connection she had made with a part of herself.*
>
> *To see if this process is occurring within you, I suggest that you reread your dreams from one or more years ago. Look specifically at dreams with similar images. Are there subtle differences in the nature, feelings, or outcome of the dreams?*

C. G. Jung, *The Archetypes and the Collective Unconscious*, ed. Herbert Read, Michael Fordham, Gerhard Adler, & William McGuire, trans. R. F. C. Hull (Princeton, New Jersey: Princeton University Press, 1975), pp. 118-120, p. 130, and pp. 135-136.

---

[1] *Psychology and Alchemy, Part II*

Alfred Adler

After his association with Sigmund Freud, the Viennese psychiatrist Alfred Adler developed an alternative to psychoanalysis, which he called "individual psychology." Adler believed that children learn they are inferior to adults in speech, strength, and knowledge before their abilities are developed, and that we tend to carry the feeling of inferiority into adulthood, always striving to gain a position of superiority. Adler's ideal adult strives to improve mastery while maintaining a realistic concept of his or her abilities.

PERSONALITY MANIFESTS IN DREAMS

... FOLLOWERS OF OTHER SCHOOLS OF PSYCHOLOGY are constantly trying to find new views concerning dreams, but our understanding of dreams has been developed along the same line as our understanding of all the integral parts manifested in the expressions and movements of the psyche.

Now just as our waking life ... is determined by the goal of superiority, so we may see that dreams are determined by the individual goal of superiority. A dream is always a part of the style of life and we always find the prototype involved in it. In fact it is only when you see how the prototype is bound up to a particular dream that you can be sure that you have really understood the dream. Also, if you know a person well, you can pretty nearly guess the character of his dreams.

Take, for instance, our knowledge that mankind as a whole is really cowardly. From this general fact we can presuppose that the largest number of dreams will be dreams of fear, danger, or anxiety. And so if we know a person and see that his goal is to escape the solution of life's problems, we can guess that he often dreams that he falls down. Such a dream is like a warning to him: "Do not go on—you will be defeated." He expresses his view of the future in this way—by falling. The large majority of men have these dreams of falling.

A specific case is a student on the eve of an examination—a student whom we know to be a quitter. We can guess what will happen with him.

He is worried the whole day, cannot concentrate, and finally says to himself, "The time is too short." He wants to postpone the examination. His dream will be one of falling down. And this expresses his style of life, for to attain his goal, he must dream in such a way.

Take another student who makes progress in his studies, is courageous and not afraid, and never uses subterfuges. We can also guess his dreams. Before an examination he will dream that he climbs a high mountain, is enchanted with the view from the mountain top, and in this way awakes. This is an expression of his current of life, and we can see how it reflects his goal of accomplishment.

Then there is the person who is limited—the person who can proceed only up to a certain point. Such a person dreams about limits, and about being unable to escape persons and difficulties. He often has dreams of being chased and hunted.

Before we go on to the next type of dream it may be well to remark that the psychologist is never discouraged if somebody says to him, "I will not tell you any dreams for I cannot remember them. But I will make up some dreams." The psychologist knows that his fancy cannot create anything other than that which his style of life commands. His made-up dreams are just as good as his genuinely remembered dreams, for his imagination and fancy will also be an expression of his style of life.

Fancy need not literally copy a man's real movements in order to be an expression of his style of life. We find, for example, the type of person who lives more in fancies than in reality. He is the type that is very cowardly in the daytime but quite courageous in dreams. But we will always find some manifestations which indicate that he does not want to finish his work. Such manifestations will be quite evident even in his courageous dreams.

THE PURPOSE OF DREAMS

IT IS ALWAYS THE PURPOSE OF A DREAM to pave the way towards the goal of superiority—that is to say, the individual's private goal of superiority. All the symptoms, movements and dreams of a person are a form of training to enable one to find this dominating goal—be the goal one of being the center of attention, of domineering, or of escape.

The purpose of a dream is neither logically nor truthfully expressed. It exists in order to create a certain feeling, mood or emotion, and it is impossible fully to unravel its obscurities. But in this it differs from waking life and the movements of waking life only in degree, not in kind. We have seen that the answers of the psyche to life's problems are relative to the individual scheme of life: they do not fit into a pre-established frame of logic, although it is our aim, for purposes of social intercourse, to make them do so more and more. Now once we give up the absolute point of view for waking life, dream life loses its mystery. It becomes a further expression of the same relativity and the same mixture of fact and emotion that we find in waking life.

Historically dreams have always appeared very mysterious to primitive peoples, and they have generally resorted to the prophetic interpretation. Dreams were regarded as prophecies of events to come. In this there was a half-truth. It is true that a dream is a bridge that connects the problem which confronts the dreamer with his goal of attainment. In this way a dream will often come true, because the dreamer will be training his part during the dream and will be thus preparing for it to come true.

Another way of saying the same thing is that there is the same interconnectedness revealed in dreams as in our waking life. If a person is keen and intelligent he can foresee the future whether he analyzes his waking life or his dream life. What he does is to diagnose. For example if somebody dreams that an acquaintance has died and the person does die, this might be no more than what a physician or a close relative could foresee. What the dreamer does is to think in his sleep rather than in waking life.

The prophetic view of dreams, precisely because it contains a certain half-truth, is a superstition. It is generally clung to by persons who believe in other superstitions. Or else it is championed by men who seek importance by giving the impression that they are prophets.

To dispel the prophetic superstition and the mystery that surrounds dreams we have to explain of course why most people do not understand their own dreams. The explanation is to be found in the fact that few people know themselves even in waking life. Few persons have the power of reflective self-analysis which permits them to see whither they are headed, and the analysis of dreams is, as we have said, a more complicated and obscure affair than the analysis of waking behavior. It is thus no wonder that the analysis of dreams should be beyond the scope of most persons—and it is also no wonder that in their ignorance of what is involved they should turn to charlatans.

It will help us to understand the logic of dreams if we compare it, not directly with the movements of normal waking life, but with the type of phenomena which we have described in previous chapters as a manifestation of private intelligence. The reader will remember how we described the attitudes of criminals, problem children and neurotics—how they create a certain feeling, temper or mood in order to convince themselves of a given fact. Thus the murderer justifies himself by saying, "Life has no place for this man; therefore I must kill him." By emphasizing in his own mind the view that there is not sufficient place on earth he creates a certain feeling which prepares him for the murder.

Such a person may also reason that so-and-so has nice trousers and he has not. He puts such value on this circumstance that he becomes envious. His goal of superiority becomes to have nice trousers, and so we may find him dreaming a dream which creates a certain emotion which will lead to the accomplishment of that goal. We see this illustrated, in fact, in well-known dreams. There are, for instance, the dreams of Joseph in the Bible. He dreamt that all the others bent before him. Now we can see how this dream fitted in with the whole episode of the coat of many colors—and with his banishment by his brothers. . . .

If we consider dreams in this manner, the task of interpretation does not become too difficult. We should remember that the selection of pictures, remembrances and fancies is an indication of the direction in which the mind is moving. It shows you the dreamer's tendency, and eventually we can see the goal at which he wants to arrive.

EMOTIONALLY INTOXICATING

THE MODERN INTERPRETATION OF DREAMS is about twenty-five years old. Dreams were first regarded by Freud as the fulfillment of infantile sex desires. We cannot agree with this, inasmuch as if dreams are such a fulfillment then everything can be expressed in terms of a fulfillment. Every idea behaves in this way—going from the depths of the subconscious up into consciousness. The formula of sex-fulfillment thus explains nothing in particular.

Later Freud suggested that the desire for death was involved. But it is certain that [*all dreams*] could not be explained very well in this way . . . .

The truth is that there is no specific formula which will explain dreams, except the general postulates which we have discussed about the unity of psychical life and about the special affective character of dream life. This affective character, and its accompaniment of self-deception is a theme with many variations. Thus it is expressed in the preoccupation with comparisons and metaphors. The use of comparisons is one of the best means of deceiving oneself and others. For we may be sure that if a person uses comparisons he does not feel sure that he can convince you with reality and logic. He always wants to influence you by means of useless and far-fetched comparisons.

Even poets deceive, but pleasantly, and we enjoy being entertained by their metaphors and poetic comparisons. We may be sure, however, that they are meant to influence us more than we would be influenced by usual words. If Homer, for example, speaks of an army of Greek soldiers overrunning a field like lions, the metaphor will not deceive us when we think sharply but it will certainly intoxicate us when we are in a poetic mood. The author makes us believe he has marvelous power. He could not do this if he were merely to describe the clothes the soldiers wore and the arms they carried, etc.

We see the same thing in the case of a person who is in difficulty about explaining things: if he sees he cannot convince you, he will use comparisons. This use of comparisons, as we have said, is self-deceptive, and this is the reason it is so prominently manifested in dreams in the selection of pictures, images, etc. This is an artistic way of intoxicating oneself.

The fact that dreams are emotionally intoxicating offers, curiously enough, a method for preventing dreams. If a person understands what he has been dreaming about and realizes that he has been intoxicating himself, he will stop dreaming. To dream will have no more purpose for him. At least this is the case with the present writer, who stopped dreaming as soon as he realized what dreaming meant.

Incidentally it may be said that this realization, to be effective, must have the aspects of a thorough-going emotional conversion. This was brought about, in the case of the writer, by his last dream. The dream occurred during wartime. In connection with his duties he was making a great effort to keep a certain man from being sent to the front in a place of danger. In the dream the idea came to him that he had murdered someone, but he did not know whom. He got himself into a bad state wondering, "Whom have I murdered?" The fact is he was simply intoxicated with the idea of making the greatest possible effort to put the soldier in the most favorable position for avoiding death. The dream emotion was meant to be conducive to this idea, but when he understood the subterfuge of the dream, he gave up dreaming altogether, since he did not need to deceive himself in order to do the things that for reasons of logic he might want either to do or to leave undone.

Contrary to Adler's assertion, contemporary sleep research has shown that everyone dreams every night (p. 135).

Alfred Adler, *The Science of Living* (Garden City, NY: Garden City Publishing, 1929), pp. 154-171.

ONGOING DEVELOPMENTS IN PSYCHOTHERAPY

The foundation laid by Freud, Jung, and Adler was built upon by myriad people who brought their own personalities and beliefs to the work. Some, including Marie-Louise von Franz, emphasize connecting to soul and emotion by intellectually exploring dreams. Others, such as James Hillman, suggest we approach a dream as we would a poem, acknowledging its mystery. Still others use physical reactions to discover dream meaning, offer step-wise approaches to dream work, or integrate all these pieces to assist us. Experiment with what you find here; play with the approaches that speak to you.

Marie-Louise von Franz

Marie-Louise von Franz was a Swiss psychologist who collaborated with Jung for more than thirty years, and was particularly clear and concise in her writings about dreams.

THE STAGES OF A DREAM

IN JUNGIAN PSYCHOLOGY, we have a technique. We compare the dream to a drama and examine it under three structural headings: first the introduction or exposition—the setting of the dream and the naming of the problem; second, the peripeteia—that would be the ups and downs of the story; and finally, the lysis — the end solution or, perhaps, catastrophe. And if I don't understand a dream, I use that scheme. First I say to myself, "Now, what is the introduction?"

The first sentence of a dream generally gives the setting and introduces the major characters. For example, a dream might begin, "I am in my childhood home with my friend Bob." You take the first sentence and ask the dreamer for his associations. "What was your childhood home like? How did you feel there? Were you happy there? How long did you stay there?" And then you ask about the friend, "How is your friend Bob? What was he like? . . . Oh, I see, he was a bore, but you did all your childhood mischief together." And then you insert these *associations* into the text, which then becomes, "I am psychologically still in my boyhood situation, and I am with a part of myself which is boring, but also mischievous."

Once you have that translation, you have naturally to think about how it applies to the moment of the dream and to the dreamer's life. In what way does the dreamer still have one leg in his childhood home? Where in his life situation is he still reacting as he reacted as a boy? You have to assume that the dream is speaking about that corner of his personality.

After you've looked at the exposition in this way, you then go on to the *naming of the problem*. Let's say a car comes up the driveway and two dark burglars jump out. Now you have a dramatic development, which means a specific story is now being told. The two dark men would be an invasion, something which is breaking in. Burglars very often represent something breaking into one's conscious system. So the dream would then translate, "In the corner of his psyche where the dreamer still has childish reactions, something from the collective unconscious is breaking in."

In this way we slowly go through the whole dream. Now the ending of a dream, the *lysis*, is always what the dream is driving at: a solution or a catastrophe. I know these rules of interpretation so well that I follow them half unconsciously. But I always pay particular attention to the last sentence of the dream, which gives the unconscious solution if there is one. Some dreams just peter out and they are not favorable.

> *Although von Franz finds those dreams that end without a solution to be unfavorable, I find them useful in indicating movement toward resolution. If the solution was not presented in the dream on a particular night, the next dream, or the next, may fill in the blank.*
>
> *In the preceding selection, von Franz outlines three dramatic sections of a dream: the setting, naming the problem, and solution. See Gerhard Adler's concept of the sections of a dream on page 30.*

DEATH

> *Here von Franz addresses one of the most disturbing images that can arise in a dream or nightmare—death. She views death in a dream as a positive indicator of some aspect of the self that must die if psychic balance is to be achieved. My clients have found this concept comforting; more importantly, it often seems to fit their circumstances.*

[*Interviewer*] I REMEMBER A DREAM in which I was shot dead, stone cold dead, with one shot right through the heart. But my murderer fired four more shots. Each bullet he fired killed me anew. I remember thinking in the dream that it was pointless for him to continue, for I was already dead. He'd killed me with his first shot. What does it mean when the dreamer actually dies or is killed in a dream?

[*von Franz*] It always means that the ego attitude as it is at that moment has to go. I have had many dreams in which I was officially executed, generally by being beheaded. They stated very clearly that the head had to come off, that some intellectual attitude had to be sacrificed. But if you are shot, that's rather like being hit by something and means you need a shock to wake you up. The death of the dreamer in dreams means a radical, complete change where absolutely nothing of the old person or the old attitude is left. So if one dreams of being killed, executed, or shot or hanged or whatever the form of death, it always points to the coming of a radical change.

Fraser Boa, *The Way of the Dream: Conversations on Jungian Dream Interpretation with Marie-Louise von Franz* (Boston: Shambhala, 1994), pp. 33-34, and pp. 46-47.

Karen Walker
SUMMARY OF KEY VON FRANZIAN CONCEPTS

In a review of The Way of the Dream: Conversations on Jungian Dream Interpretation with Marie-Louise von Franz, *Karen Walker summarizes several of von Franz's key ideas.*

IN INTERPRETING OUR OWN DREAMS, von Franz warns us that usually we project what we already know into the dream. The purpose of the dream is to show us what we don't know. Jung would tell his dreams to his students or to someone who knew nothing of dream interpretation. If they could not say what the dream meant, at least they could give him a sense of what it did not mean.

For von Franz, dreams are like letters delivered to our conscious mind from our Self. In Jungian terms, the Self is that which guides our psychic life. It could be called our divine center. Dreams give us direction, predict future events, and show us the way towards harmony with our Self.

It is when we are out of harmony with the Self that the energies, unexpressed emotions and unrealized potentials of our lives result in neurosis or neurotic symptoms. Restlessness is the most general neurotic symptom today, according to von Franz. This restlessness, a bottled-up energy in the unconscious which we do not tap and do not integrate into consciousness, "can take the form of an all-pervading anxiety, a fear that somewhere, something dark is lurking and might happen at any minute. Then one is anxious about nothing all the time.... Irritability, aggressiveness, oversexiness, or a feeling of complete meaninglessness or emptiness—all the symptoms of different neurotic diseases come from that restlessness."

The Self, along with the shadow, animus and anima, can be seen as dream figures. Each dream figure can personify aspects of our total personality. The shadow figure usually appears in the dream as a person of the same sex as the dreamer. Whether a positive or negative figure, it is a part of ourselves we'd rather not take a look at, a part we haven't integrated into our lives. . . .

Von Franz comments . . . . "If we reject or split off some complex of our psyche, then it begins to sap our energy secretly behind our back. . . . They come into analysis and they say 'I feel listless, I just feel tired, I just don't want to do anything. I wake in the morning already depressed. Nothing means anything to me any more. I have no interest or anything.'"

The animus dream figure appears in the dreams of women as a male figure. It is a woman's inner man. In a chapter [of The Way of the Dream] entitled "The Tyrant," von Franz discusses the dream of a woman in which her father appears as the chief of police. The dreamer is stroking a cat.

. . . the cat often is an image of something feminine, independent and sure of itself, just what modern women so often lack . . . the chief of police is that animus in woman who wants orderly, conventional behavior that will not be shocking to anyone. Just the opposite of a cat."

Von Franz warns that the dream world can be dangerous. "It can suck us away from reality and spin us into a neurotic or even psychotic unreality. The dream world is only positive if it is in a living, balanced dialogue with a lived, actually lived, life."

Review by Karen Walker of *The Way of the Dream: Conversations on Jungian Dream Interpretation with Marie-Louise von Franz* (Boston: Shambhala, 1994), *Electric Dreams* 5, no. 1 (January 1998), www.Dreamgate.com.

DIRECT AND UNIQUE EXPERIENCE

... EVERY ENCOUNTER IS AN ADVENTURE and the dream is that direct encounter. Among the thousands of dreams I've interpreted, I've never met the same dream twice.... Its' a message from the powers of the instinct, the powers of the collective unconscious, a message which comes at a specific moment during a particular night which is meant specifically for the dreamer. The alchemists would say it's a message from the unique to the unique. Namely, from the divine center of the psyche to the unique individual pertaining to the unique situation one is in. That's why you can never predict dreams....

So at the source of a dream is a creative mystery which we cannot rationally explain.... They are something unique which you can only marvel at.

The next time you remember a dream, ask yourself, "Why this dream, why dream this now?"

Fraser Boa, *The Way of the Dream: Conversations on Jungian Dream Interpretation with Marie-Louise von Franz* (Boston: Shambhala, 1994), p. 73.

Gerhard Adler

Gerhard Adler (not to be confused with Alfred Adler) practiced analytical psychology in London and was an editor of the most comprehensive collection of Jung's work in English (The Collected Works of C.G. Jung). The following two selections, presenting Adler's interpretation of a patient's dream, were taken from a series of lectures Adler delivered between 1936 and 1945.

CASE EXAMPLE: ARCHETYPES AND THREE-PART DREAMS

In the first paragraph, below, Adler gives us background about the patient whose dream he will then recount and interpret.

As to the analysis, this soon revealed the fact that except for their first meeting twelve years ago, his so-called love affair had no foundation in fact whatsoever.... the girl was to all intents and purposes a creature of phantasy, functioning merely as a figure on which to project his emotions. The relation, therefore, was not the expression of genuine feeling but a symptom of his negative mother-fixation. For this had driven him into such violent opposition to everything connected with the opposite sex that he had built up an imaginary love relation in order to confirm and intensify this antagonism, and thus avoid ever really facing up to the genuine problems of love and the emotional side of life. His situation was very acute, and the first three months of the analysis were spent in discussing this and in unraveling the main threads of his elaborate system of infantile reaction. After three months of analysis the patient brought the following dream ...

"I am present at a party which I find very boring. I pass into an adjoining room. There I see in a corner two toy animals with which I begin to play. One of the animals is an ordinary sized teddy bear, the other is a wolf. The wolf is about a quarter the size of the teddy bear, and his pads are furnished with very sharp claws. It occurs to me that these claws render him very life-like, and at the same time extremely dangerous, so that he should be firmly seized by the scruff of the neck. This I proceed to do in order to prevent him turning round and clawing me. Then I allow the wolf to claw the bear's fur, telling the latter that he need not be afraid as I will see to it that the wolf does him no harm. Suddenly the wolf escapes from under my hand. He immediately runs out of the room and out of the house, and I know that once outside he will quickly grow into a large and dangerous animal. Someone says that what I am here experiencing is the primeval worm, the giant serpent encircling the world, or, as might equally well be said, the dragon, the adversary of man."

The patient was very much impressed by this dream, although quite unable to furnish any associations. In order to set his unconscious reactions going, I suggested that he should try to make a picture of the "giant serpent encircling the world" and he promptly adopted my suggestion. Two days later, he brought me not only one drawing, but a series of five, and informed me that when he had finished painting the first picture he experienced an irresistible impulse to continue drawing, so much so that he spent the entire night making this series of pictures. He said they were quite spontaneous, and were drawn without any conscious volition or control on his part, as if indeed the pictures had drawn themselves, a condition typical of the processes of active imagination. It was only after he had completed the fifth picture that he experienced a sense of fulfillment and relief which allowed him to stop working. As for the meaning contained in the pictures, this was, if anything, even more of a riddle to him than the dream.

The patient could not supply associations either to the dream or to the pictures. From this we may conclude that the symbolism of the dream, as well as that of the pictures, originated in a psychic level beyond the ordinary reach of the dreamer's consciousness; that is, it does not contain personal contents, but rather archetypes, which are the manifestations of the collective unconscious. Faced with such a special situation, we are justified—in contradistinction to our usual practice of using the patient's associations—in intervening ourselves because of our knowledge of collective symbolism; indeed, such intervention on our part is essential if we wish to discover the meaning of such a content. I will, therefore, apply in the following interpretation our method of *amplification*, that is of making use of parallels drawn from mythology and folklore.

The dream may be divided into three episodes, as follows: (1) a party at which the dreamer is very bored; (2) an adjoining room in which he finds the animals—this forms the main action; (3) "outside," where the wolf changes into the primeval worm—the serpent—the dragon.

We look on dreams as "the spontaneous self-revelation in symbolical form of the actual state of the dreamer's unconscious."[1] Our main problem is always to discover what one-sided and therefore unsatisfactory attitude in conscious life is being *compensated* by the dream, because we believe that the relation of the unconscious to the conscious psyche is compensatory. Therefore a knowledge of the actual situation of the patient, as described earlier, is necessary. From the discussion of the dream with the patient the meaning of the *boring party* became clear, namely, that it revealed in the unconscious the compensatory factors to his sterile social attitude. A "party" may symbolize either that one is well adapted to social and communal life, or, on the other hand, that one is being submerged in it. A "party" also personifies everyday life, that is, the part of our life and psychology which is completely covered by the field of our ego complex, and hence it may symbolize the ego. The development of the ego consciousness is certainly an essential concomitant of every psychological advance, but it should not be achieved at the expense of the instinctive and natural powers of the individual. . . . No life is complete that is identified with the limited area of social life, or what one might call the collective consciousness; and therefore the comment made by the unconscious on the dreamer's one-sided attitude finds vivid expression in his condition of boredom. We find a situation boring if it offers us nothing new, or stimulating, or constructive. This is the dreamer's situation in his everyday life, which it is his duty to set about changing. The dream, however, does not rest content with mere criticism, it points the way to new and vital experiences.

At this juncture, we can with advantage make use of a fact discovered through long experience in the interpretation of dreams, namely that

---

[1] Jung. *Ueber die Energetik der Seele*, p. 157.

these can often be divided into three parts corresponding to a *threefold chronological pattern* consisting of past, present and future. Our dream shows this threefold division very clearly; the party, the room adjoining and the outside. The party, therefore, states the original problem with which the patient starts, that is, the cause of his neurosis rooted in his past history; the subsequent step, when he enters the adjoining room, represents his present critical situation; that is, it states his present problem which is crying out for a solution, and we may assume that the third act which takes place "outside" foreshadows the future in which the patient may attain to a new insight and to a more mature attitude to life once his present acute difficulties have been overcome. The immediate and urgent need, therefore, is that the patient, convinced of the barrenness of his present completely one-sided attitude, with its resultant nervous disturbances, should make up his mind to take the next step. What does this further step imply? He moves out of the region of social boredom, and of his one-sided intellectualism, into the "adjoining room," which is empty, except for two toy animals, with which he begins to play. During this game, or rather, to give the dynamic potency of the dream its due, because of and through this game, the two playthings come to life. This coming alive occurs in play, as it were casually and almost inadvertently; for through "playing" with them the objects are supplied with psychic energy and life. Through playing the activity of phantasy is stimulated, and in this way new potentialities are created.[2]

> *Adler believed the three parts of a dream represent the past (the origination of the dream conflict), the present (the conflict in life today), and the future (the direction of change). Marie-Louise von Franz presents another hypothesis as to the three-part structure of dreams (see*

---

[2] "*Play*" conveys first and foremost the idea of something done simply as a game, almost without intention and, as it were, by the way. But in addition to this, to play with something means to give oneself up to the object with which one plays; one so to speak infuses one's own libido into the thing played with. As a result of this the play develops into a magic action which conjures up life. It has long been known that the play of primitives and children represents a magic action which for them possesses absolute reality, though on a different level from so-called "concrete" reality. To play means to bridge over the gap between phantasy and reality by the magical action of one's own libido ...

p. 25). I find it helpful to try on either Adler's or von Franz's approach, or both, to see if they fit one of my own dreams or a client's.

MYTHS AND MEANING

Still working with the dream recounted in the previous selection, Adler here shows how mythology can be used to amplify the meaning of dream images.

IT WILL BE READILY UNDERSTOOD that animals in dreams represent the level of the instincts. An animal is "subhuman," and stands for the animal side of our nature; animals express the instinctual libido and, in general, the unconscious.[3] But why in particular a bear, a wolf and a snake? In order to answer this question in the absence of all associations on the part of the dreamer, it is necessary to draw on our knowledge of collective psychic material. To begin with the bear. From very ancient times the bear has been used as a symbol of motherhood. It plays a prominent rôle in Greek antiquity, and, choosing from an immense number of examples, I will confine myself to an account of a few specially characteristic ones. The bear plays an important part, for instance, in the cult of Artemis, the goddess most closely associated with the typical functions of the feminine sex: she is the tutelary deity of childbirth and is intimately concerned with the care of children. It was customary for young girls before marriage to bring her as votive offerings their tresses, or jewelry or playthings.[4] Artemis and her priestesses were often represented as she-bears; at an annual initiation ceremony in Athens little girls between five and ten years old performed symbolically the rites of the priestesses of Artemis; they were dressed in bearskins and were known as arktoi or the bears. This cult of the she-bear, referring particularly to the ethical side of maternity, is found in all parts of the ancient world where the cult of the Magna Mater exists.

---

[3] Cf. Jung, *Modern Man in Search of a Soul*, p. 29.
[4] Preller-Robert, *Griechische Mythologie*, 4th edition, Weidmann, Berlin, 1894. Vol. I, p. 319. ·

To mention another instance from quite a different quarter, we may recall the bear goddess Artio of Celtic origin, whose fame is probably perpetuated in the coat of arms of the Swiss town of Berne. Such examples could be multiplied at will. This symbolism is based on the well-known fact of natural history that bear cubs are particularly helpless young animals, and that she-bears are noted for the tender and self-sacrificing care they lavish on their young. In any case, ancient writers such as Pliny and Plutarch lay great stress on this characteristic, and there is no doubt that the she-bear is pre-eminently a mother symbol, a fact fully borne out by much psychological material.

The symbolism of the *wolf* is not quite so straightforward. To begin with, the wolf like the bear represents a mother symbol, but in this case the emphasis is chiefly laid on the maternal instinct as shown in care for the stranger and the outcast, that is, those who are in danger of destruction. The best-known example occurs in Roman mythology where the she-wolf suckles the twin founders of the Eternal City. It is, however, a remarkable fact that the wolf plays a very alarming and uncanny rôle in most other mythologies. Even in Rome the wolf did not always bear a benign aspect. Lupa, or she-wolf, was a common term for harlot, which is the exact antithesis of the maternal aspect of woman. This name for harlot obviously arises from the predatory nature of wolves. To Dante the wolf is the symbol of avarice and of the greed for material possessions.[5] In Greek mythology the wolf, that fierce denizen of dark and wintry forests, personifies devouring plagues, or the "pestilence that walketh in darkness,"[6] and is opposed by the god of light, Apollo, another name for whom is Lykios (from *lykos*, wolf), that is, the god who scares away the prowling wolf from the herds and flocks. In Nordic mythology the wolf plays an especially characteristic part. He is the diabolical inhabitant of the wilderness, he is the Fiend. As such, he has the power of the evil eye. The sinister rôle of the wolf as "werewolf," or wolf-man, a shape much

---

[5] Cf. *Divina Commedia, Inferno* I, 49, *Purgatorio*, XX, 10.

[6] It is interesting that e.g. to the Red Indians of North America the wolf is the representative of the waning or dark moon; it is opposed to the power of light (ci. Krickeberg, *Indianermärchen* aus *Nordamerika*, Diederichs, Jena, 1924. p. 373).

affected by sorcerers and witches, is well known. Echoes of this rôle can still be found in the fairytale of Red Riding Hood.

The strongest expression of the uncanny and destructive nature of the wolf is to be found in the Edda, in the saga of the Fenris wolf. The giantess Angreboda, harbinger of evil, bears to Loki the following three monsters who bring destruction on gods and men: Hel, the goddess of the underworld; Jörmungand, the serpent of Midgard, and most terrible of all the ruthless Fenris wolf. At the end of the world when gods and giants meet in mortal combat, it is the Fenris wolf who swallows the highest god Odin. Together with Hel and the Midgard serpent it is the dangerous adversary of the gods, and as such the symbol of the end of the world.[7] An interesting parallel to the events in our dream is afforded by the fact that in Nordic mythology, immediately after birth, the three monsters Hel, the Midgard serpent and the Fenris wolf rapidly grow to monstrous proportions, just as in the dream the wolf quickly grows into a large and dangerous animal. Another point of similarity is that in the dream the wolf appears closely related to the snake and to its equivalents the primeval worm and the dragon: this is another remarkable parallel to the Nordic myth in which the Fenris wolf and the Midgard serpent are brother and sister. The meaning of the wolf in the dream is clearly connected with its fierce and predatory nature; it represents the dark, uncanny principle of the underworld.

In order fully to grasp the symbolism of the bear, and even more especially of the wolf, one must keep in mind the latter's transformation into the snake. The *snake* is one of the most pregnant symbols of the unconscious, so much so that it often stands for the unconscious itself.

Gerhard Adler, *Studies in Analytical Psychology*, (New York: W. W. Norton & Company, Inc., 1948), pp. 93-100.

---

[7] The wolf plays a similar rôle in the Persian *Avesta*, where it is said that after the victory of Ahuramazda—the good principle—the time of the Wolf will have passed and that of the Lamb is to begin. (Cf. Chantepie de la Saussaye, *Lehrbuch der Religionsgeschichte*, Mohr, Tubingen, 1925, Vol. II, p. 253.)

Marion Woodman

Marion Woodman is a contemporary Canadian Jungian analyst and writer; many of her books explore aspects of the feminine in women and men. Her innovative therapeutic approach integrates analytical psychology, dream work, art, mask making, voice, body work, and forms of movement.

DREAMS AND THE BODY

Here Woodman describes her understanding of dreams, and also warns us to balance our dream work with awareness of the messages from our physical body.

WHAT IS IMPORTANT TO REALIZE is that releasing the body into spontaneous movement or play constellates the unconscious in precisely the same way as does a dream. For this reason, I came to the conclusion that for many of my analysands a body workshop was as necessary as dream analysis. Since most of my analysands were suffering in one way or another from a deep psyche/soma split, I saw that the exclusion of the body in the exploration of the unconscious was at least as one-sided as would be the exclusion of the dream. In its spontaneous movements the body is like an infant crying out to be heard, understood, responded to, much as a dream is sending out signals from the unconscious.

The great advantage of body movement ... is that the individuals involved become participating agents in their own dreaming in ways that are far less apparent when they are asleep or when they are alone. It is therefore easier to work more directly with the waking dream (i.e., body movement) than with the all too easily forgotten sleeping dream, for which the only witness is the dreamer. A dream cannot be verified, cannot participate directly in the concrete waking world. Unlike the body, which does not lie, a dream can be forgotten, half-remembered, reduced to a fragment of itself, or even grossly distorted in the waking re-creation of it. The attempt to make prose sense of a dream subjects the dream to a grammatical logic that may be alien to the symbolic logic of the dreaming state, which is closer to poetry than prose. Although the dream is and will remain our richest source of information from the unconscious, body movement can bring us closer to the actuality of the dream, even as the dream may deepen our understanding of the psychic dimension of the musculature of the body. The two work together because they belong together. The body is the unconscious in its most immediate form and continuous form; the dream is also the unconscious, though as a body of images it lacks both the immediacy and continuity of the physical body.

The unconscious per se is unknowable; it is a reality that is inferred from such things as spontaneous or involuntary body movement and dreams. Ultimately we may come to think of body movement or the dreaming state as a manifestation not of unconsciousness, but as a consciousness that operates upon us and within us. Certainly there are many who believe that what we now think of as the unconscious is equivalent to the traditional concept of God as an unsleeping Being within, an omniscient inner presence. Similarly, I speak of Sophia or the Virgin because they are divine womanly beings associated with the feminine side of God.

THE DEMON LOVER

Many of us remember a stifling or oppressive relationship that we were too bewitched to leave. Woodman gives a vivid description of one cause, and the emotions and dream images that accompany it.

THE GIRL MOST VULNERABLE TO THE DEMON LOVER is the one who adores or fears the idealized father. (If he is absent through divorce, alcoholism or death, her adoration may be even more intense.) Having accepted his anima projection from infancy, she has lived to please him, to share his intellectual pursuits and to meet his standards of perfection. In the dynamics of such a relationship, the mother is experienced either as absent or as a rival. While the daughter experiences herself as the beloved of the father, consciously she knows she dare not share his bed, yet instinctively her energies remain incestuous. Thus her love is split off from her sexuality. In fantasy she dreams of her spiritual lover; in reality, she remains unconscious of her sexuality, acts it out without love, or fears it as some explosive power that can destroy her. She tends to "fall helplessly in love" with a man who cannot marry her and around whom she creates an ideal world in which she is either adored or dramatically rejected. In life, she lives without her body; in dreams, she appears behind glass, or in a plastic bag or glass bottle.

... From her prison, the tiniest details of living take on a mystical beauty. In her aloneness, she fantasizes her emotions, but she has no "I" with which to experience real feeling. Life does not flow through her. Having been filled with her father all her life, she has learned exactly how to mirror a man, but she remains a reflector. . . . She is her father's walking doll, yet sweet and erotic as she unconsciously may be, she has a pseudo-male psychology. Consciously she is a good buddy, a great friend for a man, and as a wife she is capable of sacrificing her life to serve her husband. If he matures, however, he will be bored with her lack of individuality and the ectoplasmic body that surrounds her. He can never quite reach her.

Marion Woodman, *Addiction to Perfection: The Still Unravished Bride* (Toronto: Inner City Books, 1982), pp. 78-79, and p. 135.

James Hillman

James Hillman is an American Jungian-trained psychologist and founder of "archetypal psychology." An expansion of Jungian psychology, archetypal psychology objects to literal and reductionistic views of the human psyche, focuses on the soul and poetic perspectives, and emphasizes access to the soul through the myriad gods, goddesses, and mythic images that shape and are shaped by our psyches.

SOUL MAKING

Hillman's ideas are difficult to convey in short excerpts. But here he suggests some clear and important questions we can all bring to our dreams.

The underlying aspirations of its work archetypal psychology has called "soul-making," taking the phrase from the poets William Blake and, particularly, John Keats: "Call the world if you please, 'The vale of Soul-making,' Then you will find out the use of the world. . . ." For all its emphasis upon the individualized soul, archetypal psychology sets this soul . . . squarely in the midst of the world. . . .

So the question of soul-making is "what does this event, this thing, this moment move in my soul? What does it mean to my death?" The question of death enters because it is in regard to death that the perspective of soul is distinguished most starkly from the perspective of natural life.

. . . the dream is taken as the paradigm of the psyche—where the psyche presents itself encompassing the ego and engaged in its own work (dream-work). From the dream, one may assume that the psyche is fundamentally concerned with its imaginings and only secondarily concerned with subjective experience in the day world which the dream transforms into images, i.e., into soul. The dream is thus making soul each night. Images become the means of translating life events into soul, and this work, aided by the conscious elaboration of imagination, builds an imaginal vessel, or "ship of death" (a phrase taken from D. H. Lawrence), that is similar to the subtle body . . . . The question of the soul's immortality is not directly answered by a metaphysical statement. Rather, the very nature of the soul in the dream—or at least the perspective of soul toward the dream—shows its inattention to and disregard for mortal experience as such, even for physical death itself, receiving into its purview only those faces and events from the mortal world that bear upon the opus of its destiny.

James Hillman, *Archetypal Psychology: A Brief Account* (Dallas: Spring Publications, Inc., 1983), pp. 26-28.

ABANDON ATTEMPTS
TO FIND A DREAM'S WORLDLY USE

In this densely written selection, Hillman radically contends we should not force the dream to fit our waking world, but instead, to interpret a dream, we must see from the perspective of the dream. The approach and ideas are so unique that you might find it helpful to read twice.

FREUD . . . called the dream a royal road, the *via regia* to the unconscious. But because this via regia, in most psychotherapy since his time, has become a straight one-way street of all morning traffic, moving out of the unconscious toward the ego's city, I have chosen to face the other way. Hence my title [*The Dream and the Underworld*], which is a directional signpost for a different one-way movement, let us say vesperal, into the dark. . . .

This little book attempts a different view of the dream from those we are used to. Its thesis does not rely on ideas of repression (Freud) or of compensation (Jung), but imagines dreams in relation with soul and soul with death. I have come to believe that the entire procedure of dream interpretation aiming at more consciousness about living is radically wrong. And I mean *"wrong"* in all its fullness: harmful, twisted, deceptive, inadequate, mistaken, and exegetically insulting to its material, the dream. When we wrong the dream, we wrong the soul . . . .

. . . the dream is made of scraps that belong to the Goddess who makes sacred the waste of life, so that it all counts, it all matters. Offering the dream to "the mysteries of Hekate and the night" (*King Lear*, act 1, scene 1) means giving back the regurgitations that "come up" in dreams without attempts to save them morally or to find their dayworld use. The junk of the soul is primordially saved by Hekate's blessing, and even our trashing ourselves can be led back to her. The messy life is a way of entering her domain and becoming a "child of Hekate." Our part is only to recognize that there is a myth in the mess so as to dispose of the day residues at the proper place, that is, to place them at Hekate's altar. . . .

By locating the dream among these impalpable fundamentals in Hades, we will begin to find that dreams reflect an underworld of essences rather than an underground of root and seed. They present images of being rather than of becoming. We will learn that a dream is less a comment on life and an indication as to where it is growing, than it is a statement from the chthonic depths, the cold, dense, unchanging state—what we so often today call psychopathic because, as Freud saw, the dream does not show morality, human feelings, or the sense of time. We can no longer turn to the dream in hopes of progress, transformation, and rebirth. . . .

What one knows about life may not be relevant for what is below life. What one knows and has done in life may be as irrelevant to the underworld as clothes that adjust us to life and the flesh and bones that the clothes cover. For in the underworld all is stripped away, and life is upside down. We are further than the expectations based on life experience, and the wisdom derived from it. . . .

So, if our therapeutic job is to walk the ego back over the bridge of the dream, to teach the dreamer how to dream, we . . . must reverse our usual procedure of translating the dream into ego-language and instead translate the ego into dream-language. This means doing a dream-work on the ego, making a metaphor of it, seeing through its "reality." Let us then suspend an entire series of ego-operations, the ego-work, the modes by means of which the ego has been approaching the dream and performing its translations. . . .

As the ego sees a set of pejorative factors at work in the dream (regression, distortion, displacement), so the underworld perspective sees a set of pejorative attitudes (humanism, personalism, literalism) at work in the ego. It is these attitudes which must first be suspended before we can approach the dream in an altogether new style.

. . . we imagine that the dream is digesting certain bits and pieces of the day, converting its facts into images. The dream is less a comment on the day than a digestive process of it, a breakdown and assimilation of the dayworld within the labyrinthine tracts of the psyche. The dream-work cooks life events into psychic substance by means of imaginative modes—symbolization, condensation, archaisation. This work takes matters out of life and makes them into soul, at the same time feeding soul each night with new material. . . .

The right work with dreams aids this transferring or dying process that goes on anyway in the dream itself. It is a work that parallels what the dream is already doing. Interpretation, like dreaming, becomes a dying to the dayworld by ruminating it from literal realities into metaphorical realities.

> *Here Hillman has told us to abandon the day-world use of dreams and instead let the dream use us. To look at the dream only intellectually, he says, is to sever its connection to the soul. To foster that connection, we must enter the world of the dream. How can you foster your experience of soul in the dream? What if you speak the words out loud? What if you draw the images with a thick crayon —not to achieve photographic realism, but rather a childlike engagement?*

James Hillman, *The Dream and the Underworld* (New York: Harper & Row, Publishers, 1979), pp. 1-2, pp. 40-41, p. 43, and pp. 95-96.

Arnold Mindell

Trained as a Jungian analyst Arnold Mindell is now known as the developer of "process oriented psychology," which attempts to foster awareness at three levels: concrete (consensus) reality; dream reality; and essential, non-dualistic reality. He currently practices in Oregon.

DREAM AND BODY

Normally dream work is not included in body therapies—probably because of two main factors. The first is that the interpreter may be insufficiently informed about the state of the patient's body. Only when the body's specific condition and the dreamer's individual description of body processes are taken into account is it possible to understand the connection between dreams and body processes.

A second reason for deleting dream work in body therapy may be due to inadequate knowledge of the physiological significance of symbols.... Hence we tend to focus only on the mental or verbalizable contents in dream work. We tend to assume that dreams do not deal with the body unless there are dream images of arms, legs, livers, kidneys, cancers, and bacteria, that is, consciously defined diseases and organs. I now want to present some dreams which include more or less direct references to the body.

A man whom I see very infrequently and hence whose conscious problems therefore remain somewhat foreign to me brought the following dream fragment. It was the end of the world and everyone who was left had to swim for his life. The one chance for survival was to slip through a pipe into the world below. The pipe was narrow, and moving through it involved risk and danger. Nevertheless, he managed to arrive in the underworld and began to swim in the waters there. He associated the word "water" to the fact that he did not like to swim because he had trouble breathing while doing the crawl. To the word "pipe" he associated a shaman's instrument used to catch spirits. The interpretation which grew from these personal associations and which connected with his conscious problems was that he now had to become what he had projected onto the spirit, an unpredictable fluid being. His "spirit catcher" is still too narrow because his relationship to the imaginal world needs development.

Archetypal amplifications to his dream tell us that the end of the world means that his consciousness has now run out of fuel, in part because he—like the people in the Noah's Ark story—has not followed the designs of the creator. A new way of being is pressed upon him. Since this way is water, the old way must have been too dry or rational. The water scene belongs physiologically to the Swadhistana chakra, the second or water center located around the bladder in Indian subtle body theory. Trouble in this chakra means that there are flow problems, blood flow disturbances, menstrual or hormonal difficulties, trouble in passing water, kidney ailments, bladder infections, etc. The inner experience of the water center includes fluidity, depth, and abysmalness which is why the whale or alligator appears in this chakra. The dreamer's spirit-catcher or pipe also appears in subtle body symbolism as the *nadi* or conduit which connects the different centers. If the pipe is too narrow, meditation that increases awareness of this area is indicated.

These archetypal ideas clicked immediately with the dreamer, who reported that he had chosen not to discuss certain physical problems even though they were forcing him into the hospital. He had prostate difficulties and could not urinate. Other dreams gave him specific meditational methods for contacting his body, or the spirit in the body.

> *Mindell, Like Marion Woodman, stresses the importance of including the body in our efforts to connect with the soul, and, like Hillman, Mindell urges us to approach our dreams as if they contain messages from the mysterious and intuitive parts of our psyches. We can take Mindell's cue and ask questions about our dreams as they relate to body. Does the dream remind me of recent physical experiences? If this dream were about my body, what would it be saying? What do I feel in my body as I tell or read the dream?*

Arnold Mindell, *Dreambody: The Body's Role in Revealing the Self* (Boston: Sigo Press, 1982), pp. 193-196. www.aamindell.net & www.processwork.org.

COMPASSION AS INSPIRATION

A man I know told me of a time he was ill and tired during his session with Arnold Mindell. Mindell encouraged him to lie down on the floor, and then Mindell lay down next to him as they continued to talk. Mindell's unusual willingness to join with the client comes through in this interview with Stephan Bodian, American counselor and former editor of Yoga Journal.

STEPHAN: So you don't simply take some technique and apply it. Rather, it comes from within you in the context of love and caring toward others.

ARNOLD: That's right. When you have a compassionate attitude toward people, you automatically start picking up their feedback and responding to it. Someone with a severe inner critic may start out by saying, "I'm hearing inner criticism all the time." So I might say, "Do you want to listen to it right now?" If she says, "No, I hate it. I hear it all the time," I might respond to her negative feedback by saying, "OK, then let's talk about something else." After a while, she may come back to the criticism, and I'll again suggest going into it. If she gives me positive feedback at this point, I'll have her listen to the inner critic for a while, asking who it is, whether it's a man or a woman, her mother or her husband or her boss, etc.

Then she might say, "Oh, my stomach hurts." Now she's switched to the proprioceptive channel. "What does that feel like?" I might ask. "Well, it feels bad." she says, making a fist at the same time. So we focus on the fist, which is a kinesthetic or movement expression of the same process. Then I might have her amplify the fist by making a muscle in her bicep, tightening her neck, and tensing her face. Suddenly she says, "Now I look like my father." "What does he look like?" I ask. "He looks like you!" At this point, I would probably say, "Can't we take this inward? Does it have to be projected outward? Are you really criticizing me? I think you just don't like me."

STEPHAN: Now you're in the relationship channel.

ARNOLD: Exactly. This is what I call "dreaming up," which is relationship work. Then as a therapist I have to look inside myself and see whether a part of me isn't in fact critical of her. There may be, in which case I need to recognize and talk about that part. We may go back and forth until the person realizes that I'm not like her father, but the father-like part is in her.

> *Mindell's fluidity in taking the cue of his client about the direction of their work together is a quality we all would do well to emulate in our dream work. Every dream presents a number of images and possible directions to pursue. It is respectful to trust the dreamer to make the appropriate choices.*
>
> *I believe that Mindell's receptivity simultaneously leads to and derives from the honesty and vulnerability that he demonstrates here. He was willing to talk to a client about ways she didn't like him, and consider ways he might be critical of her. It takes a strong rapport to hold the relationship through that discussion.*
>
> *Mindell also suggests a way to bring the body into dream work. If you made a fist in your dream, does your experience of the dream change if you also make a fist as you tell it? What if you amplify the experience further by assuming the posture of the dream?*

Stephan Bodian, "Field of Dreams: An Interview with Arnold Mindell," *Yoga Journal* (March/April 1990).

D. W. Winnicott

DREAMING VERSUS FANTASY

Winnicott practiced psychoanalysis in the Freudian tradition. His ideas were also shaped by his work with the traumatized children of London during the Second World War. Here Winnicott presents his client's central issue, which is the subject of the therapy, and then relates the client's dreams to that issue.

AS SOON AS THIS PATIENT began to put something into practice, such as to paint or to read, she found the limitations that made her dissatisfied because she had let go of the omnipotence that she retained in the fantasying. This could be referred to in terms of the reality principle* but it is more true, in the case of a patient like this, to speak of the dissociation that was a fact in her personality structure. Insofar as she was healthy and insofar as at certain times she acted like a whole person she was quite capable of dealing with the frustrations that belong to the reality principle. In the ill state, however, no capacity for this was needed because reality was not encountered.

Perhaps this patient's state could be illustrated by two of her dreams. . . .

1. She was in a room with many people and she knew that she was engaged to be married to a slob. She described a man of a kind that she would not in fact like. She turned to her neighbor and said: "That man is the father of my child." In this way, with my help, she informed herself at this late stage in her analysis that she has a child, and she was able to say that the child was about ten years old. In point of fact she has no child, yet she could see from this dream that she has had a child for many years and that the child is growing up. Incidentally this accounted for one of the early remarks she made in the session, which was to ask: "Tell me, do I dress too much like a child, considering that I am middle-aged?" In other words, she was very near to recognizing

---

* [*Winnicott said, "The Reality Principle is the fact of the existence of the world," in his book,* Home is Where We Start From: Essays by a Psychoanalyst.]

that she has to dress for this child as well as for her middle-aged self. She could tell me that the child was a girl.

2. There was a previous dream in a session a week earlier in which she felt intense resentment against her mother (to whom she is potentially devoted) because, as it came in the dream, her mother had deprived her daughter, that is herself, of her own children. She felt it was queer that she had dreamed in this way. She said: "The funny thing is that here I look as if I am wanting a child, whereas in my conscious thought I know that I only think of children as needing protection from being born." She added: "It is as if I have a sneaking feeling that some people do find life not too bad."

Naturally, as in every case, there is a great deal else that could be reported around these dreams which I omit because it would not necessarily throw light on the exact problem that I am examining.

The patient's dream about that man being the father of her child was given without any sense of conviction and without any link with feeling. It was only after the session had lasted an hour and a half that the patient began to reach to feeling. Before she went, at the end of two hours, she had experienced a wave of hate of her mother which had a new quality to it. It was much nearer to murder than to hate and also it felt to her that the hate was much nearer than it had previously been to a specific thing. She could now think that the slob, the father of her child, was put forward as a slob to disguise from her mother that it was her father, her mother's husband, who was the father of her child. This meant that she was very close to the feeling of being murdered by her mother. Here we were indeed dealing with dream and with life, and we were not lost in fantasying.

These two dreams are given to show how material that had formerly been locked in the fixity of fantasying was now becoming released for both dreaming and living, two phenomena that are in many respects the same. In this way the difference between daydreaming and dreaming (which is living) was gradually becoming clearer to the patient, and the patient was gradually becoming able to make the distinction clear to the analyst. It will be observed that creative playing is allied to dreaming and to living but essentially does *not* belong to fantasying. . . .

The patient posed the question: "When I am walking up on that pink cloud, is that my imagination enriching life or is it this thing that you are calling fantasying which happens when I am doing nothing and which makes me feel that I do not exist?"

For me the work of this session had produced an important result. It had taught me that fantasying interferes with action and with life in the real or external world, but much more so it interferes with dream and with the personal or inner psychic reality, the living core of the individual personality.

It could be valuable to look at the subsequent two sessions in this patient's analysis.

The patient started with: "You were talking about the way in which fantasying interferes with dreaming. That night I woke at midnight and there I was hectically cutting out, planning, working on the pattern for a dress. I was all but doing it and was het-up. Is that dreaming or fantasying? I became aware of what it was all about but I was awake."

I found this question difficult because it seemed to be on the borderline in any attempt one might make to differentiate between fantasying and dreaming. There was psychosomatic involvement. I said to the patient: "We don't know, do we!" I said this simply because it was true.

We talked around the subject, how the fantasying is unconstructive and damaging to the patient and makes her feel ill. Certainly working herself up in this way restricts her from action.

Winnicott points out that the dreamer in this session did not begin to attach feeling to her dream until an hour and a half had passed. We, too, can bring this patience to our dreams. If you are having trouble engaging with your dream, ask yourself are you allowing enough time for it to work into your awareness? Or in Hillman's language, are you letting the dream use you?

To Winnicott's suggestion that fantasying can be avoidance, I would add that I have found it helpful to take clients' fantasies as I would dreams, and use them to ask, "What need does this fantasy serve?" For Winnicott's client, a more concrete question might have been, "When did you find yourself traveling to the pink cloud, and what was going on at the time?"

D. W. Winnicott, *Playing and Reality* (London: Routledge, 1971), pp. 30-32.

Viktor Frankl

DREAM, LIBERATION AND HOPE

Viktor Frankl survived the Nazi concentration camps and became a leading voice in existential psychology. He believed that our need to find or create meaning in our activities and life itself is key to fulfillment and joy, and that the meaning we ascribe to events can even tip the balance between living and dying.

I ONCE HAD A DRAMATIC DEMONSTRATION of the close link between the loss of faith in the future and the dangerous giving up. F—, my senior block warden, a fairly well-known composer and librettist, confided in me one day: "I would like to tell you something, doctor. I have had a strange dream. A voice told me that I could wish for something, that I should only say what I wanted to know, and all my questions would be answered. What do you think I asked? That I would like to know when the war would be over for me. You know what I mean, Doctor – for me! I wanted to know when we, when our camp, would be liberated and our suffering come to an end."

"And when did you have this dream?" I asked.

"In February, 1945," he answered. It was then the beginning of March.

"What did your dream voice answer?"

Furtively he whispered to me, "March thirtieth."

When F— told me about his dream, he was still full of hope and convinced that the voice of his dream would be right. But as the promised day drew nearer, the war news which reached our camp made it appear very unlikely that we would be free on the promised date. On March twenty-ninth, F— suddenly became ill and ran a high temperature. On March thirtieth, the day his prophecy had told him that the war and suffering would be over for him, he became delirious and lost consciousness. On March thirty-first, he was dead. To all outward appearances, he had died of typhus.

Those who know how close the connection is between the state of mind of a man – his courage and hope, or lack of them—and the state of immunity of his body will understand that the sudden loss of hope and courage can have a deadly effect. The ultimate cause of my friend's death was that the expected liberation did not come and he was severely disappointed. This suddenly lowered his body's resistance against the latent typhus infection. His faith in the future and his will to live had become paralyzed and his body fell victim to illness—and thus the voice of his dream was right after all.

> *Was the dream prophetic? Were the events literal and without mystery? There is no answer to the question at this time, nor do we need one. Without direct contact with the dreamer, we cannot hope to interpret Frankl's friend's dream, but we can talk about how we might consider such a dream if it were mine or yours. If it were mine, I'd consider all the meanings of the words "liberation," and "free from suffering." Liberation for me may just as well refer to the freedom of mind that Henry David Thoreau referred to when he was jailed; he considered himself freer in spirit than the townspeople walking outside.*
>
> *However you or I might understand the dream of Frankl's friend, we can be moved by the role of the dream in the man's story.*

Viktor Frankl, *Man's Search for Meaning* (New York: Pocket Books, 1985), pp. 96-97.

Clara Hill

Clara Hill is a teacher and researcher in the University of Maryland
Department of Psychology. Her presentation of dream work uses
everyday language and is elegant in its accessibility. She integrates
early and recent approaches in her model of dream interpretation.
Her use of association is similar to the practices of the early developers
of psychoanalysis, but her emphasis on action comes from a recent
behavioral technique that assists us in taking the lessons from dreams
into our daily lives.

   Whether you're working with your own dreams or those of a friend,
try stepping through Hill's stages (which will be described in detail in the
next several excerpts).

A THREE-STAGE MODEL: EXPLORATION, INSIGHT, AND ACTION

THIS DREAM INTERPRETATION MODEL is an integration of Freudian, Jungian, experiential and behavioral theories into a basic three-stage model of therapy proposed by Carkhuff (1969) and Egan (1986). This model assumes that cognitions, experience, insight, and action are all essential components of therapy.

   … The model uses common therapist interventions that work well in either short- or long-term approaches. It is a collaborative model that is based on the premise that only the client has the key to the dream and the therapist's job is to work with him or her to decipher the meaning. I believe that dreams are personal and cannot be interpreted with a dream dictionary or standard symbolic interpretations.

   The dream interpretation model involves three stages: exploration, insight and action. In the Exploration Stage, therapists first ask clients to retell the dream. They then go back through the dream sequentially, with clients first describing each image more thoroughly to reimmerse themselves in the experience of the dream, and then associating (saying whatever comes to mind) to the image. Reimmersing themselves in the dream and associating to the images leads directly to the waking conflicts and the associated memories that caused the dreams to occur. Following the thorough exploration of the images, waking conflicts, and memories, the therapist moves to the Insight Stage, in which the therapist facilitates the client coming to a new understanding of the meaning of the dream. The dream can be understood on several different levels: the dream itself, current waking life, past experiences, or the dream representing parts of oneself. Once the person comes to a new understanding of the dream, the therapist helps the client move to the Action Stage, in which they decide what the client could do differently now that he or she has attained some new self-understanding. Action often arises naturally after exploration and insight but sometimes has to be stimulated by the therapist so that the client does not get stuck in endless experiencing of sterile insight. The action may be related to changing the dream, continued work on the dream, or actual changes in the person's life.

Clara E. Hill, *Working with Dreams Psychotherapy* (New York: Guilford Publications, Inc., 1996), pp. 7-8.

FOUR WAYS TO EXPLORE

Now Clara Hill guides us through the exploration stage of her three-stage model.

THE ACRONYM DRAW can be used to describe the steps we use to help clients explore each major image. The therapist should go through each of the DRAW steps for one image and then move to the next image, with a thorough exploration of each image taking about five minutes. The therapist should be curious and try to learn as much as possible about the client's thoughts and feelings in relation to each image. . . .

DESCRIPTION:

. . . We ask the client to provide a thorough description of the dream image, verbally re-create the scene for us, live inside the image, and give us a tour of the scenery. . . .

T: Tell me about the man with the blond hair.

C: He is cute. I like him in the dream.

T: Tell me more about how he looks in the dream. Paint the picture for me so that I can see him through your eyes.

C: He has the 70's style feathered hair look. He has bad skin and pronounced features. He isn't much taller than me. . . .

RE-EXPERIENCING:

Therapists should always be alert for opportunities to help the client talk about and experience feelings because of the importance of getting the client maximally involved in the dream affect. For each image, therapists want clients to focus on what they are feeling at that moment in the dream so that the feelings become more immediate, real, and significant for the client. Therapists typically ask open questions to probe for the feelings (e.g., "What are you feeling at this moment in the dream?") and then follow up with reflections of feelings (e.g., "You sound a bit pensive as you talk") to help clarify the feelings as well as expand on and deepen the feelings. . . .

T: What are you feeling at this moment in the dream when you see this man?

C: I'm attracted to him.

T: How are you feeling, though?

C: I think I'm happy. I'm certainly curious.

T: You sound a bit apprehensive as you talk about it. . . .

ASSOCIATIONS:

Gathering associations to the image is a very important part of the exploration stage, because it provides clues for what the image is related to. Therapists cannot assume that they know the meaning of images for clients . . . . Rather, they want to help clients search their memory banks for what the images mean. . . .

It is not possible to know which associations are going to be crucial ones for helping the client construct an understanding about the dream, so therapists need to go for as much depth as possible for the five to ten chosen images, hoping to stimulate recollections of critical issues for the client....

WAKING LIFE TRIGGERS:

We assume that each image is connected to some issue in waking life (past, present, or future), so we ask the client to explore possible waking life triggers to each image. The therapist should ask for waking life triggers for the *particular* image rather than for what might have triggered the whole dream, because he or she is still focused on the individual image and is gathering the building blocks to use in constructing meaning for the whole dream in the insight stage....

T: What might have triggered the image of your mother at this particular time?

C: My mother is a constant presence in my life. We are changing roles right now from her being the mother to my taking care of her more. She wants me to take care of all the business matters. And she gets much too intrusive in my love life.

T: Tell me more about that.

C: She just recently asked me if I had met anyone yet. She really wants me to get married ...

CONSTRUCT MEANING

In the insight stage, the therapist assists the dreamer in finding meaning in the dream. Clara Hill describes a collaborative process in which the therapist is constantly aware of the experience, needs, and expertise of the dreamer in divining his or her own dream. If you are working with your own dream, ask your waking mind to bring the same respect to your dream as would Clara Hill. Try asking questions and wait for the feeling sense to tell you that the meaning you find fits your dream.

I BELIEVE THAT THE THERAPIST AND CLIENT work together to develop or create the meaning that makes the most sense at the moment, given the information that they have at hand. . . .

Listening to the client's initial interpretation can also provide clues as to the appropriate level of interpretation for the client. If the initial interpretation is about an intense fantasy-type experience (e.g., flying), the therapist might aim for the experiential level. If the initial interpretation closely reflects waking life (e.g., concern about an upcoming presentation), the therapist has a clue that it would be important to start with the waking life level. If the initial interpretation seems more related to deep-seated personality conflicts or existential concerns, the therapist might orient the subsequent work toward looking at inner conflicts. . . .

Reik (1935) wrote that the meaning of the dream should come as a surprise to both the client and therapist, and I heartily agree. The key is to recognize that the client is an expert on him- or herself. The therapist, rather than stating what the dream means, can say something like, "I wonder if it might mean . . ." and encourage the client to modify and correct the meaning. By working together, therapists and clients can often construct a better interpretation than either could alone. The client is ultimately the arbiter of the meaning of the dream, so the therapist needs to listen very attentively for client disagreement or feelings of being misunderstood. . . .

Another method that works well comes from Ullman (1979, 1987, 1993; Ullman & Zimmerman, 1979). The therapist says something like, "If it were my dream, it might mean. . ." In this way, the therapist owns that the interpretation may be a projection and hence may not be accurate or work for the client. Clients often feel more permission to refute an interpretation phrased tentatively (e.g., "No, it's not quite that; it's more. . .") than if the therapist states "the" meaning. . . .

Another issue to note is that it is wonderful and exhilarating for therapists and clients when clients have breakthrough "aha" insight experiences . . . . However, not all clients, not even those who are psychologically minded, have breakthrough insights during every dream session. . . .

Whatever comes out, comes out. Therapists should not keep pushing for more insight after a certain amount of concerted effort (i.e., 15-20 min) but should go on to the action stage.

ACT ON INSIGHTS

THE PURPOSE OF THE ACTION STAGE is for therapists to help clients extend what they have learned during the previous stages to thinking about changes that they might want to make in waking life. Some clients spontaneously move to action after the insight stage. For example, one client had a dream in which she was wearing a see-through dress while walking down a dark alley in a bad section of town. By going through the insight stage, she recognized that she was engaging in some risky behaviors because of some self-destructive tendencies. She thought she had worked through these self-defeating attitudes but realized that they had come up again as she was becoming involved in a new relationship. She saw the dream as a message that she needed to be more careful in how she dressed, where she went, and with whom she got involved. She did not need the therapist's guidance to move her along to the action stage because her insight led her directly to want to change her behavior. . . .

Other clients, however, need more help . . . .

The action stage can begin with the therapist asking the client to change the dream or create a sequel to the dream (i.e., continue the dream and give it a different ending). Because the client created the dream initially, she or he can change it or extend it. Encouraging clients to change dreams is important for three reasons. First, the task emphasizes that clients are the creators and directors of their dreams and can change their dreams, which can facilitate a sense of empowerment for the client. By realizing that they are not passive recipients of their dreams but rather are active players, clients can learn to take more responsibility for themselves. Second, making changes in the dream is often a fun and creative way to get the client started in thinking about making changes and can lead to specific behavioral changes.

Third, hearing what clients say about changing their dreams allows therapists an opportunity to assess readiness for change. Some clients immediately gravitate toward the idea of changing the dream, whereas others resist changing the dream because it seems silly or irrelevant. If clients act helpless and cannot change their dreams, chances are that they are not going to be willing to make changes in their lives. However, if clients readily think about changes that they could make in their dreams, they are more likely to be willing to make changes in their lives....

T: If you could change the dream in any way, how would you change it?

C: There wouldn't be a snake in it.

T: Why not?

C: It feels like the snake is restricting me ....

C: I don't like being so paralyzed by this stupid snake. It's my room. I want to feel more comfortable there.

T: What would you like to do?

C: I'd like to tell my roommate that she can't have a snake in the room.

T: Go ahead and tell her....

The therapist can choose to help the client explore how changes in the dream parallel actual changes the client wants to make in his or her life. For example, if a client wants to change his or her behavior in the dream to be more assertive with male authorities, the therapist might conduct some assertiveness training with the client and practice specific situations in which the client could be more assertive. Clients often lack specific skills for making changes, so therapists can use behavioral techniques (e.g., behavioral rehearsal, feedback, reinforcement) to help clients learn how to behave differently....

T: Let's translate the changes that you made to the dream into how you would change things in your waking life. The first thing you said was there wouldn't be a snake. The snake represents restricting you, trapping you. So how would you translate that? So there's something restricting or trapping you.

C: Saying what's on my mind to my roommate about what a slob she is.

T: How would you do that?

C: Being more aggressive.

T: What would that be like for you?

C: It would be very different.

T: Is it something that would be easy or difficult?

C: Very difficult. I save everything up, and then I'm just furious and blow up.

T: It sounds like you're so worked up at that point, there's no choice. . . .

T: How would you like it to be?

C: Not as confrontational, not as angry. Just talk it out. Say it sooner. . . .

Clara E. Hill, *Dream Work in Psychotherapy*, ed. Clara E. Hill (Washington D.C.: American Psychological Association, 2004) pp. 26-34, pp. 41-60, and pp. 71-81.

Kristin Heaton

DEFUSING NIGHTMARES

Kristin Heaton is a psychologist with the U.S. Army in Massachusetts. Here she integrates research on helping people with nightmares with Clara Hill's approach to dreams (see p. 53).

In general, nightmares fall into one of two broad categories: (a) non-recurrent (unique each time it occurs) or (b) recurrent (with at least part of the nightmare repeated over time). Evidence from sleep laboratory studies and other research has suggested that both recurrent and non-recurrent nightmares tend to occur late in the sleep cycle, often during REM sleep, and are generally characterized by the absence of gross motor movements (see Hartmnan, 1984; Hobson, 1998; Solms, 1997). However, nightmares have been reported during non-REM sleep across the entire sleep cycle, particularly for nightmares that occur after traumatic waking life experiences (e.g., Hartmann, 1984; Ross et al., 1994b). Some recurrent nightmares also have been associated with movements of large muscle groups, especially in people diagnosed with PTSD (e.g., Ross et al., 1994a) and REM behavior sleep disorder (e.g., Olson, Boeve, & Silber, 2000). . . .

Treatment approaches that address nightmares, either as a discrete entity or as a symptom of a specific disorder, have been developed primarily from psychoanalytic-psychodynamic, behavioral, and cognitive-behavioral perspectives. However, most empirical investigations of nightmare-focused treatments have emerged from the cognitive-behavioral literature and have involved imagery rehearsal (e.g., Krakow et al., 2001), eye movement desensitization and reprocessing (e.g., Silver, Brooks & Obenchain, 1995), and other exposure-based treatments (e.g., Burgess, Gill & Marks, 1998).

Another method of working with dreams in therapy, the Hill cognitive-experiential approach, has received considerable empirical attention over the last ten years . . . . Although this method has been used with a wide variety of dreams, research has only begun to document its use specifically with nightmares. . . .

The goals of dream work using the Hill approach are the same for all clients, regardless of the valence (pleasantness) of their dreams. These goals include collaborating with clients to develop a deeper, more complete understanding of the dream or nightmare, helping clients use this understanding to inform and clarify problems in daily lives, and helping clients use what they have learned about the dream or nightmare and themselves to develop clear, realistic plans for cognitive or behavioral change.

In the case of nightmares, clinical experience indicates that the pace of work tends to be slower and is met with greater client resistance and emotional distress than when working with more pleasant dreams. Research has suggested that nightmares have been associated with central conflicts and fears or traumatic events in the dreamer's life . . . .

The inherent flexibility of the Hill approach makes this model well suited to working with nightmares in therapy. In our work with nightmares, my colleagues and I (a) incorporate several techniques from the trauma literature (e.g., imagery rehearsal, grounding) into the treatment process, (b) explore a single nightmare in two or more sessions, (c) allow a full 90 minutes for each session, and (d) complete the full three-stage model in each session. We believe that by using the Hill method in this manner, therapists enable clients to work with their nightmares in a safe and manageable way, develop a sense of mastery over their nightmares, and have time to create and refine plans for using new insights and understandings to effect meaningful change in their lives....

> For a description of imagery rehearsal therapy, see p. 63.
>
> Perhaps it is too much to ask of yourself to work alone with your own nightmare. Is there someone who will accompany you as you try using Hill's exploration, insight, and action stages on your nightmare? See also page 26 for Marie-Louise von Franz's comments on dying in a dream.

Kristin J. Heaton, "Working with Nightmares," *Dream Work in Psychotherapy*, ed. Clara E. Hill (Washington D.C.: American Psychological Association, 2004) pp. 204-207.

Gary Tucker

NIGHTMARES & PTSD TREATMENT WITH IMAGERY REHEARSAL THERAPY

As editor of Journal Watch Psychiatry, *Gary Tucker summarized research for physicians. In the following selection he summarizes research done with women survivors of sexual violence who suffered from post-traumatic stress disorder (PTSD) and nightmares, but this approach to dream work is applicable more generally. You could try this practical intervention for your own nightmares.*

RECURRENT NIGHTMARES are common in patients with post-traumatic stress disorder (PTSD), but rarely are nightmares treated directly. These researchers randomized 168 women with chronic nightmares and DSM-IIIR-diagnosed PTSD to receive imagery rehearsal therapy (IRT) or to be placed on a wait list (control group). Of the participants, 79 percent were receiving concurrent psychotherapeutic or pharmacologic treatment.

Initially, the IRT sessions (two 3-hour group sessions a week apart plus 1 hour of follow-up 3 weeks later) provided participants with information about nightmares associated with traumatic experiences. Participants were taught methods of developing pleasant imagery and drawing on old nightmare images to slowly create a new dream, which they were instructed to rehearse 5 to 20 minutes per day. Standardized interviews and self-reports conducted 3 and 6 months afterwards showed that the treatment significantly decreased the weekly incidence of nights with nightmares and the weekly number of nightmares per week. Treatment also was associated with improved sleep and fewer PTSD symptoms compared with the wait-list status. Improvement in these measures was not associated with any concomitant treatment.

Comment: Although the use of wait-listed participants as controls may have exaggerated the differences between groups, the effectiveness of this intervention in both reducing bothersome nightmares and improving other PTSD symptoms is remarkable. Decreased PTSD symptoms, however, could also be related to improved sleep. The effectiveness of this therapy may have implications for psychotherapeutic techniques that rely on dream interpretation: The content of nightmares—and dreams—apparently can be manipulated and changed by continual rehearsal.

The research Tucker summarized was published by Barry Krakow in the Journal of the American Medical Association. *Krakow went on to describe the process of imagery rehearsal therapy. Participants first practiced holding pleasant imagery in their minds. They were then asked to write down a nightmare as they had dreamed it, then rewrite it with any changes they wished to make. Finally, they spent 10-15 minutes using imagery to mentally "rehearse" the changed dream. They were asked to rehearse new dreams for at least 5-20 minutes a day but not to rehearse more than 2 new dreams a week.*

Gary Tucker, "Controlling Nightmares with Image Rehearsal Therapy," *Journal Watch Psychiatry*, no. 7 (September 5, 2001): p. 77. Summary of Barry Krakow, et al., "Imagery Rehearsal Therapy for Chronic Nightmares in Sexual Assault Survivors With Posttraumatic Stress Disorder," *Journal of the American Medical Association*, 2001; 286:537-545.

Walter Bonime

Walter Bonime trained psychiatrists and psychoanalysts in New York. His book, renowned for its practical (clinical) approach and absence of theoretical discussion, addresses the role of action, feelings, setting (surrounding), and the characters in dreams. Excerpts of his ideas on dream action and setting are shown in the next two selections.

ACTION

IN EVERYTHING with which both therapy and dreams are concerned, process is invariably present or inherent. The action of the dream (although not the action alone) symbolizes part of the total living process of the patient. Although only fragments of a dream may be preserved, although the dream may be no more than a flash, a tableau, a sensation, a sound, a word or a pain, process is implied.

Throughout analysis the question is always present: What kinds of movement or movements describe the patient? Are these parallel, coordinated, or conflicting movements? What is the direction, the intensity? What is the nature of his thinking activity, his feeling activity, his behavior toward other people and behavior in response to them? Is pathology disappearing or merely moving into obscurity? Is new pathology developing or an old pathology moving into view? Is health evolving or is the patient struggling against change? Are both occurring? Is he working with the analyst or blocking him? Or is he involved in both processes? These are the problems of movement in therapy and these are the processes that are reflected and may be emphasized by the action in dreams. . . .

In . . . [a] dream a patient digs a small irrigation channel in the garden which in part represents her marital relationship. . . . This action in the dream corresponds with efforts to enrich her marriage with more open and spontaneous feelings. But suddenly in the same dream a "deluge" rises up out of the channel and she runs away. A new and conflicting type of action, running away, appears in the dream, corresponding to her anxious evasion of spontaneous expression of emotion in her marriage.

To explore the role of action in your own dream, look at the changes that occur before and after new actions are taken.

SETTING

THE SURROUNDINGS IN THE DREAM are significant to the extent they make contributions to the identity and meaning of the other dream elements—action, individuals, and feeling. The surroundings include not only the places in which action occurs and where individuals are but also all the components of nature and all the products of civilization and any realistic or unrealistic synthesis or abstraction or fragment of them which is not identifiable in the dream as any of the other elements. . . .

The terrifying height and sheer face of a mountain wall as a part of the surroundings served in a patient's dream to accentuate anxiety, the feeling element. In addition, it identified by its form the wall of an excavation for a swimming pool that was under construction at the patient's suburban home. The pool project had become a source of tension between the patient and his wife. The wall thus pointed toward the marital milieu of the problem, toward the focal item (the pool), and in addition contributed through these factors to the identification of an individual (the wife) who otherwise appeared in the dream only in obscure form.

Does the setting in a dream of yours remind you of a period of your life (past or present), or a place that has a significant role (home, work, play) in your life?

Walter Bonime, *The Clinical Use of Dreams* (New York: Basic Books, Inc., 1962), pp. 2-3, and pp. 8-9.

Eugene Gendlin

A philosopher with interest in phenomenology and a practicing psychologist, Eugene Gendlin collaborated with client-centered-psychology pioneer Carl Rogers. Here he presents a list of questions to take to your dreams, although he makes clear (in guidelines I've not reprinted here) that it isn't necessary to apply all the questions to one dream. Just start with one question and follow from there. He further suggests that the dreamer ask the questions of the body—that is feel the answer not just as an intellectual exercise, but as a physical sensation. When asking the body, don't rush it; stay with the body feeling.

I've broken Gendlin's excerpt into three selections so you can have an opportunity to try some of the ideas in your own dream work before moving on, if you so choose. The first 9 of Gendlin's 16 questions are included in the first selection, and the second has the rest. In the third selection Gendlin shows us how to work with the biases we bring to our dream interpretation.

[Except for the standard centered and underlined headings and, my prefatory remarks in the Bias selection, the typography (including capitalization, boldface, and italics) is Gendlin's, not mine.]

ASSOCIATIONS, STORY, AND CHARACTER

1. WHAT COMES TO YOU?
   What are your associations in relation to the dream?
   What comes to mind as you think about the dream?
   Or pick a part of the dream. What comes to you in relation to that?
2. FEELING?
   What did you feel in the dream?

Sense the feel-quality of the dream. Let it come back as fully as possible.

Choose the most puzzling, oddest, most striking, or most beautiful part of the dream. Picture it to yourself and let a felt sense of it come in your body.

Or pick one part of the dream.

Then ask: What in your life feels like that?

Or: What does this feel-quality remind you of? When did you ever feel like that?

Or: What is new for you in that felt sense?

3. YESTERDAY?

What did you do yesterday? Scan your memory of yesterday. Also recall what you were inwardly preoccupied with.

Something related to the dream may come up.

Questions #1, #2, and #3 offer three ways to get associations. . . .

4. PLACE?

Visualize and sense the lay-out of the main place in your dream.

What does it remind you of?

Where have you been in a place like that?

What place felt like that?

5. STORY?

First summarize the story-plot of the dream. Then ask yourself: What in your life is like that story?

Summarize the events of the dream in two or three steps: "first . . . and then . . . and then . . ." Make it more general than the dream. . . .

Example: Crossing the River Dream

I had to cross this river, there was no way across, then I saw a bridge further down but when I got there it was only to an island in the river.

The story-summary might be: "First there seems to be no way, then there is one, but only part way. What in your life is like that?"

Or: "First you're discouraged, then it's better but not all O.K. What in your life is like that?" ...

6. CHARACTERS?

Take the unknown person in your dream. Or, if you know them all, take the most important. (Or take them up in turn.)

What does this person remind you of? What physical feel-quality does this person in the dream give you?

Even a person whom you didn't see clearly may give you a bodily sensed quality.

With familiar people: Did the person look as usual?

Questions #4, #5, and #6 can be remembered together as Place, Story, and Characters. . . .

7. WHAT PART OF YOU IS THAT?

According to some theories, the other people in your dreams are parts of you. We aren't sure that's true, but try it out:

What feel-quality does this person give you? What sense comes in your body? You needn't name it, just have it.

If no quality comes, ask yourself: What is one adjective I could use for that person?

Now think of that adjective or feel-quality as a part of you. If that is a part of you, what part would that be?

You may or may not like this part of you, or know much about it. But let it be here for the moment, anyway.

Does the dream make sense, if you take it as a story about how you relate to that part of you? ...

8. BE THAT PERSON?

Stand up or sit forward on the edge of the chair. *Loosen your body.* Now imagine that you are preparing to act in a play. The play is tomorrow. Now you are just getting ready, feeling yourself into the role. You are going to play that character from the dream. *Let the feel-quality of being that person come in your body.*

You can actually do this now, or just imagine it, but *be sure to do it in your body.*

How would you walk on stage? With a stomp, or stiffly, or how? How would you stand or sit? How would your shoulders be? Don't decide. Let your body do it of its own accord. . . .

9. CAN THE DREAM CONTINUE?

Vividly visualize the end, or any one important scene of the dream. Feel it again. When it comes back as fully as possible, just watch it and wait for something further to happen.

Wait for it, don't invent anything.

Later: What impulse do you have, if any, to do something back at the image once it has done something of its own accord? . . .

Questions #7, #8, and #9, can be remembered as three ways to work further with the characters. . . .

DECODING AND DEVELOPMENT

THE NEXT THREE QUESTIONS ARE ABOUT DECODING:

10. SYMBOLS?

What is that kind of thing anyway?

Some people think there are common symbols. Others don't agree. Try this out, and see if it opens something in this dream. What does some object in your dream "stand for"?

Take one of the main things in your dream, and ask: What is such a thing?

What is it used for? Say the obvious.

Examples:

A bridge: it crosses from one side to the other

A river: it is a natural barrier

A policeman: an enforcer of the law

A letter: it brings a message

A tractor: it is used to plow the earth

A car: it goes somewhere

A train: it transports and can take you somewhere, but you don't control its moving

Baggage: your clothes as well as what you take with you

Then substitute that into the story of the dream. . . .

11. BODY ANALOGY? ESPECIALLY: HIGH, LOW, AND UNDER

Something in a dream may be an analogy for the body. For example, a long object may be a penis, a purse may stand for a vagina. The car may be your sexual activity. A house may be your body.

Does this fit? The attic or other high place can mean thought, being in your head, far from feelings.

Downstairs, ground level, can mean feelings, being in your body lower down, grounded.

The basement, underground, or underwater can mean the unconscious, or what is not visible.

Odd-looking machines and diagrams often make sense if viewed as body analogies.

12. COUNTERFACTUAL?

What in the dream is specifically different from the actual situation?

Exactly what has the dream changed?

Example: Wall Dream

A wall (which isn't really there) ran the whole length of my apartment, dividing it in two long halves.

If the dream went out of its way to change the situation in just certain respects, ask: Why would it make just these changes?

Or: Does the dream picture something different in value, opposite from how you evaluate it in waking life? Does someone you think of as stupid appear unusually large and impressive in the dream? Is someone pictured small, silly, or disheveled whom you in fact admire? Is something you consider worthless represented as hauntingly beautiful? See if the dream "corrects" your waking attitude. If so, try out a more moderate attitude in between. . . .

Questions #10, #11, #12, are three decodings: Symbols, Analogy, and Counterfactual. . . .

13. CHILDHOOD?

What childhood memory might come in relation to the dream?

If you think of your childhood, what comes?

In your childhood, what had this feel-quality from the dream?

What went on in your life at that time? What was it like for you?

14. PERSONAL GROWTH?

How are you developing, or trying to develop?

What do you struggle with or wish you could be or do?

In what way are you a one-sided, not a well-rounded, person? Could the dream or the characters in it represent what you still need to develop?

Suppose the dream were a story about that? What might it mean?

15. SEXUALITY?

Try the dream out as a story about whatever you are currently doing or feeling about sexuality.

Or: If it were a story about your ways of being sexual, what would it be saying?

16. SPIRITUALITY

What creative or spiritual potential of yours might the dream be about?

Are there dimensions of being human in the dream that you don't take much account of in your life? . . .

BIASES

Gendlin warns us that our first impulse in interpreting our own dream is to bring to it all the biases of our waking mind. To control for these biases, he suggests a brilliant technique of postulating the opposite interpretation, action and character.

He believes that no matter how scary they are when we dream them, dreams are always "friendly," pointing toward growth. From the example below, we can see that he finds a useful and positive message in the root of a nightmarish image.

Mountain Cabin Dream

I was up in the mountains with Sandy. *She was in a cabin that stood all alone, further down. I was walking toward it. From behind me a man came with a knife. I knew he was dangerous. I was hoping to reach the house before he got there, but he started running. He ran past me, toward the cabin. I woke up.*

"I can feel that that's my anger at Sandy. I'm scared it will get out of control I guess. I am scared it will get to Sandy and I won't be able to stop it. It will break us up. I can feel that the dream is a warning to me about blowing up at her."

This example is typical of how people interpret their own dreams. It is very natural with one's own dream. And such an interpretation fits convincingly. He is probably right that the dream is (at least partly) about that. He can sense that it is about his anger which threatens to blow. But he interprets the dream in the same way that he views the situation. He controls his anger. Resentful remarks slip by him, and he wishes he could stop those too. He thinks the dream warns him not to blow up and break the relationship. After the dream he feels no different than before.

His interpretation was, "The dream is warning me about blowing up at her."

His reaction *in* the dream is the same as his reaction *to* the dream. He runs away from the man with the knife and wants to keep him away from Sandy.

Now he applies Part 1 of the BIAS CONTROL, as he makes room for an opposite interpretation.

a) "The opposite of my interpretation? It would be that I ought to blow up at her, maybe end the relationship."

b) "The opposite of my action in the dream-story? I guess I would turn and fight him, or check him out."

c) "What character or thing is most opposite to me in the dream? Well, that guy, of course. What characteristic of his is most opposite to me? Violence. I've never wielded a knife. It's not like me. I never hit anybody."

"So the opposites in a, b, and c come to the same thing: anger, violence, I guess. I'm supposed to stay open to something I need in this. The character has too much of it. Could I try saying I need some of that in a different form?"

Now, notice: It isn't too hard to think this far, but then it's a struggle to keep that open!

His thought: "Sure, there might be some mature form of anger or aggressiveness that I could use more of. But the way my anger is, it's no good. The dream can't be telling me to let that anger loose. It's immature, resentful, and destructive. I have lots of that, I don't need more. I say things to Sandy because I feel resentful. It makes our interaction bad, and then I feel bad. And the dream warns me that it could all blow up."

Here he got right back to his first interpretation. That happened because he tried accepting the simple opposite (letting his anger loose). He forgot that the point of the BIAS CONTROL is not to adopt the opposite but to stay open in that direction.

The growth step is not violence or breaking up with Sandy. Nor will it be the simple opposite of controlling his anger.

We won't make the mistake of asking: Who is right, he, himself, in the dream, or the man with the knife? Neither is likely to be just right.

We expect a *new step from the anger side, a better way than he now knows. Something like that. For example, he might stand his ground more often, become more confident, express more bad and good feelings. Who knows? He needs to leave it blank.*

Eugene Gendlin, *Let Your Body Interpret Your Dreams*, (Wilmette, IL: Chiron Publications, 1986) pp. 9-17, and pp. 73-75.

Stanley Krippner

LUCID DREAMS

Stanley Krippner is an American professor of psychology and a writer who has conducted seminars on dreams in countries around the world. Here he discusses lucid dreaming: becoming aware of the dream while dreaming, and sometimes controlling the dream content.

RESEARCH

IN 1978, KEITH HEARNE (a British investigator) and Stephen LaBerge independently discovered that lucid dreamers could communicate with the outside world by moving their eyes, clenching their fist muscles, or flexing their arm muscles in a predetermined pattern during a lucid dream. During REM sleep, there are the "phasic" period when the muscles, especially those around the eyes, are more active, and the "tonic" period, which is more placid. Most lucid dreams appear to take place in the phasic portion. Some lucid dreams occur in non-REM sleep. Furthermore, the events experienced in lucid dreams produce effects in the brain and the body that are remarkably similar to those that would be produced if the events were experienced while awake. . . .

Although lucid dreams are fairly common phenomena, research studies indicate that people who are frequent dream recallers have more lucid dreams. Meditators tend to have more lucid dreams than non-meditators, as do individuals who have somewhat androgynous gender role identities. People who have a better sense of balance tend to have more lucid dreams.

Frequent lucid dreamers also tend to be "field independent" on personality tests, that is, they do not need to rely on context to move about in physical or psychological space. Field independence can be of great assistance in lucid dreaming, since a person who can stand back from the events of the dream has a better chance of being able to realize the actual nature of the events than one who is fully embroiled in the plot.

When lucid dreams and ordinary dreams are compared, lucid dreams tend to occur more frequently in the early morning. In addition, lucid dreams contain more auditory and kinesthetic imagery. Most dreams are basically visual in nature and involve considerable movement, probably because the visual-motor cortex of the brain is stimulated during REM sleep. In lucid dreams, there is more conversation, but fewer dream characters. In one study, ordinary dreams had happier and more successful endings than lucid dreams. However, in most comparisons, lucid and ordinary dreams were similar despite individual differences.

Pierre Weil, a French-Brazilian psychologist, has written a fascinating account of his study of "dream yoga" with a Tibetan lama. By practicing various types of meditation, visualization, and breathing during wakefulness, Weil was able to attain lucidity in his dreams. Weil kept a dream diary in which he recalled his dreams each morning. Not only did he have more lucid dreams during the three years he studied with the lama, but also he recalled more dreams in general. However, once his studies stopped, so did his dream recall and his dream lucidity. For example, in 1983, Weil recorded nineteen lucid dreams; he recorded thirty-seven in 1984 and thirty-one in 1985. During the two years following the end of his work with the lama, his dream lucidity dropped to zero. He was still able to recall dreams, but at a lower frequency than before. Nevertheless, Weil felt that the work was worthwhile, and that he had been able to incorporate the elements of lucidity into his daily life.

Many lucid dreamers report spiritual experiences in lucid dreaming. Scott Sparrow, author of *Lucid Dreaming: Dawning of the Clear Light*, reported a lucid dream that changed the direction of his life. After becoming lucid in a dream, he wrote: "I stand outside a small building that has large black double-doors on its eastern side. I approach them to enter. As soon as I open them, a brilliant white light hits me in the face. Immediately I am filled with intense feelings of love."

Fariba Bogzaran's study, "Experiencing the Divine in Lucid Dreaming State," showed that the mere intention of wanting to have a spiritual experience in lucid dreaming can actually lead to such experiences. Incubation and intention prior to sleep are the two most important elements in cultivating spiritual experiences in lucid dreaming. Transpersonal experiences in lucid dreaming vary with each individual; however, there are common reports of visiting one's spiritual teacher or contacting spiritual figures who appear in a personalized form. Also, there are reports of spiritual encounters with white light or dark light, geometric shapes, non-representational forms, unrecognizable images and events, and multidimensional spaces during the lucid dream.

George Gillespie, author and a lucid dream explorer, has experimented and reported several transpersonal experiences in his own lucid dreams. He describes in detail powerful imagery and mystical experiences that occur while he is lucid in his dreams. Sometimes he sees "light patterns, with color and movement." At other times, he has encountered "disks of light," which often appear in the shape of a moon or planet, either stationary or moving. If he can lose the sensation of his dreaming body, he may enter a state that he calls "total elimination of objects of consciousness."

Gillespie also describes his encounters with "the Light," which he claims appears only in his lucid dreams. Often the Light appears while he is in darkness or engaged in some religious activity. The experience of the Light, according to Gillespie, is a moment of bliss and joy, or "union with the spiritual world."

For their book, *Control Your Dreams*, Jayne Gackenbach and Jane Bosveld interviewed a professor of physics and long-time practitioner of transcendental meditation. In the interview the professor, who preferred to remain anonymous, explained five stages from lucidity to witnessing. These five stages, similar to those in a categorization Gillespie set up, start with awareness of dreams and images as something outside the self, then proceed to recognizing that the images are inside the dreamer. The last stage is the entrance into the transcendental state, which is referred to as "pure consciousness."

In this state, the professor claims that he encounters forms not seen in a non-lucid dream. "They will be much more abstract and have no sensory aspects to them, no mental images, no emotional feelings, no sense of body or space. There is a quality of unboundedness to them. One experiences oneself to be a part of a tremendous composite of relationships."

Another of Bogzaran's studies, "Images of the Lucid Mind," suggests that when one moves from ordinary lucid dreaming to a multidimensional dream, images slowly transform into more abstract patterns such as light lines or energy lines, spheres, dots, and circles. In this state of consciousness that she calls "hyperspace lucidity" lucid dreamers often experience the transformation of their dream bodies into particles of light, or the dream body slowly or suddenly disappears but awareness continues.

KEELIN'S DREAM

After two weeks of attempting to incubate a spiritual dream, Keelin experienced the following dream during which she became lucid:

> I become aware of being in a vast limitless darkness that is at the same time brilliant with countless stars and very much alive. Something emerges from darkness. It looks like some kind of living, molecular model/mathematical equation—extremely complex, three-dimensional, fluorescent, neon-orange in color—very thin lines, very clear and sharp visually. It seems to unfold itself, multiplying, constantly changing, forming more complex structures and inter-relationships. It is filling up the Universe. This growing movement is not erratic, but consistent and purposeful—rapid but at the same time determined. . . . This is the best way I can describe the space. It is rapid, yet there is a feeling that the knowledge or reality of it already exists, or that it is being born, exists in its entirety and visually manifest all in the same one moment.

When Keelin awoke from this dream, she experienced a tingling sensation throughout her body. She described the sensation as the opening of the energy centers in her body. She referred to this experience as a powerful and transformative experience of her life.

WORKING WITH LUCID DREAMS

THERE ARE MANY WAYS TO ENHANCE DREAM LUCIDITY, but one of the simplest methods is to pay attention to every dream. The more dreams that are recalled, the more likely one is to remember an occasional lucid dream. Self-suggestion will often enhance lucidity in dreams. Before going to sleep at night, simply repeat this suggestion: "Tonight I will become aware that I am dreaming and will remember that dream when I wake up." Repeat this suggestion twenty or thirty times; do not be discouraged if it is not effective immediately, as this technique rarely works during its first few applications.

Carlos Castaneda wrote that his purported mentor, the Yaqui sorcerer don Juan Matus, had instructed him in lucid dreaming. Before sleep, Castaneda was told to place his hands in front of his gaze. Eventually, he reported that he had found his hands in a dream and had lifted them to the level of his eyes. At this point he realized that he was dreaming. Castaneda used this technique of looking for his hands in his dreams to become lucid on a regular basis. From this vantage point he claimed to be able to perform wondrous feats.

Several years earlier, Kilton Stewart claimed that the Senoi tribal people in the Malay peninsula had developed dream lucidity; when they encountered a terrifying creature or situation in their dream, they would become lucid, would face their fear directly, and either conquer it, make friends with it, or surrender to it. The consensus of contemporary anthropologists is that neither Castaneda nor Stewart accurately presented the practices of the native groups they claimed to have studied. Nevertheless, the techniques they describe actually seem to be effective for some people.

Charles Tart used Kilton Stewart's procedure whenever he had a nightmare, and he taught the technique to his young son. In both cases, the occurrence and severity of their nightmares abated, although Tart stated that "Stewart dreamwork" is probably a more accurate title for the procedure than "Senoi dreamwork." Castaneda's approach has also been effective with some dreamers although it probably has little to do with Yaqui Indian practices. Stanley Krippner practiced the Castaneda technique, placing his hands at eye level before falling asleep. After a few nights, he became aware of his hands in a dream and immediately obtained lucidity. Once lucid, he was able to make choices in his dream. He talked with plants and animals, and instructed other people in his dream to become lucid as well.

Practicing lucidity during waking fantasy has increased lucidity in dreams for some individuals. The basic procedure is to "re-dream" a dream while awake, pretending to be asleep. During this period of re-entry, one can attempt to work with the problems presented in dreams by facing the problems and working through them to gain more insights. Eventually, this procedure may evoke lucidity during nighttime dreams.

The "critical question" technique, utilized by a variety of dreamworkers, differs from the "intention" technique of self-suggestion and from the "re-dreaming" technique involving daytime fantasy. The "critical question" involves asking, am I dreaming? One can ask this question at regular intervals during the day (for example, every thirty minutes) or whenever observing an item that frequently appears in dreams, for example, food, water, a timepiece. In the latter instance, one would ask the question, am I dreaming? whenever looking at a clock or a watch during the day. Then one would make a "reality check" to test waking consciousness. A "reality check" involves looking away from the timepiece then looking back at it again and noting whether the timepiece has changed. If changes are noted in the timepiece, this indicates that one is indeed in a dream.

Using this exercise, one slowly builds a conditioned response in waking that allows the mind to remember to ask the "critical question" in the dream. For example, when the timepiece appears in a dream, the dreamer is likely to automatically ask, am I dreaming? and then make the reality check. If there is still any doubt, the dreamer can look around the environment to see if it is familiar. The dreamer then can observe the people in the dream to determine whether or not their behavior is bizarre. If so, the answer is, yes, I am dreaming, the dream becomes lucid.

The process of becoming lucid in the dream often involves some of the following experiences:

- Waking up due to excitement caused by becoming aware in a dream.
- Being actively involved in the dream while fully lucid.
- Witnessing the dream event without being involved in the dream activity.
- Deliberately changing objects in the dream.
- Leaving the dream scene by intending to be in another space or time.
- Confronting nightmarish characters and working therapeutically with the fear.
- Visiting deceased relatives and friends.
- Having transpersonal experiences; contacting a higher being, God, or spiritual entity.
- Entering a multidimensional space, "hyperspace," either spontaneously or by incubation.

One simple technique to foster lucid dreaming is to fall asleep on the right side. On the average, lucid dreams were three times more likely while sleeping on the right side of the body than on the left, in a study reported by Lynne Levitan. There were no gender differences, and those people sleeping on their backs also reported more lucid dreams than individuals sleeping on their left sides. This research finding corroborated the advice given to yogic adepts for many centuries by Tibetan Buddhist instructors.

As is the case with other dreams, we can gain insights from the power of the lucid dream experience and the resulting symbols and metaphors. The following dream is an example of how a lucid dream can assist in self-awareness and insights.

STEVE'S DREAM

Steve, one of our students, went camping by himself on Mount Shasta in California to meditate and enjoy the wilderness. He incubated a dream every night to guide him toward the next step in his life. On the fifth night, he had the following lucid dream:

I am in a cave with a group of old men. They are drinking water from an old bowl that is being passed around. As the bowl comes closer towards me I realize that this must be a dream. An old man with dark skin and dark hair sitting next to me hands me the bowl. I take it and drink the water. As I am drinking the water the sensation feels more real than waking reality. I suddenly hear a humming sound and as I look up the men have disappeared and a beautiful white deer is walking in the light in the far distance. I awake feeling ecstatic.

I once told a Jungian analyst a lucid dream of mine. She approached it as she would any dream—asking me what associations I had with the realization that I was dreaming while in the dream—considering lucidity in a dream just another expression of Jung's "all-unifying world of the psyche." (Page 9)

Stanley Krippner, Fariba Bogzaran, and Andre Percia de Carvalho, *Extraordinary Dreams and How to Work with Them*, (New York: State University of New York Press, 2002), pp. 37-42.

Leland Shields

QUESTIONS FROM NARRATIVE THERAPY

Narrative therapists believe we use our stories to understand and organize our lives. Together with those around us, we create these stories through the meaning we attribute to our experiences. Narrative therapy is based on fostering the telling and re-authoring of our stories. To do so, narrative therapists have developed the art of nonjudgmentally asking questions to help draw out clients' stories. While this style of therapy is not focused on dream work, I can't imagine a more natural fit for it.

Jill Freedman and Gene Combs are American narrative therapists who, in their book Narrative Therapy, *have identified five categories of questions. Those that help to deconstruct the dream story; open space to explore unrecognized possibilities; reveal preferences regarding the process; develop the dream story; and reveal what holds meaning for a client.*

Each of these categories offers a rich cache of tools for dream exploration, which I have developed here.

DECONSTRUCT THE STORY

DECONSTRUCTION QUESTIONS can be used to help unpack dreams, or see them from another perspective. They aim to illicit the dreamer's implied beliefs, attitudes, and feelings. Deconstruction questions can be broken down further into types, each of which is designed to illuminate an aspect of the beliefs, approaches, attitudes, and feelings portrayed in the dream. The types were identified by Freedman and Combs and paraphrased by me. I have included examples showing application of the questions to hypothetical dreams.

Explore memories or previous experiences similar to the dream events.
- What was going on in your life at the time you knew that man (in a hypothetical dream)?

- The dream includes evocative images, yet you didn't mention emotional reactions. Have there been times of your life when you found it helpful to maintain distance from your emotions?
- When have you felt those feelings?
- When have you seen a cake like that before?
- Have you ever seen someone respond to fear like the old woman did in the dream?

Look for influences related to the context of events.
- Do the events of your dream remind you of anything going on in your waking life?
- Are there settings in which you are more likely to react like that in your waking life?

Consider the effects of actions taken or results of decisions made.
- What happened to you in the dream when this character confronted you?
- How did the man in the black jacket react when you yelled at him?
- What effect does the fatigue shown in this dream have on your waking life?

Find interrelationships between images (characters, feelings, objects and events).
- Which people did you find supportive in this scene, and which were not?
- Were there images that struck you as out of place or surprising?
- Was your anxiety in this scene in keeping with the calm events?

Examine the tactics or choices made in the dream.
- What worked to save you in this dream?
- What actions of yours resulted in your ending up in the alley?
- How did you manage to be so convincing to your boss?
- What did the man do to make you so afraid?

DEVELOP THE STORY

Story development questions invite dreamers to relate the process and details of a dream experience and to connect it to a timeframe, to a context, and to other people. They allow the dreamer to re-experience the dream while consciously including those parts of the dream that could otherwise be neglected, forgotten, or misunderstood.

Notice the sequence of events and transitions of the dream.
- Can you give a summary of the dream story as it would look in a few frames of a cartoon?
- What occurred before each scene change?
- In your dream, what were you feeling before the scene switched to your driving fast?
- Did the discomfort you described resolve after the scene switched?

Remember the details to try and regain the immediacy of the dream.
- What was the look on his face when you said that?
- Show me how you were standing when that happened. Where were the others?
- What do you think your waking self would have noticed if you had been there watching?
- What were the others doing while you were looking for your shoes?

Find the role of time in your dream. Images of past events can help us reclaim parts of ourselves that have been neglected. Future events can give dream solutions to current problems or show our fear of what is coming. Questions can also contrast past, present, and future events to highlight changes over time.
- When in the past has your sister stood by your side and protected you?

- Have there been times when you spoke out so forcefully?
- What age are you in the dream?
- How old were you when you lived in that house?
- Is it unusual for you to sit down calmly rather than run around looking for the exit?
- In this dream you seemed pretty content working in the hospital. Is the dream showing how you would feel if you made that career decision? How does that fit?

Examine the geographical, social, and cultural contexts that influence the dream.
- The argument scene is in a mall. Do you have a harder time with your children in public?
- Have you ever walked along the Seine in Paris? If you were French, how do you think you would have greeted your brother?
- You said the place was your office but also could have been Bill's house. Is there something similar about those two places that could be represented here?

Consider the characters in the dream. People can represent themselves and a role they play in our lives, the parts of us that are like them, or both. Indistinct people in the dream can be a generalized male or female figure, or that male or female part of ourselves. We learn as much from the information that is missing as we do the information available.
- Who in your waking life might react in the way you reacted in the dream?
- When the floor collapsed, your brother pulled you to safety. Is he an anchor for you when the ground shifts under your feet?
- Is the part of you that is like your brother helpful when things fall apart?
- How would you and your brother have related if this had happened in waking life?

- You couldn't tell anything more about the figure chasing you than that it was a man. Is there something about men in general that is frightening or disturbing?
- Or, is there something about your own masculine side that you want to avoid? For instance, do you think you're too aggressive?

BROADEN THE PERSPECTIVE

These questions can expand the dreamer's perspective on the dream beyond the immediate and the obvious interpretation. They help us see what is just outside of view, what else may be possible, or even points of view we shun.

Notice unique outcomes, events, behaviors or processes.
- Has there ever been a time when your mother said things similar to those things that made you angry in the dream, but you did something other than yell back at her?
- In what waking situations do you find you can be as decisive as this?
- What do you think gave you the strength to resist the bear?
- What led to your trusting the man who at first looked so forbidding?

Use hypothetical questions to find alternate approaches or experiences.
- If you hadn't responded to her anger with your own anger, what do you think would have happened?
- What would have happened if you had reacted angrily instead of being accommodating?
- Is there anything you could have offered that would have satisfied the woman?

See the dream through someone else's eyes.

- What would your grandmother have done if she were in your position in the dream?
- Can you think of anyone who would have been able to find his or her way home from the park?
- What was the dog trying to do when it strained at the chain and barked?
- When you put yourself in the role of the terrifying man, what do you imagine a man like him would want, and why? What sort of background might he have?

Notice when you or others in the dream react differently than your waking mind would expect. These instances may indicate perspectives on your psyche that your waking mind has missed.

- Is your waking mind bothered by something your dream self seems to take in stride?
- In this dream you were much calmer talking to your ex-husband about parenting than you've been describing lately. How did your dream self do that? Or was your dream self holding back emotion?
- Your dream self responded to the broken glass with intense emotions; is that different from what you would expect of your waking mind?

Imagine future events past the end of the dream.

- If you could repeat this dream in which you were lost, what would you do differently?
- What would you like to say to her next time she asks for your help?
- What would impede you from responding in the way you wish to respond?

OTHERS' DREAMS

There are always numerous directions a dream interpretation can take. When talking to a friend, a dream group colleague, or a psychotherapy client, it is important to pause and frequently check that the questions are those that fit the dreamer and address issues of interest to the dreamer. In asking for the dreamer's preferences, we are at once respecting the dreamer as the expert of his or her own dream, and allowing the dreamer to commit to a direction of his or her own choosing. Choosing the direction is in itself an important component in approaching the dream. Here are examples of preference questions in dream interpretation.

- I can think of many associations related to a frog: a prince waiting for a kiss; an amphibian able to live in more than one world; green, slimy skin; eating bugs; and living in swampy places. Are there any associations that stand out for you with respect to this dream?
- This dream seems to address very personal issues. Are you comfortable discussing them now?
- When you told the dream, you laughed and seemed most animated in describing the part with the old woman. Do you want to start with that image, or is there another part that stands out in your mind?
- Or, more simply, of all these images, are there parts that stand out most in your mind?
- Does that association make sense for you?

EXPLORE MEANING

ON PAGE 57, the psychologist Clara Hill called the moment in dream work when meaning takes hold the "aha" experience. Viktor Frankl, on page. 51, described the centrality of meaning to life itself. Discovering meaning in a dream is not just an intellectual exercise, but a visceral engagement in finding out who we are, what we believe, and how we are living now. Meaning questions are intended to help us knit answers to all the previous questions into a cohesive whole: "That is what this dream is about." Clara Hill also warned that we should not expect to have an "aha" with every dream (page 57). On the other hand, we can sometimes find more than one meaning for some dreams.

Explore the implications, qualities, and characteristics of dream images, motivations, goals, and values.

- What is the significance of your father's being in the room while you tried to resolve the issue with your colleague?
- What motivated the dog to snarl like that?
- If the snarling dog was part of you, what would that tell you about yourself?
- Do you see your relationship with your sister in the dream as being like your relationship in the waking world? What does that say about the role she plays in your life? Does this change your view of some of her characteristics?
- What underlying needs or values were the basis of the decisions you made in this dream? What was important to you? How do you express those needs or values in your waking life?

Leland Shields, adapted from by Jill Freedman and Gene Combs, *Narrative Therapy: The Social Construction of Preferred Realities* (New York: W.W. Norton Company, Inc., 1996), Chapter 5.

SCIENCE, SLEEP, AND DREAMING

We are products of our rational and analytical culture, no doubt, but I find that even people inclined to subjective insight still crave an understanding of what science can tell us about dreams. Sometimes people want to know something concrete, such as the biological reason why it is difficult to remember dreams. Others want to understand the science if only to answer skeptical friends or family members. Scientific methods have been applied to dream work from Asclepius' use of snakes in ancient Greece to researchers' use of brain scans today.

Jeanne Achterberg

DREAM THERAPY IN ANCIENT GREECE

Early Western medical (healing) traditions feature a strong mind-body connection and associate physical health with states of mind and dreaming. Our Greek ancestors suggest that we look to our dream images not just as metaphors of psychic phenomena, but as potential indicators of our physical condition.

IN SEPARATING FACT FROM FANCY, it is apparent that Asclepius was indeed an influential mortal. Over 200 temples were eventually erected throughout the area of Greece, Italy and Turkey to honor him and the practices of medicine which he fostered. These *Asclepia*, as the temples were called, were the first holistic treatment centers. . . .

Within the Asclepia, dream therapy or divine sleep, later to be called incubation sleep by Christian practitioners, reached perfection as a healing tool. Dream therapy is a prime example of the imagination as diagnostician and healer. Most of the patients to receive this therapy were severely ill, and all the usual medicines had proven ineffective. At night, the patients went to the temple or outlying buildings to await the gods. In preparation, "the priests take the inquirer and keep him fasting from food for one day and from wine for three days to give him perfect spiritual lucidity to absorb the divine communication."

The diagnosis and healing took place during that special state of consciousness immediately prior to sleep, when images come forth automatically like frames of thought projected on a movie screen. (We now call this "hypnogogic sleep.") During this sensitive, susceptible time, Asclepius purportedly would then appear as a handsome, gentle and strong healer, who either cured or advised treatment. He held a rustic staff with a serpent entwined about it—resembling the symbol of the medical profession known as the *caduceus*. (The caduceus actually has been identified much earlier even than the ancient Greeks, and the snake emblem itself is richly endowed by cross-cultural myths with significance as a healing partner.) During the dreamlike experiences in the Asclepian temples, the snakes were reported to slither over to the patient and lick on their wounds and their eyelids—an event that in most of us would at least activate the adrenal glands!

Since the temples were established well after Asclepius' lifetime, the rituals were performed by physician/priests, dressed as Asclepius, accompanied by a retinue representing his family, and even by animals such as geese, which, in addition to the serpent, were believed to have some healing ability. Moving from patient to patient, the group carried the accoutrements of the physician, such as medicines and surgical tools, and performed, or perhaps just playacted, both the standard medical treatments as well as magical rites. In the semidarkness, in the presence of the earthly representatives of healing deities, with music playing in the background, and surrounded by all the pomp and circumstance of the magnificent shrines, whatever innate healing ability the patients possessed in the face of their grave illnesses was greatly enhanced. It was a perfect situation for the imagination to go to work; and go to work it apparently did. . . .

Aristotle, Hippocrates, and even Galen were trained in the Asclepian tradition, and all of them were able to articulate the role that the imagination played in health. Aristotle believed that the emotional system did not function in the absence of images. Images were formed by the sensations taken in and worked upon by the *sensus communis*, or the "collective sense." These images caused changes in bodily functions, and affected both the cure and production of disease. Aristotle also suggested that the special images of the dream state were vital. He wrote in the *Parva Naturalia*, "Even scientific physicians tell us that one should pay diligent attention to dreams, and to hold this view is reasonable also for those who are not practitioners but speculative philosophers."

Hippocrates, the "Father of Medicine," symbolized the change in the practice of medicine from mystical to naturalistic principles. He believed that the physician's role was essentially to understand and assist nature, to know what humans were in relation to food, drink, occupation, and what effect each of these had upon the others. He, too, espoused the Asclepian mode of gentleness and concern, love and dignity.

Galen, whose dictums influenced the practice of medicine for no fewer than forty-five generations, was the last important pillar in the millennium of Greek medical preeminence. In fact, medicine had already begun its decline from glory some years prior to Galen, so that what was captured and practiced by medieval Europe was by no means the crowning achievement of the Greek physicians, but rather something less. . . .

Galen was the first, however, to record a full-fledged description of the effect of the imagination on health, indicating that he understood the relationship between body and mind in quite a modern sense. In the absence of laboratory tests, the patient's imagery or dream content was believed to offer clinically important diagnostic information. For example, images of loss or grief related to an excess of melancholy (black bile), and images of terror or fright reflected a predominance of choler. . . .

Jeanne Achterberg, *Imagery in Healing: Shamanism and Modern Medicine* (Boston: Shambhala, 1985), pp. 54-57.

Hippocrates

DREAMS AND DIAGNOSIS

The writings attributed to Hippocrates, the Greek founder of Western medicine, were considered authoritative in their time (between 430 and 330 BCE). In his textbook on medical treatment, Hippocrates included a section on using dreams for diagnosis and treatment because, to him, dreams represent the voice of the soul.

Hippocrates classified two categories of dreams: those with activities and images that are consistent with our waking life, and those with activities and images that are not. When inconsistent dream images arose, he concluded there was some physical imbalance for which he prescribed treatments.

86. Accurate knowledge about the signs which occur in dreams will be found very valuable for all purposes. While the body is awake, the soul is not under its own control, but is split into various portions each being devoted to some special bodily function such as hearing, vision, touch, locomotion and all the various actions of the body. But when the body is at rest, the soul is stirred and roused and becomes its own master, and itself performs all the functions of the body. When the body is sleeping it receives no sensations, but the soul being awake at that time perceives everything; it sees what is visible, it hears what is audible, it walks, it touches, it feels pain and thinks. In short, during sleep the soul performs all the functions of both body and soul. A correct appreciation of these things implies considerable wisdom.

87. There are special interpreters, with their own science of these matters, for the god-given dreams which give to cities or to individuals foreknowledge of the future. Such people also interpret the signs derived from the soul which indicate bodily states; excess or lack of what is natural, or of some unusual change. In such matters they are sometimes right and sometimes wrong, but in neither case do they know why it happens, whether they are right or wrong, but nevertheless they give advice so you shall "beware of taking harm." Yet they never show you how you ought

to beware, but merely tell you to pray to the gods. Prayer is a good thing, but one should take on part of the burden oneself and call on the gods only to help.

88. The facts about dreams are as follows: those that merely consist of a transference to the night of a person's daytime actions and thoughts, which continue to happen in normal fashion just as they were done and thought during the day, are good for they indicate a healthy state. This is because the soul remains true to its daytime cogitations, and is overcome neither by excess nor by emptiness, nor by any other extraneous circumstance. But when dreams take on a character contrary to daytime activities and involve conflict or victory over them, then they constitute a sign of bodily disturbance. The seriousness of the conflict is an indication of the seriousness of the mischief. . . .

> *As we look at our dreams today, we might ask ourselves about those images that are inconsistent with our waking life. Are they expressions of our soul that we do not feel or allow ourselves when we are awake? Is the dream telling us that the way we think about the situation when awake is deficient in some way? What questions can you bring to these images in your dreams?*
>
> *In the balance of this excerpt, Hippocrates uses specific celestial dream images for diagnosis. We no longer accept the objective accuracy of his diagnostic practice, but the celestial imagery may still be relevant to the symbolism of the dream. For example, Hippocrates concludes that a dream showing disturbance of the stars represents a disturbance of our "outermost parts," while an image of the moon represents a disturbance internally. Just as Gerhard Adler used myths to explore meaning in images of animals (p. 34), you can use Hippocrates' medical texts to explore the symbolic meaning of celestial images.*

89. It is a good sign to see the sun, moon, sky and stars clear and undimmed, each being placed normally in its right place, since it shows that the body is well and free from disturbing influences. But it is necessary to follow a regime which will ensure that such a condition is maintained. On the contrary, if any of these celestial bodies appear displaced or changed,

then such a sign indicates bodily disease, the severity of which depends upon the seriousness of the interference.

Now the orbit of the stars is the outermost, that of the sun is intermediate, while that of the moon is nearest to the hollow vault of the sky. Should one of the stars seem to be injured, or should it disappear or stop in its revolution as a result of mist or cloud, this is a weak sign. If such a change be produced by rain or hail, it is stronger and signifies that an excretion of moisture and phlegm has occurred into the corresponding outermost parts.

Hippocrates, *Hippocratic Writings*, ed. G.E.R. Lloyd, trans. J. Chadwick and W. N. Mann (London: Penguin Books, 1978), pp. 252-254.

Ilan Kutz

BRAIN CHEMISTRY
AND DREAM RECOLLECTION

Jumping ahead now to modern Western medicine, I am interested to see Israeli psychiatrist Ilan Kutz's explanation of how difficulty in remembering dreams and dreams' symbolic nature serve as protective mechanisms: we only remember and understand those dream messages that we are ready to receive.

ACCORDING TO DREAM PHYSIOLOGY, the freshly awakened brain forgets dreams because it is still under the influence of the neurotransmitter system (the acetylcholine system) that operates during sleep and inhibits memory. Memory physiology may also explain why telling the dream content to someone, or writing it on a piece of paper, enables one to capture it in memory. During the awake activities of talking or writing, the brain switches gears to the opposing transmitter system (dominated by the noradrenergic and serotonergic systems), which enhances the preservation of memory. Thus, the activity of writing or talking one's dream not only secures a witness to its content but also shifts the brain into a better mode for remembering it. . . .

The natural properties of the dreaming brain, i.e., the absence of memory function during sleep and the condensed symbols of the dream that create a puzzling code, unite together to form an excellent safety valve. That we do not remember most dreams is probably the most common and surest way of avoiding, while awake, mentally threatening "dream stuff." As for those dreams that have managed to cross the sleep barrier into waking memory but contain information that is too "risky," they will not be understood by the dreamer once he is awake. He/she will disregard with vehemence or indifference any interpretation of the plot or symbols for which he is unready. He/she will use other defenses, notably rationalization, to explain away unwanted conclusions, and will not interpret correctly a dream whose message he/she isn't ready to handle. Only when the dreamer is ready to tap deep-seated emotions and expose hidden premonitions and passions, will he/she do so.

Ilan Kutz, *The Dreamland Companion: A Bedside Diary and Guide to Dream Interpretation* (New York: Hyperion, 1993), p. 7 and p. 11.

Siri Carpenter

BRAIN SCANS AND FREUDIAN DREAM THEORY

Brain scans have shown which areas of the brain are at work during REM sleep, the time when dreaming is common. This has led to a reexamination of some of Freud's ideas.

FREUD'S THEORY that dreams are the "royal road" to understanding the unconscious mind has come under fire over the past thirty years as scientists have probed the neural bases of dreaming. But new findings from brain imaging studies are beginning to show that there may be some truth behind Freud's hypotheses.

The results have narrowed the gulf between basic researchers' beliefs that dreams are merely the byproduct of random neuron firings and psychoanalysts' stance that dreams reveal people's deepest instincts and impulses. . . .

Freud's dream theory began to unravel in the 1960s, when scientists discovered that REM sleep, the phase in which dreaming most often occurs, is controlled not by the brain's emotion or motivation centers but by the pons, the part of the brainstem involved in automatic jobs such as respiration, thermo-regulation and cardiac activity. . . .

NEW SUPPORT FOR AN OLD IDEA

The advent of imaging techniques that reveal the brain at work have given researchers a fresh look at what's happening when people dream. Positron emission tomography (PET) and functional MRI techniques have revolutionized dream research, says neurologist Allen R. Braun, MD, of the National Institute on Deafness and Other Communication Disorders (NIDCD).

Using PET, Braun and his colleagues found that the limbic and paralimbic regions of the brain—areas that control emotion and motivation—were highly active during REM sleep. In addition, areas of the prefrontal cortex, which sustain working memory, attention, logic and self-monitoring, were inactive, the researchers reported in *Science* (Vol. 279, pp. 91-95).

Suppression of the prefrontal cortex during REM sleep may help explain several of the cardinal features of dreaming, such as bizarre imagery, loss of critical insight and logic, diminished self-reflection, inability to shift attention, morphing of time, place and identity and forgetting of dreams, says Braun.

His team also found that the primary visual cortex—the point of entry for visual information from the external world—was deactivated during REM, but regions of the brain that conduct higher-level visual processing remained activated, perhaps explaining why people continue to "see" while dreaming, even while the brain is cut off from the outside world.

"The data are consistent with a number of elements of classical Freudian theory," Braun says. Deactivation of the prefrontal cortex may be consistent with Freud's ideas of encoding of wishes into dream imagery, emotional disinhibition and instinctual needs, he says.

In research that complements the brain imaging findings, Solms [*a London neuropsychologist*] studied patients who had damage either in the pons region of the brainstem or in areas of the forebrain involved in motivation. Although the REM sleep of people with damage in the pons was disrupted, dreaming was not. In contrast, people with damage to motivation centers in the forebrain reported a loss of dreaming even though their REM sleep was not disturbed.

... Solms says. "Dreams are evidently produced by motivational, emotional, memory and perceptual systems of the forebrain. It is, in short, the 'wishing system,' to allude back to Freud. Nothing that we know about in the brain comes closer to being the neurophysiological equivalent of what Freud described as the libidinal wish or libidinal drive."

Siri Carpenter, "Freud's dream theory gets boost from imaging work: Meaning in dreams may be less disguised than commonly believed," *American Psychological Association Monitor*, volume 30, number 7 (July/August, 1999).

William Dement

William Dement founded Stanford University's Sleep Disorder Clinic in 1970 and is now one of the world's foremost sleep researchers. For decades he has studied sleeping people in laboratory settings.

DREAMING, HYPNOSIS, AND IMAGE PERCEPTION

[SUBJECTS WERE PLACED UNDER] deep hypnosis with suggested hallucinations. We instructed these deeply hypnotized subjects to "see" an object—a pair of shoes, for example—and to examine it very carefully, reporting to us exactly what they saw. Our subjects had no trouble focusing their attention on the specified object. But it was almost always perfectly clear from the subject's spontaneous account and responses to interrogation that the hallucinated object was always substantially different from its real counterpart. Often the hypnotized subject would express puzzlement over the strangely incomplete and flawed image. Such distorted images are common to imaginings that occur in the waking state, to sleep onset imagery, and to various kinds of hallucinations, whether psychotic or drug induced. On the other hand, we believe, the images we report ourselves to have seen in the dream world are identical to our perceptions in the real world.

DREAMING IS NOT A RANDOM PROCESS

REGARDLESS OF THE SEMANTICS, I disagree with the random-process theory; I cannot accept that the creation of the dream is a product of chance. Tell me if you think this next dream—one of my personal favorites—was random. It dates back to 1968, when my colleagues at Stanford and I were working with PCPA, an experimental drug that appeared to have profound effects upon the basic sleep processes. We were working with furious intensity to study all the changes. About one year into the project, I developed a serious suspicion that the chemical we had been purchasing from a manufacturer was not PCPA, but something else. I experienced tremendous uneasiness: Was the rug about to be pulled out from under us? Would a whole year of work go down the tubes? I resolved to get samples of the compound analyzed in a lab; but the weekend was approaching, so nothing could be done until the following Monday. I could only wait and hope I was wrong.

Friday afternoon I went to a party at the home of artist and Stanford professor Nathan Oliveira. He was talking about a recent trip to Sweden, where he had had a show. During this trip, he said, someone had asked him if he was Jewish (he is, in fact, Portuguese), and he had responded in jest: "There are no Jews in Portugal."

That night I had a lengthy, vivid dream. It took its theme from the movie *Around the World in 80 Days* and from the day's events. In this dream, I was on the trail of the lost tribe of Portuguese Jews. I would pursue them over mountain and plain and arrive at the warm ashes of a campfire, only to realize that the lost tribe was still ahead of me. With considerable intensity, I followed them across the United States, across the Atlantic Ocean, across Europe and Asia—always arriving, after considerable hardship, a little too late. Eventually I got to Vladivostok, where, upon learning they had sailed for California, I requisitioned a boat and set out to sea.

There were raging storms, and toward the end of the voyage the boat sank. Buffeted by waves, I struggled through the surf and was finally thrown up onto a California beach, totally exhausted and bereft of everything. As I crawled up on the sand totally defeated, my head bumped something. It was a signpost. I looked up and read on the sign: "Ha, ha! We were here all the time! (Signed,) The Portuguese Jews." I awoke with a feeling of overwhelming loss and failure.

Certainly the dream was humorous, at least in retrospect, but what did it "mean"? To me it clearly depicted the fear that we had gone all the way around the world—that is, had worked a whole year—and had accomplished absolutely nothing. It reflected the intensity of the work and, at the end, a tremendous sense of loss and waste. (As it turned out, my harrowing world tour was unnecessary—lab results on Monday showed that the PCPA was, in fact, PCPA.) Its significance aside, the dream was a coherent and meaningful whole. How could it possibly have occurred as a random process?

William C. Dement, *Sleepwatchers* (Stanford, CA: The Portable Stanford Book Series, 1992), p. 108 and pp. 117-118.

Charles Fisher

INSANE

The American psychiatrist and psychoanalyst Charles Fisher worked with sleep-researcher William Dement.

DREAMING PERMITS EACH AND EVERY ONE OF US to be quietly and safely insane every night of our lives.

"Perchance to Dream," *Newsweek* (November 30, 1959), p. 104.

Andrea Rock

Andrea Rock is an American investigative reporter noted for her coverage of medical topics.

DREAM CONTENT ACROSS THE WORLD

AN INNOVATIVE SCIENTIST, [Calvin] Hall first began collecting dream reports in the 1940s from college students at Case Western Reserve University, where he was head of the Psychology department. Rather than analyzing dreams and trying to interpret what they meant, he was focused on simply quantitatively describing what it is we dream about and which emotions most often accompany dreams. Over the next three decades, Hall expanded his efforts, gathering dream reports from children and adults, including dreams collected by anthropologists from people living in remote traditional cultures throughout the world. When he died in 1985, Hall had amassed the world's largest and most systematic body of findings on dream content, drawn from his collection of 50,000 dream reports. The quantitative coding system he developed with collaborator Robert Van de Castle . . . has been used by researchers . . . to compare how dreams differ from culture to culture and to see how women's dreams compare to men's or how a single individual's dreams change as he or she ages.

Thanks to [G. William] Domhoff's efforts, much of Hall's data on comparisons of dreams across cultures became available publicly for the first time in the mid-1990s. The results show that there are more similarities than differences in dream content among all people regardless of where or how they live. Throughout the world, women's dreams contain an equal number of male and female characters, but in men's dreams, nearly 70 percent of characters are other men. Both sexes have dreams that feature more misfortune than good fortune, more negative than positive emotion, and more aggression than friendliness, but men generally have more physical aggression in their dreams than do women. Children's dreams contain little aggression, but that element begins to increase during teenage years. . . .

Among industrialized societies studied . . . Americans ranked highest for aggression in dreams, with scores of 50 percent for U.S. males (34 percent for females) versus 29 percent for Swiss men and 32 percent for Dutch men. . . .

The chief character in our nightly dramas is nearly always the dreamer, but about 95 percent of our dreams involve other characters too. The rest of the cast consists of people, animals, and mythical figures, with adults dreaming mostly of other adults. Animals feature more prominently in the dreams of children and people living in more primitive societies. Homes or other buildings are the most common dream settings, and automobiles or other conveyances also frequently pop up as scenes for dream action. The majority of dreams during REM sleep are filled with motion, especially walking or running, while dreams in other phases of sleep are less action oriented.

The popular idea that dreams are chock-full of sexual experiences—stemming in part from Freud's views that all dreams were fulfillments of wishes, usually sexual in nature—is in large measure wishful wakeful thinking. The Hall–Van de Castle content analysis data indicates sexual activity crops up in no more than ten percent of dreams, while other studies have shown no more than a third of dreams contain explicitly sexual content, with men more likely to dream of sex with strangers while women tend to dream of partners that they know. . . .

Content analysis also reveals that there is remarkable consistency in what an individual dreams about over time. . . . For instance, a woman Hall called Dorothea . . . provided more than five hundred dreams in a dream journal she'd begun at the age of twenty-five in 1912 and continued through the age of seventy-six. Using content analysis to examine the dreams, he found that six elements appeared with the same frequency throughout that fifty-year time span. For instance, one of every six dreams involved loss of an object, usually her purse; being in a small or messy room or a room that was being invaded by others featured in ten percent of the dreams; and another ten percent focused on interactions between the dreamer and her mother. Being late or missing a bus or train was a theme in one of every sixteen dreams. As she grew older, being left out or ignored was the only theme that significantly increased in frequency for Dorothea, a schoolteacher who remained single throughout her life. . . .

> Hall's approach is elegantly simple and can be applied to our own dreams in at least two ways. For one, we can compare Hall's averages with how frequently key images show up in our dreams. As an example, consider that Hall found that 95% of dreams involved characters in addition to the dreamer; what might it mean if most of your dreams did not include others? Or, since children's dreams were found rarely to include aggression, what might it mean when a child has many aggressive dreams?
>
> Another method used by these researchers was to compare the frequency with which certain images arose in the dreams of the same individual over time. To apply this we might review our own dream journals occasionally to see if we notice changing patterns of images. In doing this at one point in my own life I found my dreams of aggression increased noticeably in periods during which I worked well over forty hours per week.
>
> Note: As of September 2006, there is a website (www. dreamresearch.net) that provides access to the Hall-Domhoff dream

records which you can access for your own studies by entering one of your dream images in a keyword search to find others' dreams with the same image.

CREATIVITY

. . . TSE WEN [*Chang*] was searching for a new way to treat allergies and asthma. Previous allergy drugs such as antihistamines worked by absorbing chemicals that are released in the wake of an allergy attack, but his groundbreaking notion was to use an engineered protein that would bind to substances in the body that set off allergic reactions and thereby prevent the attack from occurring in the first place. As Tanox chief executive officer Nancy Chang tells it, the out-of-the box approach came in the dead of the night. "He actually concocted that in the middle of the night in a dream, and he woke me up and told me," she recalls. "We didn't go back to sleep for the rest of the night."

Accounts of such moments of inspiration or breakthroughs during dreaming time have been reported by other scientists, musicians, athletes, mathematicians, writers, and visual artists. Many of them have been chronicled by Harvard psychologist Deirdre Barrett in her book, *The Committee of Sleep.* For Barrett, who has been a prolific and vivid dreamer since childhood, the idea that creativity can spring from a state some people don't even regard as consciousness makes perfect sense. "During dreaming, we're tuned inward, we experience vivid visual imagery, our conventional logic system is turned down, and social norms are loosened, all of which can lead to making more creative associations than we make when we're awake and our brain is censoring the illogical," she says. . . .

Similarly, when mathematician Donald J. Newman was working on a tough new theoretical math problem when he was at the Massachusetts Institute of Technology in the 1960's, he found he was completely stuck. At the time, Newman was part of a group of highly competitive mathematicians on campus, including John Nash, whose life later became the subject of the popular book and film, *A Beautiful Mind*.

As Newman, now retired in Philadelphia recalls, "I'd been mulling over this problem for a week or so and just couldn't get anywhere with it when I had a dream that I was at a restaurant in Cambridge with Nash. I asked him about this problem in the dream and I listened to his explanation of how to do it. When I woke up, I had the solution."

Newman says he's never had such an experience before or since and felt so strongly about it that when he published a paper elucidating the problem, he actually gave John Nash credit for contributing to the work . . . .

> *Newman credits Nash in the way indigenous people might, as if Nash himself were a visitor in the dream. Alternatively, von Franz (see p. 28) would ask what part of Newman is being represented by Nash in the dream. Or, she might ask Newman, "Can you think of other times when it would be helpful to invoke the part of you that is similar to Nash?"*

And out-of-the box thinking that emerges during dreams sometimes involves more mundane matters too. When Kathy Hurxthal was a Peace Corps volunteer in a Moroccan village during the 1960s, she was teaching local women how to knit. While she knew how to knit sweaters or mittens, one of the women was bent on knitting a pair of socks—something Hurxthal had never done before. "The part I couldn't figure out was how to turn the heel. I was completely preoccupied with that challenge, and finally it came to me while I was dreaming one night. . . . I woke up, went to the center, and showed them all how to knit socks exactly as I had done it in my dream." . . .

For excerpts from The Committee of Sleep, *by Deirdre Barrett, see p. 110.*

Andrea Rock, *The Mind at Night*, (Cambridge: Basic Books, 2004), pp. 62-65 and 136-140.

August Kekulé

A BREAKTHROUGH IN CHEMISTRY

*History is crowded with scientific breakthroughs that have arisen first
in dreams. Such discoveries remind us of the potential for creativity
we all have in our nightly dreaming. Here August Kekulé tells of how,
in 1858, his dream images showed the structure of carbon bonds in
organic substances—a key breakthrough in organic chemistry. This and
other dream experiences led him to say to a German Chemical Society
audience, "Let us learn to dream, gentlemen, then perhaps we shall find
the truth."*

DURING MY STAY IN LONDON I resided for a considerable time in
Clapham Road. . . . I frequently, however, spent my evenings with my
friend Hugo Muller at the opposite end of the metropolis. We talked
of many things but most often of our beloved chemistry. One fine summer evening I was returning by the last bus, through the deserted streets
of the city. I feel [*sic*] into a reverie (Traumerei) and lo, the atoms were
gamboling before my eyes! . . . I saw how, frequently, two smaller atoms
united to form a pair; how a larger one embraced the two smaller ones;
how still larger ones kept hold of three or even four of the smaller; whilst
the whole kept whirling in a giddy dance. I saw the larger ones formed a
chain, dragging the smaller ones after them but only at the ends of the
chain. I saw what our past master, Kopp, my highly honored teacher and
friend, has depicted with such charm in his "Molecularwelt": but I saw
it long before him. The cry of the conductor, "Clapham Road," awakened
me from my dreaming; but I spent a part of the night in putting on paper
at least sketches of these dream forms.

O. Theodore Benfey, "August Kekulé and the Birth of the Structural Theory of Organic
Chemistry in 1858," *Journal of Chemical Education*, vol. 35, no. 1, (1958), pp. 21-23.

Deirdre Barrett

PROBLEM SOLVING

Deirdre Barrett is a Harvard professor of psychology, a dream researcher, and a past president of the International Association of the Study of Dreams.

THE RULES OF DREAM INCUBATION

Psychologists have developed "incubation" rituals to encourage problem-solving dreams. These usually target interpersonal and emotional problems, but they are also relevant to objective creative tasks. Incubation instructions usually include the following:

1. Write down the problem as a brief phrase or sentence, and place this by your bed.

2. Review the problem for a few minutes just before going to bed.

3. Once in bed, visualize the problem as a concrete image if it lends itself to this. Visualize yourself dreaming about the problem, awakening, and writing on the bedside note pad.

4. Tell yourself you want to dream about the problem just as you are drifting off to sleep.

5. Keep a pen and paper—perhaps also a flashlight or pen with a lighted tip—on the night table.

6. Arrange objects connected to the problem on your night table . . . or on the wall across from your bed if they lend themselves to a poster . . . .

7. Upon awakening, lie quietly before getting out of bed. Note whether there is any trace of a recalled dream, and invite more of the dream to return if possible. Write it down.

One dream psychologist who applies such techniques full-time is Anjali Hazarika of India's National Petroleum Management Program. Hazarika runs creativity workshops . . . *[focused]* exclusively on dreaming. Small groups of oil executives and engineers gather for three days of instruction and experiential exercises with her. Hazarika emphasizes

solving personal problems at home that are interfering with job perfor-
mance and helping work groups get along better with each other through
dream insights. However, some of her workshop participants choose to
focus on objective problems.

Hazarika told me of one chemist who was developing enzymes
that would refine crude oil. He asked the Committee of Sleep for help
with this. That night he dreamed he was next to a road when a big truck
rumbled by with a load of rotten cabbages. He could see them heaped
over the top of the truck, and he could smell their stench as they passed
by. It was a vivid dream, but when he told it in the group, neither he nor
anyone else could make sense of it. Hazarika tried to help him interpret
it, and other members of the group offered symbolic associations to cabbages and rot, but they didn't get far.

The next Monday, when the chemist returned to his lab to work on his
oil-refinement project, he suddenly realized the dream was literally true.
As cabbages decomposed, bacteria would break them down into exactly
the kind of enzymes he sought! And cabbages were dirt-cheap—rotten
ones were simply thrown out. He proceeded to develop a technique for
crude-oil refinement using exactly the material his dream had trucked in
for him.

Deirdre Barrett, *The Committee of Sleep: How Artists, Scientists and Athletes Use Dreams for
Creative Problem-Solving* (New York: Crown Publishers, 2001), pp. 120-121.

Jeffrey Moussaieff Masson

ANIMALS DREAM

American-born Jeffrey Moussaieff Masson, a former Freudian psychoanalyst currently residing in New Zealand, has written several books on the emotional life of animals. Masson shows us that the act of dreaming is evolutionarily older than humanity: we are not the only animals that dream: when dreaming we join an ancient tradition of distant ancestors.

IN HIS BOOK *The Expression of the Emotions In Man and Animals*, Charles Darwin had dared to imagine a dog's conscious life: "But can we feel sure that an old dog with an excellent memory and some power of imagination, as shown by his dreams, never reflects on his past pleasures in the chase? And this would be a form of self consciousness." . . .

Animal behaviorists are unlikely to acknowledge that terror can return in the dreams of animals. And yet from a Kenyan "elephant orphanage" comes a report of baby African elephants who have seen their families killed by poachers, and witnessed the tusks being cut off the bodies. These young animals wake up screaming in the night. What else but the nightmare memories of a deep trauma could occasion these night terrors?

Jeffrey Moussaieff Masson and Susan McCarthy, *When Elephants Weep*, (New York: A Delta Book, 1995), p. xvii and p. 45.

David Foulkes

A RESEARCH OVERVIEW

David Foulkes is the retired director of the dream research laboratories at the University of Wyoming and the Georgia Mental Health Institute. He is a leader in the empirical study of children's dreaming. Written in 1989, this piece provides background information about natural science theories and laboratory research which may not reflect the current work.

BIOLOGICAL THEORIES

Physical or biological scientists tend to think that dreaming can be attributed to a peculiar pattern of brain functioning specific to the state of sleep. Nowadays, this view derives not only from a general frame of reference in which aberrant brain states [*sic*] but also from a particular discovery: REM sleep. Named for its accompanying rapid eye movements, REM sleep is a paradoxically aroused state that comprises about 25 percent of total sleep-time in adults. REM sleep was discovered at the University of Chicago in 1953 by Eugene Aserinsky and Nathaniel Kleitman, who also noted that adult volunteers reported detailed dreams on most awakenings from REM sleep and no dreams at all on most awakenings in the absence of REMs. The association of REM awakenings with reports of vivid dreaming has been confirmed in studies of thousands of adult volunteers worldwide.

Reverse learning hypothesis:

Thus, recent natural scientific theories have focused on observed or hypothetical peculiarities of REM sleep to explain the seemingly mysterious properties of dream experience. Often, as in the theory of Nobel laureate Francis Crick and his colleague Graeme Mitchison, the focus is on REM sleep rather than on dreaming as such. Their theory, first advanced in 1983, proposes that the REM state involves a process of "reverse learning" or "unlearning," through which unwanted or "parasitic" neutral [*sic*] patterns are purged from the brain's repertoire. Dreaming is, in some unspecified way, a reflection of this unlearning process. Thus we dream not to heighten our awareness of any mental contents but rather to obliterate such contents. Evidence does suggest that most REM dreams are not remembered unless interrupted by an awakening. For Crick and Mitchison, the remembered and dwelled-upon dream is an unwitting failure of the mind-clearing process that is inherent in "unconscious" (i.e., unremembered) dreaming.

P Hypothesis of consolidation:

Other theories have been proposed in which the REM state is imagined to involve the consolidation, rather than the obliteration, of mental associations. Thus, Edmond Dewan of the Air Force-Cambridge Research Laboratories proposed the P (for Programming) Hypothesis in 1969, according to which REM sleep should increase in organisms undergoing much novel waking experience. Although there is some evidence that this is the case for other animals, there is little support for the hypothesis among humans. And as is also true of Crick and Mitchison's theory, the P Hypothesis is very vague on how proprieties [sic] of the experienced dream reflect the underlying brain processes assumed to be occurring in REM sleep. That is, neither theory makes a serious attempt to explain the general form of specific content of dreams.

Activation-synthesis hypothesis:

More explicit is the activation-synthesis theory of Allan Hobson and Robert McCarley, first published in 1977 and publicized in Hobson's recent book, *The Dreaming Brain.* Unlike the previous neuroscientific theories, the activation-synthesis theory starts not with a presumption about REM function but rather with an observation, specifically of the brain-stem accompaniments of the REM state in experimental animals. (Almost all mammals exhibit REM sleep to one degree or another.) According to the theory, dreaming (like REM sleep) originates from random activation of specific sites in the brain stem, and this activation has "little or no primary ideational, volitional, or emotional content." The dream itself, in Hobson and McCarley's view, is "the forebrain … making the best of a bad job in producing even partially coherent dream imagery from the relatively noisy signals sent up to it from the brain stem."

In support of their theory, Hobson and McCarley have noted a number of parallels between the general form of brain activity observed in animals and the presumed form of dream experience in adult humans. Thus, the frequently bizarre nature of dream imagery is related to random patterns of brain-stem neural activation, and frequent shifts of scene or plot are related to random sequences of such activation. However, Hobson and McCarley have not demonstrated point-for-point correspondences in humans between particular physiological events and particular properties of dream experience that their theory predicts to be the consequence of these events. Indeed, their theory largely ignores researchers' failure to demonstrate convincing relationships between any discrete physiological event in preawakening REM sleep (e.g., changes in brain wave or eye-movement pattern, changes in respiration or heart rate) and any discrete property of post-awakening dream reports.

CRITIQUE OF BIOLOGICAL THEORIES

REM-REDUCTION THEORIES OF DREAMING also face more general problems. First, understanding of the REM state as a physical process is constantly evolving. We may not yet know enough to explain something as complex as dreaming, and consequently, there is a risk of focusing on physical variables currently accessible to detailed study (e.g., individual brain stem neurons) rather than on variables more likely implicated in dreaming but at present more difficult to study (e.g., patterns of higher brain activity). Thus, the brain stem neurons susceptible to detailed physiological investigation are sufficiently primitive not to have, at present, any established mental correlates.

Moreover, there is the difficult philosophical question of whether any account of the biological accompaniments of an experience can ever fully "explain" that experience. Traditionally, many psychologists who have been reluctant to embrace reductionist accounts of waking thought have been willing to accept them for dreaming. Presumably this is because of the stereotype of dreaming as an aberrant form of thought (bizarre, disorganized) and because delusional thinking seems to lend itself more readily to brain-state explanation than does thought within the normal range.

However, one of the major accomplishments of recent laboratory dream research has been to demonstrate the fallacy of this stereotype of dreaming. Remembered dreams may tend toward the unusual—in bizarreness and emotion, for example—and that may be precisely why they are memorable. But research has shown that the typical REM dream is not terribly bizarre or emotional. Nor does it involve frequent and inexplicable shifts of scene or plot. In fact, typical REM dream experience is not so very different from typical waking experience: It is more notable for its plausibility and thematic coherence than for its bizarreness.

The third and fatal problem for theories reducing dreaming to its supposed REM sleep foundations is that dreaming can and does occur in other states of sleep, and even, in more fragmentary form, in wakefulness. The evidence for this has been accumulating since the late 1950s and is now unequivocal. Aserinsky and Kleitman's original observations underestimated the occurrence of dreaming in non-REM sleep. More recently, research by John Antrobus and his associates at the City University of New York has also shown that, although there is more dreaming in REM sleep than in non-REM sleep, it is not a qualitatively different kind of dreaming. In other words, the same dreaming system seems to be engaged whether in REM sleep or outside REM sleep. This makes it impossible to explain dreaming in terms of any peculiarities of REM sleep.

THE FREUDIAN TRADITION

HOBSON AND MCCARLEY undertook a deliberate challenge of psycho-analytic theory. They argued that dreams are not meaningful; dreams do not originate in a meaningful unconscious, but rather in a meaning-free brain stem. The element of provocation here is testimony both to the staying power of Sigmund Freud's theory, formulated ninety years ago, and to the scientific community's cumulative grievances regarding its longevity. With the discovery of REM sleep and the ensuing proliferation of sleep and dream laboratories, it seemed likely that newer, more scientific theories would replace a model built more around Freud's intuition than any substantial body of original dream observations. For one reason or another, however, that did not soon happen. The received clinical wisdom survived: Dreams are meaningful; they have deep as well as manifest content; their affective sources, accompaniments, and consequences are particularly significant.

In the laboratory, as in the clinic, however, this wisdom remained more a matter of belief than of observation. Beginning in 1967 Louis Breger, then at the Langley-Porter Neuropsychiatric Institute in San Francisco, did mount a valiant effort to tie elements of received clinical wisdom to moorings in information-processing models of the newly evolved cognitive sciences. By and large, however, dream theory was, for a long time after the discovery of REM sleep, at a relative standstill, despite the fact that this discovery had generated a whole body of novel and unexpected observations about typical dream life.

Interesting research continues to be done along standard psychiatric lines. Rosalind Cartwright, a researcher at Rush Presbyterian-St. Luke's Medical Center in Chicago, and her colleagues, for example, have been studying the dreams of persons undergoing divorce, with the idea, following Breger's lead, that dreaming contributes to adaptation in the face of stress. She found significant differences in dream content between women undergoing divorce who were not depressed and both depressed women undergoing divorce and a (nondepressed) control group who never had considered divorce. The nondepressed divorce group had longer reports and reports with more negative contents and a wider time perspective, as if their dreams were being used to cope with their changing life circumstances. But this sort of research, where dream content is shown to be related to waking life circumstances, is notoriously unreliable in establishing causality. Is the dream merely reflecting current experience, or is it also helping to shape future experience? Is it an essential element in a causal chain, or simply a by-product of other casually [*sic*] significant experiences? Researchers still lack the ability to manipulate dream content experimentally (and to be able to do so without having to wake a person to establish the validity of the manipulation). Thus, waking-dreaming correlations cannot provide evidence about the effects of dreams on waking life, that is, about the function of dreams.

COGNITIVE SCIENCE THEORIES

AS NEUROSCIENTISTS best known for their studies of neurons in the cat's brain stem, Hobson and McCarley naturally enough base their alternative to Freud upon their own observations of sleep physiology. For nonreductionist modern theorists, on the other hand, a better starting point seems to be the new laboratory observations on dream psychology. If typical dream experience is more ordinary than extraordinary, then perhaps dream study should be aligned with theory and research on other, ordinary (waking) mental experiences. Fortunately, mental-science theory and research exist today in profusion, a situation quite unlike that when either Freud or Aserinsky and Kleitman began their research.

Beginning in the late 1950s, the "cognitive sciences" (e.g., cognitive psychology, artificial intelligence, contemporary linguistics, and psycholinguistics) coalesced and underwent explosive development. Their platform was, and largely remains, mentaltic (i.e., having nonreductionist explanations for mental phenomena). On the model of the modern computer, which was to play a large role in both their conceptualization and implementation, these sciences were less interested in the "hardware" of the mind than in the "program" run through that (biological) hardware.

Since their inception, the cognitive sciences have, in the judgment of at least one thoughtful observer, "discovered" more about how we human beings think than we had previously learned in all of our time on earth.

Some dream researchers have moved toward bringing dreaming within the explanatory scope of the cognitive sciences, while trying to convince these sciences that their rightful territory need not stop at the onset of sleep. So far, these efforts have been necessarily tentative and pretheoretical; what they have produced are more like programs for research than theories. One thing common to their efforts is the use of concepts and frameworks found useful in cognitive science analysis of waking mental life (e.g., short-term vs. long-term memory, mental "production systems"). Another is their abandonment, either on principle or for strategic reasons, of the orienting assumptions of the Freudian tradition (e.g., the unconscious, the latent dream, the primacy of affect over reasoning), assumptions that have not been found necessary in the analysis of ordinary waking mental life. Finally, most researchers in this tradition start with what may be the major empirical finding of dream research since the 1950s: The typical dream is a well-organized sequence of novel experience with substantial narrative continuity and real-life plausibility.

This finding, along with any theory built around it, implies that dreaming depends on, in the broad sense of the word, "intelligence." In other words, dream phenomena can be predicted directly neither from what an organism does (its responses) nor from its environment (its stimulation). Rather, dream experience should depend on (a) an organism's ability to represent and organize its experience in memory and (b) its ability to access, reorganize, and experience memories and knowledge in the absence of current and related environmental stimulation. In terms of the concepts of the great Swiss child psychologist Jean Piaget (1896-1980), dreaming should occur only where there is "representational intelligence." Thus, neither most subhuman animals nor human infants should be capable of dreaming, since their waking behavior gives scant evidence of this level of intelligence.

The (currently unanswerable) question about animal dreaming thus provides a kind of litmus test for belief in the usefulness of a cognitive-psychological approach to dreaming. Is dreaming like seeing and acting? If so, any organism capable of either should dream, and representational intelligence is not involved. Is dreaming more like thinking, reflecting, and remembering? If so, only organisms capable of demonstrating such capacities in their waking lives should be able to dream. Belief in the perceptual basis of dreaming is widespread and an obstacle to acceptance of cognitive psychology's relevance to dream phenomena. As one cognitive psychologist wistfully remarked, people who would never imagine that birds sitting on a wire were engaged in waking rumination or reflection are quite capable of believing that these same birds must dream.

A relevant test case is the dreams of persons rendered totally blind after six to eight years of life. These people no longer see a visual world, but they still are capable of creating mental imagery in their "mind's eye." How do they dream: non-visually, as they currently perceive, or visually, as they still are able to think? The answer, according to both surveys and laboratory research, is that they dream as they are able to think. Research by Nancy Kerr and associates at the Georgia Mental Health Institute in 1982 indicted [sic] that they even can experience visual realizations of persons they have known only since losing their sight. They dream as they think or imagine that these people must look.

CHILDREN'S DREAMS

STILL MORE RELEVANT DATA in favor of the cognitive approach came from longitudinal studies for children's dreams conducted at the University of Wyoming in the late 1960s and early 1970s. In one of these studies, children were studied in a laboratory nine nights per year over a five-year period between ages 3-4 and 8-9. Like adult volunteers, they too were awakened from REM (and non-REM) sleep and asked to report their dreams. The results suggested little dreaming at ages 3-5, while both the quantity and quality of dreaming were subject to later improvement. Three stages of dream development were identified: ages 3-5, infrequent dreaming, and no narrative or plot and no active self-representation when dreams were described; ages 5-7, infrequent dreaming, with rudimentary narrative structure but self-representation still absent; and ages 7-9, increased dreaming, with complex narrative structure and active self-representation. Thus, there were changes in the apparent incidence and nature of children's dreams as they matured intellectually. In fact, waking cognitive measures (e.g., from the Wechsler Preschool and Primary Scale of Intelligence) were the best predictors of children's dream phenomena.

It can be objected that it might not be the children's dreaming that changed, only their ability or inclination to remember or describe their dreaming. The Wyoming researchers tried to determine if this might be the case by examining what kind of cognitive measures best predicted children's dreaming. If memory or verbal skill measures did, then maybe it was only their remembering or describing of dreams that changed. The researchers found, however, that neither memory nor verbal skill measures predicted the incidence or recall of dreams well. Rather, the best predictors of growth in dreaming were visual and spatial skills that could well be imagined to be implicated in the act of dreaming itself. Their conclusion, then, was that both the very possibility of dreaming and the nature of the dream a child can create depend on the child's waking intelligence. Young children dream as they are able to think.

Although important in their significance, the results of this study were based on repeated observations of only 14 children (7 girls and 7 boys). However, a cross-sectional study (different children studied at different age levels) of 80 children aged 5-8 at the Georgia Mental Health Institute has just successfully replicated the findings of the Wyoming study. Both the same stages of dream development and the same patterning of waking cognitive correlates of dream phenomena were observed.

Thus, there is empirical support for considering dreaming as another activity that we do with the same mind and intelligence we use in waking life. Most cognitive-psychological theories base the uniqueness of dreaming in its origins. In the absence of patterned stimuli from the environment and lacking active mental intention, there is nothing to constrain mental activity in some single direction. Hence, organized, meaningful memories and knowledge of diverse sorts are simultaneously active. The experienced dream has consciousness doing just what it does in wakefulness: trying to make sense of current information in a way that organizes it and makes it cohere with real-life knowledge and expectations. Thus, most dreams are coherent and plausible. That all are not and that most dreams are slightly off center by waking criteria are hardly surprising, given the diversity of the information available to dream consciousness.

What is remarkable is how smoothly and creatively consciousness works, given the information available to it. The cognitive psychologist would conclude that we are right to be fascinated with our dreams: They are among the most impressive and remarkable things we do with our minds.

David Foulkes, "Understanding Our Dreams," *The World and I*, article no. 15471, (1989), http://www.worldandi.com.

PHILOSOPHY, PHILOSOPHERS, AND DREAMING

Dreams are so vivid and compelling that philosophers from East and West have wondered how to tell whether dream or waking experiences can be called "real." Some have also found dreams to be a source of creativity and inspiration, and a means of learning about hidden parts of themselves. Articulate thinkers of past and present have recorded the roles that dreams have played in their lives. This section contains little direct advice about dream work, but you may find that these philosophers' thoughts resonate with yours.

Chuang Tzu

AM I AWAKE OR DREAMING?

Chuang Tzu was a Taoist in 4ᵗʰ century BCE China. Here he portrays the difficulty in discriminating between dreaming and "reality." If you consider dreams "real" or not, does it change how you hold them?

THOSE WHO DREAM OF A GREAT FEAST may weep the next morning. Those who dream of weeping may enjoy the hunt the next day. While they dream, they do not know they are dreaming. They may even interpret their dreams while still dreaming. Only after they awake do they know it was a dream. By and by, there will be a great awakening; then we will know that this is all a great dream. All the while, the fools think they are awake, appearing to understand things, calling this man ruler and that man herdsman. How stupid! You and Confucius are both dreaming. When I say you are dreaming, I am dreaming too. These words may sound like double-talk. Yet after ten thousand generations, we will meet a great sage who can explain all this. Or it may happen any time now. . . .

Once upon a time, I, Chuang Tsu, dreamed I was a butterfly flying happily here and there, enjoying life without knowing who I was. Suddenly I woke up and I was indeed Chuang Tsu. Did Chuang Tsu dream he was a butterfly, or did the butterfly dream he was Chuang Tsu? There must be some distinction between Chuang Tsu and the butterfly. This is a case of transformation.

An alternate translation has the last line as, "This is what is meant by the transformation of things." For similar ideas about dream reality, see Nietzsche, page 127.

Chuang Tsu, *Chuang Tsu: Inner Chapters*, trans. Gia-Fu Feng and Jane English (New York: Vintage Books, 1974), p. 45 and p. 48.

Kai-wing Chow

CONFUCIUS' DREAM INTERPRETATION

Kai-wing Chow is a professor of history at the University of Illinois. He tells of a time when early Chinese philosopher Confucius (551-479 BCE) found insight from a dream.

WHEN CONFUCIUS WAS ABOUT TO DIE, he had a dream. He found himself sitting in between two pillars. When he woke up, the dream so touched him that he exclaimed: "I am after all a man of Yin!"

Kai-wing Chow, "Identity and Cultural Pluralism: Confucius in Early Narratives" (Association for Asian Studies, Annual Meeting, 1998).

Plato

INSPIRATION FROM THE IRRATIONAL

More than 2,300 years ago in Greece, Plato admired the creativity of dreams while the rational mind is relaxed. Deirdre Barrett has made the same observation (p. 107) in our times.

NO MAN ACHIEVES TRUE AND INSPIRED DIVINATION when in his rational mind, but only when the power of his intelligence is fettered in sleep ... But it belongs to a man when in his right mind to recollect and ponder both the thing spoken in dream or waking vision ... and by means of reasoning to discern about them all wherein they are significant.

Ilan Kutz, *The Dreamland Companion: A Bedside Diary and Guide to Dream Interpretation* (New York: Hyperion, 1993), p. 135.

Friedrich Nietzsche

The highly influential 19th century German philosopher Friedrich Nietzsche was credited with influencing the existentialist writers and philosophers that followed.

DREAM REALITY/WAKING REALITY

Here Nietzsche describes the dual nature of dreams and waking life; both appear to be vivid, he says, and both carry a quality of illusion. Nietzsche's words are very similar to a passage from the Diamond Sutra attributed to the Buddha: "All composite things are like a dream, a fantasy, a bubble . . . they are thus to be regarded." Similar ideas were also expressed by Chuang Tzu on page 125, and by Refik Algan about Sufis on page 228.

THE BEAUTIFUL APPEARANCE of the world of dreams, in whose creation each man is a complete artist, is the condition of all plastic art, indeed, as we shall see, an important half of poetry. We enjoy the form with an immediate understanding, all shapes speak to us, nothing is indifferent and unnecessary.

For all the very intense life of these dream realities, we nevertheless have the thoroughly disagreeable sense of their illusory quality. At least that is my experience. For their frequency, even normality, I can point to many witnesses and the utterances of poets. Even the philosophical man has the presentiment that this reality in which we live and have our being is an illusion, that under it lies hidden a second quite different reality. And Schopenhauer specifically designates as the trademark of philosophical talent the ability to recognize at certain times that human beings and all things are mere phantoms or dream pictures.

SOCRATES THE LOGICIAN

Nietzsche portrays Socrates as an uncompromising rationalist whose dream interpretation served only to support how he wished to see himself and the world. Then in his final days, Socrates relented and accepted that his dream was pushing him beyond his logic.

WHERE CULTURE IS CONCERNED, that despotic logician [*Socrates*] now and then had the feeling of a gap, an emptiness, a partial sense of reproach for a duty he might have neglected. As he explains to his friends in prison, often one and the same dream apparition came to him, always with the words, "Socrates, practise music!" He calmed himself, right up to his last days, with the interpretation that his philosophizing was the highest musical art, and believed that it was incorrect that a divinity would remind him of "common, popular music." Finally in prison he came to understand how, in order to relieve his conscience completely, to practice that music which he had considered insignificant. And in this mood, he composed a poem to Apollo and rendered a few of Aesop's fables in verse.

What drove him to this practice was something like the voice of his warning daemon. It was his Apollonian [*rational*] insight that, like a barbarian king, he did not understand a divine image and was in danger of sinning against a divinity through his failure to understand. That statement of Socrates's dream vision is the single indication of his thinking about something perhaps beyond the borders of his logical nature. So he had to ask himself: Have I always labeled unintelligible things I could not understand? Perhaps there is a kingdom of wisdom which is forbidden to the logician? Perhaps art is even a necessary correlative and supplement to scientific understanding?

Friedrich Nietzsche, "The Birth of Tragedy," trans. Ian C. Johnston (Nanaimo, British Columbia: Malaspina University-College, 1871). http://www.mala.bc.ca/~Johnstoi/ Nietzsche/tragedy_all.htm

RESPONSIBILITY FOR YOUR DREAMS

You would wish to be responsible for everything except your dreams! What miserable weakness, what lack of logical courage! Nothing contains more of your own work than your dreams! Nothing belongs to you so much! Substance, form, duration, actor, spectator—in these comedies you act as your complete selves! And yet it is just here that you are afraid and ashamed of yourselves . . . From this I must conclude that the great majority of men must have dreadful dreams to reproach themselves with.

C.G. Jung's expressed the same idea (see p. 9).

Friedrich Nietzsche, *The Dawn of the Day*, trans. J. M. Kennedy, (New York: Gordon Press, 1974), pp. 131-132.

Søren Kierkegaard

INSIGHT IN THE NIGHT

The Danish philosopher and religious thinker Søren Kierkegaard laid the foundation for the existentialist movement in the 19th century. Here in his journal he projected himself and his father into the roles of Solomon and King David. He imagined a dream of Solomon's that showed a darkness of David's character not visible in the light of day.

Solomon's judgment is already well known: it succeeded in distinguishing truth from deceit, and the judge became renowned as the wisest of princes; his dream is less well known. . . .

Solomon, thus fortunate, was living with the prophet Nathan. His father's strength and his father's achievements did not spur him to action, for they left him no opportunity, but it drew from him admiration, and admiration made him a poet. But while the poet was almost envious of his hero, the son was happy in his devotion to his father.

Once the young *[Solomon]* went to visit his royal father *[David]*. He woke in the night at the sound of movement, where his father slept. Terror seized him, and he feared that some miscreant was seeking to murder David. He stole near—he saw David with broken and contrite heart, he heard the cry of despair from the penitent's soul.

Powerless, *[Solomon]*sought again his couch; he slumbered but he did not rest, he dreamed; he dreamed that David was cast out by God, an ungodly man, that his royal majesty was the anger of God upon him, that he wore the purple as a punishment, that he was condemned to rule, condemned to hear the praise of his people, while the hidden justice of the Lord secretly condemned his guilt; the dreamer suspected that God was not the God of the pious, but of the ungodly, and that only the ungodly were chosen of God; and the terror of the dream lay in that contradiction.

As David lay upon the ground with contrite heart, Solomon stood up from his couch, but his understanding was broken. Terror seized him when he thought what it meant to be marked out by God. He suspected that the saint's intimacy with God, the uprightness of the pure before the Lord, was not the explanation, but that secret guilt was the mystery that explained all.

And Solomon became wise, but he did not become a hero; and he became a thinker, but not a man of prayer; and he became a preacher, but not a man of faith; and he could help many, but he could not help himself; and he became sensual, but not repentant; and he became contrite, but he was not raised up again, for the power of his will was strained by the weight which had been above the powers of his youth. He staggered through life, and was knocked down by life; he was strong, unnaturally strong, that is with feminine weakness, in the daring illusions of the imagination, and the ingenious explanations of the mind. But there was a rift in his nature; and Solomon was like a weakling who cannot bear his own weight. He sat in his harem like an enfeebled old man, till desire should wake in him once more, and he called out: strike the cymbals and dance before me, ye women! But when the Queen of the East came to visit him, drawn by his wisdom, his soul was rich, and wise sayings poured from his lips like the precious myrrh which flows from the trees of Arabia.

> *Kierkegaard described how deeply painful and limiting it can be when we have not found a way to reconcile the conflicting light and dark aspects of our selves. His journal entry ends where our dream work begins—in the slogging work of integrating even those parts of ourselves and others we find most repulsive (see C.G. Jung on the shadow archetype, p. 11; and Robert Bly's poem on p. 254).*

Søren Kierkegaard, *The Journals of Søren Kierkegaard*, ed. and trans. by Alexander Dru (New York: Oxford University Press, 1959), pp. 565-566.

Ilkka Niiniluoto

PHILOSOPHY AND DREAMING

Ilkka Niiniluoto, professor of philosophy at the University of Helsinki, delivered a lecture at the 11ᵗʰ European Congress on Sleep Research in 1992. Here I excerpt three sections of that talk on the philosophical history of dreams from prehistoric times to the present.

PERSPECTIVES ON DREAMS FROM PREHISTORY TO FREUD AND JUNG

FOR OUR PREHISTORICAL ANCESTORS, who had waken [sic] to self-consciousness and to awareness of their mortality, dreams were a puzzling and frightening phenomenon. Magical and religious explanations were given to the strange visions that fall upon a sleeping man in the darkness of night: Perhaps our soul is able to depart from our body and travel to another reality, where the living and the dead meet each other? Perhaps dreams are messages sent to us by gods and demons who rule our destiny? Such magical and occultist beliefs explain the social power of medicine

men and shamans, who are able—by using drugs or self-suggestion techniques—to reach a dream-like trance in the daytime. The fatalist belief
in dreams as omens or portents of future events gave also a special social
status to those who claimed to be able to interpret the content of dreams
(priests, oracles). In the ancient world, "dream books" became as popular
as another method of divination, astrology.

The Ancient philosophers in Greece favored a more rational natural-
ist approach. Plato characterized, in *Timaeus*, dreams as "visions in us, . . .
which are remembered by us when we are awake, and in the external
world." Aristotle defined, in *De somniis*, the dream as "a sort of presentation" (φαντασια, imagination), "more particularly, one which occurs in
sleep."

In *De somno et vigilia*, Aristotle argued that sleeping and waking
belong necessarily to all animals: sleeping is a privation, but also potential-
ity, of waking. Dreams occurring in sleep have natural causes: persisting
impressions derived originally by sense-perception from external objects
or from causes within the body. In *De divinatione per somnium*, Aristotle
further argued that "dreams are not sent by God," nor designed for the
purpose of predicting the future. Yet, sometimes dreams may be tokens
or causes of future events, if a remembered dream-movement paves the
way for a later daytime action.

Plato, who was more imaginative than his always sober pupil Aristotle, was concerned with the shameless nature of dreams. Plato expelled
poets from his ideal Republic, since they tell lies, and don't seek genuine
knowledge. Similarly, he compared sleepers to madmen: both "think
falsely," when they imagine, e.g., that they can fly (*Theaitetos* 158b). More
seriously, Plato stated in *Republic* that "in all of us, even the most highly re-
spectable, there is a lawless wild-beast nature, which peers out in sleep":

> . . . when the rest of the soul—the reasoning and human and ruling pow-
> er—is asleep; then the wild beast within us, gorged with meat or drink, starts
> up and having shaken off sleep goes forth to satisfy his desires; and you know
> that there is no action which at such a time, when he has parted company with
> all shame and sense, a man may not be ready to commit; for he does not, in his
> imagination, shrink from incest with his mother, or from any unnatural union
> with man, or god, or beast, or from parricide, or the eating of forbidden food.
> And in a word, no action is too irrational or indecent for him.

Plato's view anticipates Freud's account of the many-layered structure of human psyche in *The Interpretation of Dreams* (1900) and *Introductory Lectures on Psychoanalysis* (1914). According to Freud, the function of sleep is rest, which would be best achieved in a dreamless sleep. But when the control or "censorship" characteristic to our daytime consciousness ("superego") is relaxed in sleep, our subconscious mental process [*sic*] continue their operation on an "archaic" or infantile level. Dreams are "regressive": they return to a language of visual images, which give expressions to primarily sexual desires. What Freud added to Plato is his theory of "dream-work": dreaming attempts to "guarantee" sleep and "fool the censorship" by revising or transforming the original "latent" dream-content into the disguise of "manifest" dream-content. The aim of *Traumdeutung* is then to decipher or interpret this manifest dream in terms of its latent content in the language of desire.

The Plato-Freud conception of man gains plausibility also from the theory of evolution. As Ernst Cassirer put it, man is *animal symbolicum*. He differs from other animals primarily through his ability to construct conventional languages, and to think and communicate with such languages. This enables him to develop a conception of himself as a spatio-temporally continuous but finite being and thereby to become self-conscious.

Even though we modern men may in our dreams act in the role of self-conscious agents with linguistic capacities, it seems correct to say that dreams contain archaic features—traces from the earlier, more "primitive" stages of human evolution.

Here the school of Carl G. Jung agrees with Freud, even though Jung believed that dreams express their contents or "messages" directly without disguise. They both claim further that the same patterns of thinking can be found, besides [*in*] dreams, in myths, religions, works of art, day dreams, jokes, and neuroses. Their main difference is in Jung's thesis that this old primitive" instinctive" mode of thinking is somehow "wiser," more originally "human," better tied with useful and healthy valuations, than the rational soul of the modern enlightened man.

Here Jung seems to return at least partly to a magical conception of dreams. He asserted that dreams may be predictive: our subconsciousness, which operates with "archetypes," may in some cases "know" in advance a future event (e.g., the death of the dreamer), whose later occurrence then "explains" the content of the dream. Where Aristotle appeals to mere coincidences, Jung seeks to find metaphysical significance in the occurrence of causally independent "synchronic" events.

CURRENT PERSPECTIVES ON DREAMS

Next Niiniluoto discusses the equivocal distinction between dreaming and not dreaming, and how philosophers and the medical community define dreams.

LET US NEXT PROCEED to discuss the ontological issues about the definition and existence of dreams.

The Received View of modern psychology follows the Aristotelian account: dreams are sequences of experiences produced by imagination during sleep. Thus, to define dreams we need two distinctions, between sleeping and waking, and between imagination and perception (see Fig.1).

	sleeping	waking
imagination	dream	phantasy daydream hallucination
perception	subliminal perception	veridical perception perceptual illusion

Figure 1

The borderlines are not always very sharp here: there are transitory states from sleeping to waking or vice versa; a real auditory stimulus (e.g., the ringing of an alarm clock) may enter a dream in a disguise.

Sometimes the context makes it clear that talk about "dreams" really means daydreams or hopes for the future: Bing Crosby singing "I am dreaming about [sic] White Christmas"; Martin Luther King reciting "I have a dream."

It is well-known how difficult it is to test by questioning, whether someone is awake or asleep. Any response to the question "Are you sleeping?" counts as an indicator of waking, but no reply does not distinguish between genuine and pretended sleep. Even the trick of an old fairy tale does not always work. When one of his friends pretended to sleep, the Rabbit loudly explained that anyone genuinely sleeping raises his left foot and says "Wahoo"—and in the tale, of course, the foot raised with the scream "Wahoo."

However, it seems relatively unproblematic to assume that a sharp dichotomy between sleeping and waking can be drawn by means of external physiological criteria (respiration, EEG, etc.). But, as all sleeping does not include dreaming, it is much more problematic to think that the same could hold for the distinction between dreaming and non-dreaming. As dreaming in the primary sense is a psychological concept, identified by our subjective introspective awareness of these experiences, the attempt to find physiological correlates to dreaming leads us directly to the classical *mind-body problem*.

The success of REM research since the 1950s (Kleitman and Dement) has lead [sic] to the suggestion that there are neurophysiologically definable periods of dreaming in everybody's sleep every night, but in many cases we don't recall them. This thesis might be construed as a *reductionist type-identity* theory which was fashionable among materialist philosophers in the1950s (Smart, Armstrong): mental predicates can be explicitly defined by physical predicates. This kind of reductionism was rejected by the *functionalists* (Putnam, Fodor) and the *emergent materialists* (Popper, Davidson): even if each mental event is "token-identical" with a physical brain event, i.e., there is no mental life without a material basis, there is no hope to correlate types of mental states with types of brain states. For example, there is no description in the physiological language of the brain states corresponding to dreaming-that-I-am-travelling-with-my-brother-in-Romania-and-eating-at-a-cocktail-party-and-walking-on-the-street-with-a-map-in-my-hand (to mention my own dream last week). This means that psychology cannot be reduced to neurophysiology—nor dream research to sleep research.

It is important to realize that most contemporary versions of materialism—in agreement with dualism—accept the *reality* of mental phenomena (Popper's "World 2"). A reductionist says that World 2 is in fact a part of the physical World 1, an emergentist claims that World 2 is an evolutionary product of World 1, while a dualist thinks that World 2 has an independent existence as a spiritual substance. A subjective idealist in turn reduces World 1 to World 2. Dualist [sic] are either interactionists (mind and body are causally related in two directions), epiphenomena lists (bodily events causally produce mental events which are causally impotent), or parallelist (body and mind are causally independent from each other).

Therefore, most philosophers today would subscribe to the Received View, which takes dreamings to be real mental acts, imaginative experiences in sleep. However, the Received View has also been challenged in three interesting ways.

Norman Malcolm's *Dreaming* (1959) relies on Ludwig Wittgenstein's remarks in *Philosophical Investigations*. Inner processes, like pains or dreams, stand "in need of outward criteria," Wittgenstein says. According to Malcolm, this means that the concept of dreaming is derived from the familiar phenomenon of telling a dream. Even though dreaming and the waking impression that one dreamt are "not one and the same thing", the only criterion of my remembering a dream is in my waking account of the dream. Malcolm concludes that dreams cannot be called experiences, illusions, or workings of the imagination: to say that a person had a thought or feeling in his sleep could only mean that he dreamt that he had one, since otherwise he was awake and not asleep at that moment.

Malcolm's argument is based upon a verificationist theory of meaning, which requires public observational criteria of application for each legitimate term. This view was made popular by logical positivism, pragmatism, and operationalism—and it still has its supporters. But the major trend of analytical philosophy of science since the 1960s, the so-called *scientific realism*, is more liberal in allowing the use of theoretical terms in explanatory theories that are only indirectly testable by observation. Thus, scientific realism mandates the move from psychological behaviorism to cognitive psychology: it is legitimate to postulate a human consciousness (with beliefs, desires, dreams, etc.) which explains manifest bodily and verbal behavior.

The second challenge to the Received View comes from Daniel Dennett. In *Brainstorms* (1981), he points out that this view assumes two processes: the presentation of the dream experiences, and the memory-loading process which allows us to recall (some of) these experiences on waking. Dennett then proposes a "cassette-library theory" which claims that there is no presentation, i.e., no dreams, but only dream recollections derived from our memory banks at the moment of waking. Even if this theory does not seem very plausible, Dennett's discussion at least has the merit that it brings forward theoretical alternatives—eventually testable—to the Received View.

The third challenge, clearly the most radical one, comes from the eliminative materialists (Paul and Patricia Churchland). Terms like belief, imagination, experience, desire, and dream belong to our everyday "folk psychology," which will eventually be replaced by scientific neuropsychology. In other words, folk psychology will not be reduced but eliminated by neuropsychology. Terms which are commonly believed to refer to psychological states or experiences, will disappear from the scientific language like talk about witches, phlogiston, and orether.

Eliminative materialism is an interesting project. But I am doubtful of its prospects in the elimination of such "folk-psychological" language as talk about dreams. It is a fact that we have access to our mental life from an internal, subjective, qualitative perspective. In particular, dreams are not merely neurophysiological processes, but they also have an experienced content.

LIVING IN A DREAM?

*Now Niiniluoto considers some of the same questions asked by
indigenous peoples (p. 167) and Chuang Tzu (p. 125), presenting
them here in the language of Western philosophy.*

IF THERE IS A PHYSIOLOGICAL DISTINCTION between sleeping and waking, it is a third-person criterion, not applicable by *me* as a test of my own state. But without such a first-person test, it might be the case, as far I am able to know, that my present experience is only a dream, not perception of the external world.

World literature contains many touching descriptions of situations where a person feels himself uncertain, whether he is dreaming or not. "We are such stuff as dreams are made on, and our little life is rounded with a sleep," Shakespeare exclaimed in *The Tempest*. In *Hamlet*, he described an alienated outsider, beset with a weakened sense of reality and a melancholic feeling of a shady dream-like existence. This ambiguous mood of mind was expressed by romantic poets of the 19th century in well-known verses—Samuel Taylor Coleridge in *Reality's Dark Dream* (1803):

> I know 'tis but a dream, yet feel more anguish
> Than if 'twere truth. It has often been so:
> Must I die under it? Is no one near?
> Will no one hear these stifled groans and wake me?,

and Edgar Allan Poe (1845):

> All that we see or seem
> is but a dream within a dream.

The same theme, treated as an epistemological rather than existential problem, has been discussed by philosophers ever since Plato's dialogue *Theaetetus*. To refute the attempted definition of knowledge as perception, Socrates raises a question "you must often have heard persons to ask":

> "How can you determine whether at this moment we are sleeping, and all our thoughts are a dream; or whether we are awake, and talking to one another in the waking state?"

Theaetetus replies:

"Indeed, Socrates, I do not know how it could be determined, for in both cases the facts precisely correspond; and there is no difficulty in supposing that during all this discussion we have been talking to one another in a dream."

This thesis—viz. merely illusory, imagined, or dreamed experiences do not have any internal characteristic that would distinguish them from "real" presentations—has been called the *Theaetetus theorem* by the Finnish philosopher Eino Kaila (1958). Perhaps the most famous formulation of this "theorem" was given by René Descartes in his *Meditations on the First Philosophy* (1641). In exercising his method of universal doubt, Descartes ponders in his chamber:

> However, I must here consider that I am a man, and consequently that I am in the habit of sleeping and of representing to myself in my dreams those same things, or sometimes even less likely things, which insane people do when they are awake. How many times have I dreamt at night that I was in this place, dressed, by the fire, although I was quite naked in my bed? It certainly seems to me at the moment that I am not looking at this paper with my eyes closed; that this head that I shake is not asleep; that I hold out this hand intentionally and deliberately, and that I am aware of it. What happens in sleep does not seem as clear and distinct as all this. But in thinking about it carefully, I recall having often been deceived in sleep by similar illusions, and, reflecting on this circumstance more closely, I see so clearly that there are no conclusive signs by means of which one can distinguish clearly between being awake and being asleep, that I am quite astonished by it; and my astonishment is such that it is almost capable of persuading me that I am asleep now.

The Theaetetus theorem does not deny that sometimes in dreaming we may strongly feel that "this is only a dream." But Plato and Descartes hoped to find a general criterion which would exclude all doubt about my state. But if a feature of my experience is proposed as a criterion of waking, it is in each case possible to claim that I only dream that my experience has the property. For example, the familiar every day rule "Pinch yourself!" is not conclusive evidence for waking, since I could dream that I pinch myself and feel pain.

On the other hand, the more sophisticated criteria of reality, like the *scientia mensura* principle of the scientific realists, are inapplicable here: I cannot ask and wait for the ultimate consensus of the scientific community to decide whether I am awake or not.

The objections of Margaret Macdonald (1953) are not quite convincing. To say that "the content of dreams do [sic] not appear in a context of real objects" begs the question: how do I know that the context is "real"?

Kaila concluded that the Theaetetus theorem is valid. However, he argued that this does not lead to skepticism: Descartes failed to distinguish logical doubt from empirical uncertainty. Even if it is always logically possible to doubt the reality of our impressions, this does not imply that we ought to be actually or empirically uncertain about the reality of our perceptions.

Many philosophers, who accept the Theaetetus theorem for momentary experiences, have sought criteria of reality in the interrelations of longer temporal sequences of experiences. In the Sixth Meditation, Descartes concluded that "our memory can never connect our dreams with one another and with the general course of our lives, as it is in the habit of connecting the things which happen to us when we are awake." This consistency requirement is hardly so conclusive as Descartes implied, since sometimes a single dream at least seems to cover a whole life.

For a complete poem by Samuel Taylor Coleridge expressing the agony of nightmares, see p. 265.

Ilkka Niiniluoto, "Dream and Reality," 11th European Congress on Sleep Research, Helsinki, July 6, 1992.

Indigenous Peoples, Visions and Dreams

We move now from the realm of objective observations and intellectual descriptions generally associated with psychology, science and philosophy, to the more subjective and intuitive perspectives of myths, religion, and artists. The categories are not absolute; some of the Indigenous Peoples selections could be categorized as philosophical or religious, while some of the psychology selections are intuitively based.

Many pre-technological cultures believed that dreams are messages from gods, spirits, demons, or visions of other worlds. Whether or not we accept the theology or worldview of these cultures, we can still benefit from the intuitive wisdom they bring to dream work. The spirits or gods to which indigenous people refer may be seen as metaphors for that which we believe holds power, controls fate, acts malevolently, or bestows wisdom. In this section you will find simple and direct suggestions about dream work from cultures that value intuitive knowledge.

Some of the selections are direct quotes from people within the culture, and others are from people one step removed from the culture—writers, ethnographers (and one poet) who describe dream work, rather than do it.

The Oto and the Sioux

VISION QUESTS

*These quotes from the Oto and the Sioux remind us of the rich
American Indian tradition of vision questing, which includes careful
and sometimes arduous preparation.*

In Oto tradition:

WHEN A BOY WAS ABOUT TWELVE YEARS OLD he was sent out to fast
and seek a vision. "You must fast if you want to be something. Especially
this is true of boys. If you are a good boy and mind your teaching, you go
off to fast alone. But if you are not, you are sent out to fast with a brave
and a teacher, who is an old man. They make you fast so that you will be
better. They make you ask for what you want."

In Sioux tradition:

YOU MAY INVOKE THE SPIRITS [while seeking a vision] in words or songs
and you must always address them in a reverential manner. First, you
should make an offering of the smoke of the *cansasa*. Offer it first to the
Spirit of the East. . . . If this spirit does not send a vision, then call upon
[each of the other spirits of the directions]. . . . If these spirits do not send
a vision to you, then offer smoke to the Spirit of the Earth and call upon it.
If no vision is sent you by this spirit, then you may call upon the spirit of
heaven, the Great Spirit. But do not offer smoke to the Great Spirit until
after you are sure that the other spirits will not send a vision to you.

*We, too, need to prepare for our dreams. It is difficult to remember
dreams unless we get enough sleep, eat well, and have room in our lives
to pay attention to the dreams that arise. What do you need to foster
your dream search? What rituals support your inner life?*

Quoted by Lee Irwin, *The Dream Seekers: Native American Visionary Traditions of the Great
Plains* (Norman, OK: University of Oklahoma Press, 1994), p 102 and p. 114.

Lame Deer

Lame Deer, a Sioux holy man, brings passion to the seeking for dreams, and reminds us of the connection to deep spirit that dreams provide.

CRYING FOR A VISION

CRYING FOR A VISION, that's the beginning of all religion. The thirst for a dream from above, without this you are nothing. This I believe. It is like the prophets in your Bible, like Jesus fasting in the desert, getting his visions. It's like our Sioux vision quest, the *hanblecheya*. White men have forgotten this. God no longer speaks to them from a burning bush. If he did, they wouldn't believe it, and call it science fiction.

Your old prophets went into the desert crying for a dream and the desert gave it to them. But the white men today have made a desert of their religion and a desert within themselves. The White Man's desert is a place without dreams or life. There nothing grows. But the spirit water is always way down there to make the desert green again.

FIRST VISION QUEST

Lame Deer spent four days waiting for his first vision, during which he had the support of his family (his grandmother in particular), and his community, who helped him understand his experience.

I FELT THE SPIRITS OF MY LONG DEAD FOREFATHERS entering my body, felt them stirring in my mind and in my heart. Sounds came to me through the darkness: the cries of the winds, the whisper of trees, the hooting of birds. Suddenly I felt an overwhelming presence. Down there with me in my cramped hole was a big bird. The pit was only as wide as myself and I was a skinny boy, but that huge bird was flying around me as if he had the whole sky to himself. I could hear his cries, sometimes near and sometimes far away. I felt his wings touching me. This feeling was so overwhelming that it was just too much for me. I trembled and my bones turned to ice. I grasped the rattle ... [*that held*] the forty pieces of my grandmother's flesh. I shook it and it made a soothing sound, like rain falling on a rock. I took the Sacred Pipe in my other hand and started to sing and pray: "Tunkashila, Grandfather, help me!" I was no longer myself. I started to cry. Crying, even my voice was different. I sounded like an old man. I couldn't even recognize this strange voice. I used long-ago words in my prayer, words no longer used today. I tried to wipe away my tears, but they wouldn't stop. In the end I just pulled that star quilt over me, rolled myself up in it.

Then I heard a human voice, strange and high-pitched, which could not come from an ordinary being. All at once I was up there with the birds. I could look down, even on the stars, and the Moon was close to my left side. The voice spoke: "You are sacrificing yourself here to become a medicine man. In time you will be one. We are the fowl nation, the winged ones, the eagles. You shall be our brother. You are going to understand us whenever you come up here to seek a vision." I felt that these voices were good, and slowly my fear left me. I had lost all sense of time. I didn't know whether it was night or day. I was asleep, yet wide awake. Then I saw a shape before me. It rose from the darkness and the swirling fog which penetrated my earth hole. I saw that this was my great-grandfather, Tah'ca Ushte, Lame Deer, Old Man Chief of the Minneconjou. I understood that he wished me to take his name. This made me glad beyond words. Again I wept. This time with happiness.

I don't know how long I had been up there, one minute or a lifetime. I felt a hand on my shoulder gently shaking me. It was Uncle Chest who had come for me. "You have been up here for four days, hokshila," he told me. "Time to come down." I was to tell him everything that had happened to me and he would interpret my visions so that I could understand what they meant. He told me also that I was no longer a boy, that I was a man now. I was Lame Deer.

How can you bring commitment to your modern dream quest? Are there others who can support your efforts?

Quoted by Richard Erdoes, *Crying for a Dream; the World Through Native American Eyes* (Santa Fe, NM: Bear & Company Publishing, 1990), pp. 27-28.

Richard Erdoes

SIOUX DREAM PREPARATION

Richard Erdoes is an American graphic artist, photographer, and World War II immigrant from Vienna. He befriended and was befriended by Lame Deer while on a photo shoot for Life magazine, which led to his writing about the Sioux.

THE FIRST VISION QUEST I PHOTOGRAPHED occurred in 1967 at Rosebud on the dreaming hill of the Crow Dog family. The vision seeker was a middle-aged man, a relative of the Crow Dogs, who had fasted many times before. He told me that he had a problem which he hoped a vision would solve for him. At the foot of the hill stood his sister-in-law making a flesh offering, *cheh'pi wanunyanpi*. This flesh offering involved the dreamer's wife cutting 50 tiny squares of skin from her sister's arms. These were carefully put, one by one, on tissue paper, and later into a softly rattling gourd. This he was to take with him to the hilltop. Its sound was meant to comfort him during his long ordeal—a reminder that someone had undergone pain to help him in his quest.

After a ceremonial sweat, friends and relatives accompanied the "lamenter" to the vision pit atop the pine-studded butte. The pit was L-shaped, consisting of a hip-deep vertical shaft and, at its bottom, a horizontal chamber into which the man crawled, taking only the gourd, a sacred pipe, and a small bag of native tobacco. Over the pit was spread a large tarpaulin which, in turn, was covered with earth. It almost seemed as if the man were being buried alive. It brought to my mind what Pete Catches had told me:

"A man going to the hilltop for a *hanblecheya* gives his flesh and bones to the Great Spirit. And if he is accepted, he goes on living, but his soul, his ghost, his spirit is working apart from his body. He has been given a power. It is almost like dying, only you come back from this death. That's a hard thing to do."

After the pit had been smoothed over with earth, tobacco offering laid out in a square, and four colored flags, representing the four directions, had been put up, everybody left, leaving the vision seeker entombed in his pit. Four days later they returned to "bring him back to life again." I thought that it took a lot of courage and stamina to undergo a vision quest in this severe manner. Women also "go upon the hill," but in their case the fasting is done in the open, not in a pit, and limited to two days and nights.

> *The Sioux vision quest rituals are particularly arduous, physically and emotionally. There are times we, too, feel a desperate need to connect with the depths of ourselves, but most of us have no inherited rituals for calling on our dreams. Still, we can create our own rituals. What questions do you have in your life right now that would benefit from a dream vision? What are you willing to give for such a vision? How would you go about it and who would help you? For a Western approach, see Deirdre Barrett on page 110.*

Richard Erdoes, *Crying for a Dream; the World Through Native American Eyes* (Santa Fe, NM: Bear & Company Publishing, 1990), pp. 26-27.

Plenty-coups

Born in 1848, Plenty-coups was a Crow chief, a warrior who fought with the U.S. army against the Sioux, and a representative of his people in negotiations with the U.S. government. He also maintained the traditional ways of his people throughout his lifetime.

TRANSFORMATIVE DREAMS

In this long and detailed dream, Plenty-coups found he "knew" himself and was transformed. What could be a more important or more encouraging message for any of us?

THE VILLAGE WAS PREPARING TO MOVE to the Little Rockies, a good place for me, and before the women began to take down the lodges I started out alone. Besides extra moccasins, I had a good buffalo robe, and as soon as I reached the mountains I covered a sweat-lodge with the robe and again cleansed my body. I was near the Two Buttes and chose the south one, which I climbed, and there I made a bed of sweet-sage and ground-cedar. I was determined that no smell of man should be on me and burned some *e-say* [a root that grows in the mountains] and sweet-sage, standing in their smoke and rubbing my body with the sage.

The day was hot; and naked I began walking about the top of the mountain crying for Helpers, but got no answer, no offer of assistance. I grew more tired as the sun began to go toward the west, and finally I went to my bed, lying down so my feet would face the rising sun when he came again. Weakened by my walking and the days of fasting, I slept, remembering only the last rays of the sun as he went to his lodge. When I wakened, looking into the sky, I saw that The-seven-stars [the Big Dipper] had turned round The-star-that-does-not-move [North Star]. The night was westward. Morning was not far away, and wolves were howling on the plains far below me. I wondered if the village would reach the Little Rockies before night came again.

"Plenty-coups."

My name was spoken! The voice came from behind me, back of my head. My heart leaped like a deer struck by an arrow. "Yes," I answered, without moving.

"They want you, Plenty-coups. I have been sent to fetch you," said the voice yet behind me, back of my head.

"I am ready," I answered, and stood up, my head clear and light as air.

The night had grown darker, and I felt rather than saw some Person go by me on my right side. I could not tell what Person it was, but thought he beckoned me.

"I am coming," I said, but the Person made no answer and slipped away in a queer light that told me where he was. I followed over the same places I had traveled in the afternoon, not once feeling my feet touch a stone. They touched nothing at all where the way was rough, and without moccasins I walked in the Person's tracks as though the mountain were as smooth as the plains. My body was naked, and the winds cool and very pleasant, but I looked to see which way I was traveling. The stars told me that I was going east, and I could see that I was following the Person downhill. I could not actually see him, but I knew I was on his trail by the queer light ahead. His feet stirred no stone, nothing on the way, made no sound of walking, nor did mine.

A coyote yelped on my right, and then another answered on my left. A little farther on I heard many coyotes yelping in a circle around us, and as we traveled they moved their circle along with us, as though they were all going to the same place as we. When the coyotes ahead stopped on a flat and sat down to yelp together, the ones behind closed in to make their circle smaller, all yelping loudly, as though they wished to tell the Person something. I knew now that our destination was not far off.

The Person stopped, and I saw a lodge by his side. It seemed to rise up out of the ground. I saw that he came to it at its back, that it faced east, and that the Person reached its door by going around it to the right. But I did not know him, even when he coughed to let someone inside the lodge know he was there. He spoke no word to me but lifted the lodge door and stepped inside. "Come, Plenty-coups," he said gently. And I too stepped into the lodge.

There was no fire burning, and yet there was light in the lodge. I saw that it was filled with Persons I did not know. There were four rows of them in half-circles, two rows on each side of the center, and each Person was an old warrior. I could tell this by their faces and bearing. They had been counting coup.* I knew this because before each, sticking in the ground, was a white coup-stick bearing the breath-feathers of a war eagle. Some, however, used no stick at all, but only heavy first-feathers whose quills were strong enough to stick in the ground. These first-feathers were very fine, the handsomest I had ever seen, and I could not count them, they were so many.

"Why have you brought this young man into our lodge? We do not want him. He is not our kind and therefore has no place among us." The words came from the south side, and my heart began to fall down.

I looked to see what Persons sat on the south side, and my eyes made me afraid. They were the Winds, the Bad Storms, the Thunders, the Moon, and many Stars, all powerful, and each of them braver and much stronger than men. . . .

"Come, Plenty-coups, and sit with *us*." This voice was kind. It came from the north side.

"Sit," said the Person who had brought me there, and then he was gone. I saw him no more.

They, on the north side of the lodge, made a place for me. It was third from the head on the left, and I sat down there. The two parties of Persons were separated at the door, which faced the east, and again in the west, which was the head of the lodge, so that the Spirit-trail from east to west was open, if any wished to travel that way. On neither side were the Persons the same as I. All were different, but I knew now that they had rights in the world, as I had, that Ahbadt-dadt-deah had created them, as He had me and other men. Nobody there told me this, but I felt it in

---

* [*To count coups a warrior had to strike an armed and fighting enemy with his coup-stick, quirt, or bow before otherwise harming him, or take his weapons while he was alive.*]

the lodge as I felt the presence of the Persons. I knew that to live on the world I must concede that those Persons across the lodge who had not wished me to sit with them had work to do, and that I could not prevent them from doing it. I felt a little afraid but was glad I was there.

"Take these, Plenty-coups." The Person at the head of the lodge on the north side handed me several beautiful first-feathers of a war-eagle.

I looked into his eyes. He was a Dwarf-person, chief of the Little-people who live in the Medicine-rock, which you can almost see from here, and who made the stone arrow points. I now saw that all on my side were the same as he, that all were Dwarfs not tall as my knee."...

"Stick one of your feathers in the ground before you and count coup," said the Dwarf-chief.

I hesitated. I had never yet counted coup, and here in this lodge with old warriors was no place to lie.

"Count coup!" commanded the Dwarf-chief.

I stuck a first-feather into the ground before me, fearing a dispute.

"That," said the Dwarf-chief, "is the rider of the *white* horse! I first struck him with my coup-stick, and then, while he was unharmed and fighting, I took his bow from him."

The Thunders, who sat at the head of the lodge on the south side, said, "Nothing can be better than that."

"Stick another feather before you, Plenty-coups," said the Dwarf-chief.

I stuck another first-feather in the ground, wondering what the Dwarf-chief would say for it. But this time I was not afraid.

"That," he said, "is the rider of the *black* horse. I first struck him with my bow. Then, while he was armed with a knife and fighting me, I took his bow from him, also his shield."

"Enough!" said the Persons on the south side. "No Person can do better than that."

"Let us leave off counting coups. We are glad you have admitted this young man to our lodge," said the Bad Storms, "and we think you should give him something to take back with him, some strong medicine that will help him."...

I had not spoken . . . and could not understand why the Dwarf-chief had ordered me to stick the feathers, nor why he had counted coups in my name before such powerful Persons.

"He will be a Chief," said the Dwarf-chief. "I can give him nothing. He already possesses the power to become great if he will use it. Let him cultivate his senses, let him use the powers which Ah-badt-dadt-deah has given him, and he will go far. The difference between men grows out of the use, or non-use, of what was given them by Ah-badt-dadt-deah in the first place."

Then he said to me, "Plenty-coups, we, the Dwarfs, the Little-people, have adopted you and will be your Helpers throughout your life on this world. We have no medicine-bundle to give you. They are cumbersome things at best and are often in a warrior's way. Instead, we will offer you advice. Listen!"

"In you, as in all men, are natural powers. You have a will. Learn to use it. Make it work for you. Sharpen your senses as you sharpen your knife. Remember the wolf smells better than you do because he has learned to depend on his nose. It tells him every secret the winds carry because he uses it all the time, makes it work for him. We can give you nothing. You already possess everything necessary to become great. Use your powers. Make them work for you, and you will become a Chief." . . .

When I wakened, I was perspiring. Looking into the early morning sky that was growing light in the north, I went over it all in my mind. I saw and understood that whatever I accomplished must be by my own efforts, that I must myself do the things I wished to do. And I knew I could accomplish them if I used the powers that Ah-badt-dadt-deah had given me. I *had* a will and I would use it, make it work for me, as the Dwarf-chief had advised. I became very happy, lying there looking up into the sky. My heart began to sing like a bird, and I went back to the village, needing no man to tell me the meaning of my dream. I took a sweat-bath and rested in my father's lodge. I *knew* myself now.

The medicine he was given was unusual in Native American culture: not a special power, but rather the advice to focus his will and use his senses. As Plenty-coups faced his fears and accepted the role of oppositional spirits, he was able to enlist their support. In your life and dream, what might happen if you accepted the forces, events, spirits, and circumstances that seem to oppose you?

CULTIVATING THE STRENGTH
OF THE CHICKADEE

In a long and wonderful dream, Plenty-coups received another message about using his mind, attention, and presence in the world. This dream also foretold the destruction of the forests and showed him a glimpse of himself as an old man. In a part of the dream I have not presented, Plenty-coups watches as buffalo are replaced by cattle streaming from a hole in the ground.

I FOLLOWED [*a dream spirit*] back through the hole in the ground without seeing anything until we came out *right over there* [pointing] where we had first entered the hole in the ground. Then I saw the spring down by those trees, this very house just as it is, these trees which comfort us today, and a very old man sitting in the shade, alone. I felt pity for him because he was so old and feeble.

"Look well upon this old man," said the Man-person. "Do you know him, Plenty-coups?" he asked me.

"No," I said, looking closely at the old man's face in the shade of *this* tree.

"This old man is yourself, Plenty-coups," he told me. And then I could see the Man-person no more. He was gone, and so too was the old man.

Instead I saw only a dark forest. A fierce storm was coming fast. The sky was black with streaks of mad color through it. I saw the Four Winds gathering to strike the forest, and held my breath. Pity was hot in my heart for the beautiful trees. I felt pity for all things that lived in that forest, but was powerless to stand with them against the Four Winds that together were making war. I shielded my own face with my arm when they charged! I heard the Thunders calling out in the storm, saw beautiful trees twist like blades of grass and fall in tangled piles where the forest had been. Bending low, I heard the Four Winds rush past me as though they were not yet satisfied, and then I looked at the destruction they had left behind them.

Only one tree, tall and straight, was left standing where the great forest had stood. The Four Winds that always make war alone had this time struck together, riding down every tree in the forest but *one*. Standing there alone among its dead tribesmen, I thought it looked sad. "What does this mean?" I whispered in my dream.

"Listen, Plenty-coups," said a voice. "In that tree is the lodge of the Chickadee. He is least in strength but strongest of mind among his kind. He is willing to work for wisdom. The Chickadee-person is a good listener. Nothing escapes his ears, which he has sharpened by constant use. Whenever others are talking together of their successes or failures, there you will find the Chickadee-person listening to their words. But in all his listening he tends to his own business. He never intrudes, never speaks in strange company, and yet never misses a chance to learn from others. He gains success and avoids failure by learning how others succeeded or failed, and without great trouble to himself. There is scarcely a lodge he does not visit, hardly a Person he does not know, and yet everybody likes him, because he minds his own business, or pretends to.

"The lodges of countless Bird-people were in that forest when the Four Winds charged it. Only one is left unharmed, the lodge of the Chickadee-person. Develop your body, but do not neglect your mind, Plenty-coups. It is the mind that leads a man to power, not strength of body."

Plenty-coups' dream advised him directly about how to apply specific strengths to his life. In your own dream, is there a message about which of your strengths you need for your life now?

Quoted by Frank Linderman, *Plenty-Coups, Chief of the Crows* (Lincoln, NE: University of Nebraska Press, 1962), pp. 35-44 and pp. 65-67.

Fringe

DREAM GROUP OF CROW ELDERS

Fringe, an Absarokee (Crow) healer, tells a dream to the gathered elders in a sweat lodge. The meaning is discussed in accordance with the individual experience of each elder, and the symbolism they cooperatively agree upon. As the dream begins, Fringe is being guided by a dream spirit.

WE CAME TO A GREAT PAINTED LODGE that was red and black in stripes. . . . I saw many horses near. . . . An Otter was on one side and on the other was a White Bear. Both were angry because I was there and spoke crossly to me; but the Person [*dream spirit*] said: "Be quiet! This is my son."

We entered the striped lodge. . . . I saw his woman sitting. She was strangely handsome and tall. When she smiled at me, I knew she was very kind, that her heart was good. . . . The Person said, "This is all, my son.". . . the woman asked, "Why do you not give this son of yours something he may use to help his people, some power for good, if used by a good man?"

He picked up a strip of Otter skin and a picket pin [*a stake used to tie a horse*] and gave them into my hand. "Take these, my son," he said in a voice so kindly that I was not certain if it was his own. . . . The woman [said], "Will you tell him nothing?" The Person smiled. I saw his face change greatly. "Women are kind," he said, and took me by the hand. "I will tell him that this water will heal the sick among his people."

The elders agreed upon the following interpretation:

The striped lodge, painted red and black, meant that he would heal wounds, become a great Wise One among them. They said the picket pin showed that he would possess many horses, gifts from the men and women he had healed; and that the Otter and the White Bear would be his Helpers throughout his life on the world. They told him, too, that the Otter was his medicine, but said he would never become a chief, that he was too kindly to become even a great warrior. "You are like the Person who led you beneath the Medicine Water," they said.

> *The elders use Fringe's dream to identify his nature and to guide him to live in accordance with it. For more on the presence of masculine and feminine figures in dreams, see the selection on yin and yang (p. 238) and the selection about Marie Louise von Franz's work (p. 28).*

Quoted by Lee Irwin, *The Dream Seekers: Native American Visionary Traditions of the Great Plains* (Norman, OK: University of Oklahoma Press, 1994), pp. 142-143 and p. 180.

Oglala Dakota dreamer

BRING THE DREAM TO LIFE

A 68-year-old Oglala Dakota man retells the dream he had as an uninitiated 13-year-old boy. The dream became the basis of his initiation rite.

ONE TIME WHEN I WAS ABOUT THIRTEEN YEARS OLD, in the spring of the year, the sun was low and it threatened rain and thunder, while my people were in a camp of four tipis. I had a dream that my father and our family were sitting together in a tipi when lightning struck into their midst. All were stunned. I was the first to become conscious. A neighbor was shouting out around the camp. I was doubled up when first becoming conscious. It was time to take out the horses, so I took them.

As I was coming to my full senses I began to realize what had occurred . . . . I cried some to myself. I told my father I had seen the thunder. . . . I was told that I must be a *heyoka [an initiated one]*, if so I would entirely recover. If I did not go through the ceremony, I would be killed by lightning. After this I realized that I must formally tell in the ceremony what I experienced.

I also saw in the dream a man with hair reaching to his heels, while all over his back were many birds moving about. He was painted red; on the arms and legs were longitudinal marks with forks at the ends. On his face were live tadpoles and dragon-flies. He carried a sinew-backed bow with four red arrows. In one hand he carried something covered with horse-flies; it seemed afterward to be a deer-claw rattle.

In the *heyoka* I was ordered to array myself as nearly like this dream man as possible. So I had a long-tailed bonnet made and covered the tail with feathers. On my face and body I painted tadpoles and dragon-flies. In one hand I carried a deer-claw rattle and a string of the same over the shoulder.

> *I am impressed by the Oglala Dakota tradition of bringing the dream experience into the waking mind. Rather than first talking about a dream of yours, act it out, surround yourself with the images and circumstances of the dream, and experience it again. After you have experienced it while awake, what does the dream mean to you? (See also Clara Hill, p. 56)*

Quoted by Paul Radin, *The Story of the American Indian* (New York: Liveright Publishing Corporation, 1944), pp. 308-309.

Blackfoot dreamer

FOOLED BY A DREAM

Indigenous people need reminding, as we do, that dream images are symbolic, not literal.

THE MALE HAWK CAME and put me to sleep right where I was. This hawk immediately turned into a man, wearing a buffalo robe who addressed me, "My son, leave my children alone. I will give you my body that you may live long. Look at me. I am never sick. So you will never have any sickness. I will give you power to fly. You see that ridge (about a mile away) well, I will give you power to fly there." On awakening . . . I took off my clothes, and with a buffalo robe went back some distance from the edge of the river. Then I took a run and springing from the edge of the cliff, spread out my arms with the blanket for wings. I seemed to be going all right for a moment, but soon lost control and fell. I was stunned by the fall and was drawn under a rock by the current where I went round and round, striking my head . . . . This is one time in which I was fooled in my dreams.

Cheyenne dreamer

REJECTING THE GIFT

In this selection, a Cheyenne dreamer walks away from an animal spirit, rejecting its offer of help, and affirming the dreamer's choice to say no.

THE FOURTH NIGHT I heard singing below at the foot of the mountain. I went down crying and saw an animal at the spring. It was blue, with spots of white and had horns. It said, "This water is mine. It is different. In the summer it is cooler and in the winter warmer than any other water. Whenever I breathe I cause a fog. What do you wish?" I did not speak to that animal, but returned to the top of the hill.

If you walked away from an image of strength in a dream of yours, was it because you are not ready or because it was not the one for you?

Quoted by Lee Irwin, *The Dream Seekers: Native American Visionary Traditions of the Great Plains* (Norman, OK: University of Oklahoma Press, 1994), p. 133 and p. 155.

Frank Waters

HOPI CYCLES OF LIFE

*Frank Waters wrote numerous nonfiction studies of Central American
and North American native peoples. In The Book of The Hopi,
Waters tells us the Hopi view of life is based on cycles: day to night to
day, summer to winter to summer, life to death to life, cycles of light
and dark, and cycles of plenty and sparseness. From this perspective,
anything that arises in a dream, even death, is not a "death sentence."
That is, not even death is final; it is another transition to a new life.*

*The selection below is not explicitly about dreams, but suggests
questions that we can bring to our dreams. If a dream contains images
of sunrise, sunset, spring or fall, you can ask if you are in a time
of transition, moving into light, waking, and growth; or into dark,
fallowness, or loss? Are the dream events in day (bright light, in the
open) or in night (darkness, indistinct)? Are there clues to the subject of
the cycle (job or relationship rising or falling?) or the next step?*

... THE PATH OF THE SUN and mankind's Road of Life are virtually syn-
onymous. As shown in [*the figure below*], they both describe the perfect
rounded whole with the same clockwise circuit about the dual division
of space and time.

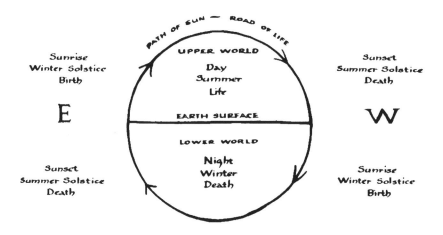

Each morning at sunrise the sun emerges from his sun-house in the east, travels in a circular path above the surface of the earth, and descends into his sun-house in the west at sunset. During the night the sun completes his circular journey, traveling west to east through the underworld. Day and night are thus reversed in the upper and lower worlds, the sun rising in the lower world as it sets in the upper world and setting in the lower as it rises again in the upper world.

This same diurnal reversal takes place during the annual shifts of the seasons. Each year at the time of the Winter Solstice, December 21, the sun leaves his winter house and travels to his summer house, where he arrives at the time of the Summer Solstice, June 21. During this period the upper world experiences increasingly longer days for planting and growing crops, which the Hopis regard as summer. Then again he returns to his winter house, the period of his journey, from June 21 to December 21, being considered as winter in the upper world. So again conditions are reversed in the underworld, which experiences winter while the surface world enjoys summer, and summer during the winter period above.

Fundamental to this concept of the year's duality is the premise that life in the underworld duplicates life in the upper world. Whatever takes place during a certain month above also takes place during the corresponding month below. . . .

Frank Waters, *The Book of The Hopi* (New York: Penguin Books, 1963), pp. 189-190.

Terri Andrews

Terri Andrews publishes The Good Red Road, a bimonthly Native American newsletter and home study guide.

LIVING BY THE DREAM

To THE NATIVE AMERICAN, dreams are their own form of reality: guidebooks for the living. Indians—of yesterday and today—hold that there are worlds that can be seen and worlds that cannot. The physical and spiritual are considered two aspects of the same presence. It is believed that the dream pulls both into the dimension of the dreamer's world, crossing the boundaries of past, present, and future.

Belief in the dream as the pathway to the spirit world gives profound importance to the efficacy of sleep's visions and the power found within their messages. It is said that "all can be found within your dreams." Thus, sacred rituals—involving abstinence from food and drink—are traditionally undertaken to pull the dream and its meaning to the dreamer.

In this view, the dream world conveys answers to the myriad problems that face both the tribe and the individual. It is not unreasonable to suggest that dreams lie at the very foundation of tribal culture. Indeed, a dream can lay the path for an entire lifetime. For many Native Americans, spiritual experience and participation provide the groundwork for their sense of being.

This is demonstrable in our history. Throughout the Plains, Native American men and women sought spiritual power through dreaming. Dreams were considered a way to connect with a higher power, the Great Spirit, creator of the universe. The dream allowed the dreamer to know a realm not traveled in the real world. Experiences of the higher power attained in sleep could lead to a greater spiritual openness when conscious.

Dreams were the most certain road to the Great One, a road that led to salvation. Several Indian communities put special emphasis on dreams as the channel to supernatural leaders in the "other realm." Attempting to connect with them, or with deceased loved ones, was common. The dreaming vessel (dreamer) who could travel to meet such greats was considered a holy person.

Reaching the spirit realm could lead to important knowledge. This came particularly in the form of prophecy. Throughout Native American history, prophecies have shaped the people's sense of their future. Dreams have warned villages of impending danger, told of death, and changed the course of tribal histories. One of the most famous prophecies tells of the coming of the white man. . . .

It is said that many years ago, in Nova Scotia, a young Micmac woman dreamed of an island floating in from the sea. The next morning the village people found that, indeed, a giant, island-like vessel was coming in to shore. The villagers thought the island was full of bears in trees, but as it came closer, the people realized there were no bears in trees at all. Rather, it was a French sailing ship with crewmen in its masts.

Another famous prophecy is that of the Sioux chief Crazy Horse. He had a remarkable dream that foretold his death ten days before it happened. The story recounts that Crazy Horse was walking on the prairie when he came upon a dead eagle. Deeply affected, he went back to his tepee and sat for many hours. He was noticeably upset. Finally, someone dared ask what was the matter.

Crazy Horse responded that he had just found his dead body on the prairie nearby. A few nights later he had a vision of riding a white pony on a plateau, surrounded by enemies armed with guns. He saw that he would be killed and his body left on the prairie, but that he would not die of bullet wounds. He would die by other means.

Several days later, Crazy Horse was surrounded by over twenty soldiers and was stabbed to death with a bayonet. A white pony was standing by, just outside the circle of soldiers.

Stories such as these, where the future had been accurately foretold in dreams and visions, are common in Native American histories. But some of the prophecies were not accurately acted upon. There are known instances of visions—retold by shamans or other tribespeople—whose meaning was misinterpreted. It wasn't until a fatal mistake had been made that the people recognized the truth behind the vision.

MISUSING SYMBOLS

Here Terri Andrews cautions us about taking traditions from another culture that we may not fully understand. We can take inspiration from other traditions, but we must realize that the symbolic meaning we attribute to them is our own and may not accurately reflect its origin.

IN MODERN SOCIETY, dreams still serve as important messengers. With the "New Age movement" that now permeates society, many native and nonnative people are realizing the power behind dreams. Books, articles, and workshops pop up all over the country, and Native American ways are gaining new respect. Shamanism, though practiced differently than in centuries past, can be found in all parts of the United States and many other parts of the world. The mixing of old and new cultural agents is gaining acceptance in many circles. For many today the dream and reality are one, just as they were for the people centuries ago.

But increased acceptance of native cultural symbols sometimes leads to their misuse or degradation. Some cultural borrowing is dreadfully superficial and sometimes little more than theft.

Cultural property includes both the tangible and nontangible. Land, beliefs, ceremonies, and religious items are all aspects of a particular culture. Misused, such elements can be utterly devalued. One item that symbolizes this problem is the dream catcher or dream net.

It was said that dreams flew around at night and could be caught with a special net, or "dream catcher." Many tribes claim to have originated the idea, including the Apache and the Oneida, but the Ojibwa/Annishnabe/Chippewa insist that it was originally their custom.

Regarded by Native Americans as a precious good luck charm and frequently hung above a crib or bed to protect infants, dream catchers are now seen hanging in the most unlikely places, from office windows to the rear windows of automobiles. Recently, I asked a young woman why she hung such an item in her car. Her reply was that it was "cool" and would bring good luck. When I asked if she knew the cultural background of the item, or why it is offensive to Native Americans to see it dangling there, she replied no to both questions.

I informed her that dream catchers such as hers, with central feathers, are for children, not adults. Adult dream catchers would have crystals or stones. The netting on her "decoration" was made with twelve strings, not eight as a genuine dream catcher would be, and hers was made of chicken feathers painted bright colors to imitate those of the Sacred Eagle.

My children commented that hanging her dream catcher from a car mirror, rather than above the person's head, removed all its cultural significance and efficacy. And most nets are eighteen inches long rather than six, as hers was. The entire meaning had been lost. The dream net had been reduced to a trinket.

Factory-made imitations like this are little better than forgeries, falsifying the artifacts of a proud society. By misappropriating an image from its cultural context, then changing the meaning and the item, one is both lying and stealing, distorting what is right and just. When a culture is turned into a commodity, crass commercialism displaces true value. So what, we asked the stunned young woman, was she really buying into?

If she wanted an authentic dream catcher, that would be fine. But to buy an imitation from the local Wal-Mart or shopping boutique was a mockery. Better to go to the culture itself, or make one by hand, researching the traditions and the meanings behind the item. Or purchase the item from a person who faithfully makes the product, whether native or not, but whose purpose in selling the item is to pass on the art, or to feed a family. And use it as it should be used.

This, I think, is the lesson of all traditional knowledge. The physical and spiritual, the practical and the symbolic, the dream and the reality, are aspects of the same presence, and the things and practices that join those realms should never be treated with indifference.

Terri Andrews, "Living by the Dream: Native American Interpretation of Night's Visions," *The World and I*, article no. 17616, (November, 1998), http://www.worldandi.com.

Tim Ingold

OJIBWA WAY OF BEING

In the selection below, Tim Ingold, professor of social anthropology at the University of Aberdeen in Scotland, attempts to bring to Western minds the Ojibwa experience of being. He quotes from an ethnographic study by A. Irving Hallowell, which describes how the Ojibwa don't experience the "self" as contained in skin, or in the mind. Instead, their perspective is empathic. For the Ojibwa, talking is not a sharing of information, but an expression of being, of self in this time, place, and circumstance.

AN OLD MAN AND HIS WIFE are sitting in their tent, and a storm is raging outside. There is thunder and lightning. The thunder comes in a series of claps. The old man listens intently. Then he turns to his wife and asks, quite casually and in a matter-of-fact tone of voice, "Did you hear what was said?" "No," she replies, "I didn't catch it." What are we to make of this?

Then Ingold comments on the story.

Certainly, so long as we remain in the Western view of the nature of sentience, volition, memory, and speech, *[that is, the nature of self]* the story seems incredible. The language of agency that we are accustomed to use posits a being, the agent, endowed with will and purpose, and whose existence and identity are given independently of any action that he or she chooses to initiate.

. . . the Ojibwa self is relational. If we were to ask where *[the self]* is, the answer would not be "inside the head rather than out there in the world." Taking this view of the person . . . it is clear that no physical barrier can come between mind and world. "Any inner-outer dichotomy," *[Hallowell]* asserts, "with the human skin as boundary, is psychologically irrelevant." But this is precisely the dichotomy, as we have seen, by which speech and similar expressive gestures are conventionally distinguished from the sounds of nature. To take Hallowell at his word means having to adopt a quite different view of speech, not as the outward expression of inner thoughts, but as one of the ways in which the self manifests its presence in the world. Thus, when I speak or clap, I myself am not separate from the sound I produce, of my voice or the mutually percussive impact of my hands. These sounds are part of the way I am, they belong to my being as it issues forth into the environment. In other words, speech is not a mode of transmitting information or mental content; it is a way of *being alive*.

If we accept this view of speech, there is no longer anything so odd about supposing, as the Ojibwa do, that thunder can speak, and that other people can hear. The rumbling of thunder is the manifestation of its presence in the world, just as the sounds of human speaking, singing, clapping, or drumming are manifestations of ours. Indeed, the world is full of such sounds, each one the signature of a particular mode of life. As people move through their environment, they constantly listen to the speech of these manifold life forms, revealing each for what it is, and respond with speech of their own. Both non-human sounds, like thunder, and human speech have the power to move those who hear them, and both kinds of sound take their meaning from the contexts in which they are heard. There is no fundamental difference here. So when the old man asked his wife, as the thunder echoed through the sky, whether she heard what was said, he was not expecting an answer in the form of some proposition, as though the Thunder Bird had been trying to send them a message coded in sound, like a telegraph. . . .

. . . the Ojibwa do not suppose that thunder is trying to transmit ideas to humans, but rather that its presence in the world, like that of other beings, whether human or other-than-human, can take an acoustic form. Responding to that presence with sensitivity and understanding is not therefore a matter of translation. It is more a matter of empathy. Total empathy is as hard to achieve as perfect translation; however, rather than shifting into another register of expression, it means taking on another way of being. Full understanding, in short, is achieved *not through translation but through metamorphosis*. And this happens, above all, in dreams.

If we adopt the Ojibwa practice, we would not be concerned with interpreting the meaning of a dream in words, but with experiencing ourselves and each of the images. The images are not separate from us, or even parts of us, but manifest a life of their own (see Jung, p. 13, and Hillman, p. 42). Questions we could bring to a dream might then be, "who am I in this image? What does it feel like to be this image?"

Tim Ingold, "A Circumpolar Night's Dream," *Figured Worlds; Ontological Obstacles in Intercultural Relations*, ed. John Clammer, Sylvie Poirier, and Eric Schwimmer (Toronto: University of Toronto Press, 2004), p. 44, p. 47, and pp. 49-50.

James George Frazer

THE SOUL'S JOURNEYS

James George Frazer began to publish his renowned studies of folklore, magic, and religion in 1890, adding to them for more than thirty years. Later anthropologists cast doubt on some of his theories, but on the whole his work is still considered to be important and scholarly. In this selection, Frazer describes cultures that consider dreams to be concretely real.

THE SOUL OF A SLEEPER is supposed to wander away from his body and actually to visit the places, to see the persons, and to perform the acts of which he dreams. For example, when an Indian of Brazil or Guiana wakes up from a sound sleep, he is firmly convinced that his soul has really been away hunting, fishing, felling trees, or whatever else he has dreamed of doing, while all the time his body has been lying motionless in his hammock. A whole Bororo village has been thrown into a panic and nearly deserted because somebody had dreamed that he saw enemies stealthily approaching it. A Macusi Indian in weak health, who dreamed that his employer had made him haul the canoe up a series of difficult cataracts, bitterly reproached his master next morning for his want of consideration in thus making a poor invalid go out and toil during the night. The Indians of the Gran Chaco are often heard to relate the most incredible stories as things which they have themselves seen and heard; hence strangers who do not know them intimately say in their haste that these Indians are liars. In point of fact the Indians are firmly convinced of the truth of what they relate; for these wonderful adventures are simply their dreams, which they do not distinguish from waking realities.

Now the absence of the soul in sleep has its dangers, for if from any cause the soul should be permanently detained away from the body, the person thus deprived of the vital principle must die. There is a German belief that the soul escapes from a sleeper's mouth in the form of a white mouse or a little bird, and that to prevent the return of the bird or animal would be fatal to the sleeper. Hence in Transylvania they say that you should not let a child sleep with its mouth open, or its soul will slip out in the shape of a mouse, and the child will never wake. Many causes may detain the sleeper's soul. Thus, his soul may meet the soul of another sleeper and the two souls may fight; if a Guinea negro wakens with sore bones in the morning, he thinks that his soul has been thrashed by another soul in sleep. Or it may meet the soul of a person just deceased and be carried off by it; hence in the Aru Islands the inmates of a house will not sleep the night after a death has taken place in it, because the soul of the deceased is supposed to be still in the house and they fear to meet it in a dream. . . . Again, the soul of the sleeper may be prevented by an accident or by physical force from returning to his body. When a Dyak dreams of falling into the water, he supposes that this accident has really befallen his spirit, and he sends for a wizard, who fishes for the spirit with a hand-net in a basin of water till he catches it and restores it to its owner. The Santals tell how a man fell asleep, and growing very thirsty, his soul, in the form of a lizard, left his body and entered a pitcher of water to drink. Just then the owner of the pitcher happened to cover it; so the soul could not return to the body and the man died. While his friends were preparing to burn the body some one uncovered the pitcher to get water. The lizard thus escaped and returned to the body, which immediately revived; so the man rose up and asked his friends why they were weeping. They told him they thought he was dead and were about to burn his body. He said he had been down a well to get water, but had found it hard to get out and had just returned. So they saw it all. . . .

It is a common rule with primitive people not to waken a sleeper, because his soul is away and might not have time to get back; so if the man wakened without his soul, he would fall sick. If it is absolutely necessary to rouse a sleeper, it must be done very gradually, to allow the soul time to return. A Fijian in Matuku, suddenly wakened from a nap by somebody treading on his foot, has been heard bawling after his soul and imploring it to return. He had just been dreaming that he was far away in Tonga, and great was his alarm on suddenly wakening to find his body in Matuku. Death stared him in the face unless his soul could be induced to speed at once across the sea and reanimate its deserted tenement. The man would probably have died of fright if a missionary had not been at hand to allay his terror.

Still more dangerous is it in the opinion of primitive man to move a sleeper or alter his appearance, for if this were done the soul on its return might not be able to find or recognize its body, and so the person would die. The Minangkabauers deem it highly improper to blacken or dirty the face of a sleeper, lest the absent soul should shrink from re-entering a body thus disfigured. Patani Malays fancy that if a person's face be painted while he sleeps, the soul which has gone out of him will not recognize him, and he will sleep on till his face is washed. In Bombay it is thought equivalent to murder to change the aspect of a sleeper, as by painting his face in fantastic colors or giving moustaches to a sleeping woman. For when the soul returns it will not know its own body and the person will die.

What did your soul do and who did your soul meet in last night's dreams?

James George Frazer, "The Perils of the Soul," *The Golden Bough: A Study of Magic and Religion*, 3rd ed., Part II, *Taboo and the Perils of the Soul* (New York: St. Martin's Press, 1976), pp. 36-41.

Mimi George

BAROK COMMUNAL DREAMS

American cultural anthropologist Mimi George wrote about the experience she had during field work with the Barok people of Papua New Guinea, when others communicated with her through dreams. I have heard too many first-hand accounts of similar experiences to deny the possibility of such mysterious events. Whatever you believe, I propose that awe is an appropriate attitude to bring to our dreams and dreaming.

THE FIRST EXPERIENCE OCCURRED IN 1979, shortly after I settled into a Barok hamlet on the west coast of south-central New Ireland. A Barok "big," or spiritually powerful, person had explained to me that before the Barok do anything important they dream about it. But I was shocked when an old woman started communicating with me in my dreams.

Kalerian was the senior female or "Big Woman" of the matrilineal Pelarau'o clan. She had adopted me as her sister just as her son, Tadi Slel, a preeminent "Big Man" of the clan, had adopted me as his clan mother. One morning at dawn, another of my sister's sons, Alek, came striding up to me. He looked me straight in the eyes and asked, "Did you understand her?"

I looked back at him for more clues then asked, "Who?" I had no idea what he was talking about. He looked blank. Nervously, I tried again: "Say what?"

Alek seemed to steel himself. "My mother was talking to you last night. She asked me to make sure that you understood what she told you." Alek kept a measured tone and watched me closely.

"I did not talk with her last night," I replied, confused.

"You do not remember when she came to see you in the night? . . . In Tokpisin, we call this griman [dreaming]."

"Oh!" I suddenly felt queasy. I remembered that she had indeed been in my dreams, though I could not recall specifically what they were about.

I just remembered a feeling that there was a problem and that she had directed me to do something about it. But even in my dream, I did not take her too seriously.

"Ah, yes," I admitted. "I do remember that she was in my dream. But I cannot remember much else."

"That is why she came to me and to Bustaman, too," Alek replied in the calm, clear manner of a kindergarten teacher. Just then Alek's brother Bustaman bounded up to us, grinning and nodding as if all three of us knew what this was about.

Alek and Bustaman then described to me exactly what was in my dream. They even repeated to me the exact words that Kalerian had said to me in the dream. While Alek and Bustaman were describing parts of my dream, I remembered everything they said and more, and I remembered with absolute certainty.

Feed your pig. The issue in my dream had to do with my decision not to give more money to their eldest brother, Bore. In fact, just the day before I had decided to be slow about giving the money because Bore had been laggardly in arranging to have a house built for me. I had told no one of my deliberation.

Yet in my dream that night Kalerian said to me, "I know what you are doing, sister, and I am upset." Her concern was that I would act without trust or respect for "our" eldest child, Bore. Even if he was not doing what he said he would, the result of my not giving him money would be bad for all of us in the future. "Feed your child," she said. "He depends on us for his lolos [spiritual strength]."

"Bore is the eldest," she continued. "This means he is the biggest Big Man of the family. ... Feed Bore."

I was taken with the way she put it. In Barok, bore means "pig of mine," which was our eldest son's name. She had effectively told me, "Feed your pig."

For some reason, I got the feeling that part of her concern actually was about pigs, though this was long before I owned any. However, some months earlier I had seen the final event of a gaba tree festival held in a

Barok village near the district border. As Kalerian had spoken to me, I had recalled the image of the young girls, called dawan, and the huge pigs they sat in front of at the feast.

"Feed Bore," Alek said, as he finished recapping the dream I had already remembered. "Now do you understand?" he pressed for confirmation. . . .

For a very long moment I could not reply, trying to grasp what had just happened. I wondered how Kalerian could have known what I had thought or felt about giving Bore money. I had not told anyone my intentions, and Kalerian was not directly involved. Of course, Bore may have told her something and she might have just decided to tell me what to do. But then, I suddenly asked myself, "How did she get into my dream to tell me anything? And how did Alek and Bustaman have the same dream?"

When this thought occurred to me, I exclaimed loudly, "Yes, what you two just told me is what was in my dream!" They were startled, and the whites of their eyes widened as they nodded nervously. I blurted out my real question: "How do you know what I dreamed? I just woke up, and I told no one anything about my dream. I did not even remember it until you started to tell me about it!"

They peered at me oddly. Then Alek said quickly, "Because your sister came to us last night, too. She talked to us, too. We watched her talk to you, and then she told us to come to you this morning to make sure you understood what she said."

"Do you always do this?" I asked.

"What do you mean?" Alek asked back.

"Can you communicate with people—visit people—in their dreams at night?" I tried to focus my question.

"Maybe it is something that big people do," Alek replied quietly. But Bustaman, in his normally ebullient way, enthused, "And it does not matter if we are over on the east coast of New Ireland, or up in Kavieng, or even over in Rabaul! If our mother wants to talk to us, she does it!"

My questions made them uncomfortable. It was clear that they were just fulfilling their mother's directive to confront me about my understanding of this dream. They realized I had trouble understanding her, and they wanted to be helpful. But I also sensed their shock at my lack of attention to her in my dreams . . . and their surprise at the degree of my ignorance about dreaming.

I wrote about what had happened in my journal—in code. Just in case anything happened to me, I did not want anyone to read about it and think that I had gone nuts in the field. But I knew there was no getting around the fact that three people had dropped in on my dream, and, according to the Barok people involved, they had done so because my sister made that happen. In my dream, Kalerian had brought to my attention that spiritual meaning and power were at stake in my dealings with Bore. Awareness of her intent and ability convinced me to change my course in non-dreaming reality. I gave Bore more money, and I looked to the future.

Mimi George, "In a Pig's Eye: Learning from Tattoos and Dreams Among the Barok," *The World and I,* article no. 13757, (1995), http://www.worldandi.com.

African dream worker

FEEL THE "CLICK"

The American writer, editor, and film producer, Marc Ian Barasch included this quote from an African dream worker in his well-researched book Healing Dreams.

AFTER A BIG DREAM you must talk to it. . . . You ask the dream in a sacred place what it wants, let it turn itself over and over. When you figure it out, it's like putting a car in the right gear—you feel a click.

Quoted by Marc Ian Barasch, *Healing Dreams; Experiencing the Dreams that Can Transform Your Life* (New York: Riverhead Books, 2000), p. 128.

Sylvie Poirier

THE KUKATJA AND DREAM SETTING

Sylvie Poirier, professor of anthropology at Quebec's Université Laval, emphasizes the importance of a dream's physical setting in this selection about the Kukatja people of Australia. The Kukatja always include a dream's location in their telling of a dream, as we should too. We can start by asking simple questions: Does this place remind me of anywhere or anything? How does the place relate to the events of the dream or my life?

THE SPIRIT-CHILD CAN . . . make its presence known to the mother or relative by way of a dream. Through dreams, the spirit-child makes known its intention to penetrate within the mother and undergo metamorphosis. At this point, it should be stressed that in the Kukatja system of thought and knowledge, dream experiences mediate between the ancestral and human realms. Dreaming is without doubt the favored space-time of exchange and communication with the ancestral beings and deceased relatives . . . It is through dream experiences that Kukatja men and women meet with ancestors at specific places falling within their country. All dream narratives are necessarily spatially located, and the dreamer will always specify the *ngurra* (country or places) where the action occurred. Dreaming also has an influence on the reproductive well-being of one's country, in terms both spiritual and material. One day, commenting on the abundance of wild food in her country near Mungkayi, Napangarti added, "This is good country, we are good dreamers." As a part of human action, dreaming is yet another form of Kukatja involvement in the landscape, as well as a form of communication with the ancestral order.

Sylvie Poirier, "Ontology, Ancestral Order, and Agencies among the Kukatja of the Australian Western Desert," *Figured Worlds; Ontological Obstacles in Intercultural Relations*, ed. John Clammer, Sylvie Poirier, and Eric Schwimmer (Toronto: University of Toronto Press, 2004), pp. 66-67.

N. Scott Momaday

THE GOURD DANCER

The Native American novelist and poet Scott Momaday was born in 1934 to the Kiowa. Here he writes about his grandfather (Mammedaty).

THE GOURD DANCER
Mammedaty, 1880-1932

l. *The Omen*
Another season centers on this place.
Like memory the blood congeals in it;
And like memory, too, the sun recedes
Into the hazy, southern distances.
A vagrant heat hangs on the dark river,
And shadows turn like smoke. An owl ascends
Among the branches, clattering, remote
Within its motion, intricate with age.

II. *The Dream*
Mammedaty saw to the building of this house.
Just there, by the arbor, he made a camp in the
old way. And in the evening when the hammers had
fallen silent and there were frogs and crickets
in the black grass—and a low, hectic wind upon
the pale, slanting plane of the moon's light—
he settled deep down in his mind to dream. He
dreamed of dreaming, and of the summer breaking
upon his spirit, as drums break upon the intervals
of the dance, and of the gleaming gourds.

III. *The Dance*
Dancing,
He dreams, he dreams—

The long wind glances, moves
Forever as a music to the mind;
The gourds are flashes of the sun.
He takes the inward, mincing steps
Describing old processions and refrains.

Dancing,
His moccasins,
His sash and bandolier
Contain him in insignia;
His fan is powerful, concise
According to his agile hand,
And catches on the sacramental air.

IV. The Give-away
Someone spoke his name, Mammedaty, in which
his essence was and is. It was a serious matter
that his name should be spoken there in the circle,
among the many people, and he was thoughtful,
full of wonder, and aware of himself and of his name.
He walked slowly to the summons, looking into the
eyes of the man who summoned him. For a moment
they held each other in close regard, and all about
them there was excitement and suspense.

Then a boy came suddenly into the circle, leading
a black horse. The boy ran, and the horse after him.
He brought the horse up short in front of Mammedaty,
and the horse wheeled and threw its head and cut
its eyes in the wild way. And it blew hard and
quivered in its hide so that light ran, rippling,
upon its shoulders and its flanks—and then it
stood still and was calm. Its mane and tail were
fixed in braids and feathers, and a bright red chief's
blanket was draped in a roll over its withers. The

boy placed the reins in Mammedaty's hands. And all
of this was for Mammedaty, in his honor, as even now
it is in the telling, and will be, as long as there
are those who imagine him in his name.

> *In this poem/dream, the dreamer is honored before the assembly of*
> *esteemed figures. They may represent internal parts of the dreamer or*
> *actual people in the waking world (see Eugene Gendlin, "What part*
> *of you is that?" p. 68). Momaday, even today, offers respect to his*
> *grandfather for and with this dream. If you had a dream in which you*
> *were honored before the assembly, do you think it came to remind you of*
> *your worth? Why now?*

N. Scott Momaday, "The Gourd Dancer," *Carriers of the Dream Wheel; Contemporary Native American Poetry*, ed. Duane Niatum (New York: Harper and Row, Publishers, 1975), pp. 94-95.

MYTH, RELIGION, AND DREAMS

Most religions share a belief that dreams are a source of insight coming from beyond ourselves. For example, when Joseph interprets Pharaoh's dreams in Genesis, he tells Pharaoh that all dream interpretations come from God (p. 200). Joseph's interpretations are still discussed in Jewish, Christian, and Islamic traditions today (p. 207, p. 214, and p. 216). Depending on your personal beliefs, you can look upon dreams as being literally true, as being intuitive wisdom with metaphoric truth, or both. It is up to each of us to discover the wisdom in dreams and in mythical and religious stories, and find their application in our lives. This chapter begins with excerpts from folk tales and myths, and concludes with sources from world religions.

Clarissa Pinkola Estes

SKELETON WOMAN

Clarissa Pinkola Estes, a Jungian analyst, researched myths, fairy tales, and folk tales for use in her writing and work with clients. Here she retells a fairy tale that offers insights about how humans interconnect. The relationship in this story begins in fear and running away, and then relaxes into sleep and dream.

SHE HAD DONE SOMETHING of which her father disapproved, although no one any longer remembered what it was. But her father had dragged her to the cliffs and thrown her over and into the sea. There, the fish ate her flesh away and plucked out her eyes. As she lay under the sea, her skeleton turned over and over in the currents.

One day a fisherman came fishing, well, in truth many came to the bay once. But this fisherman had drifted far from his home place, and did not know that the local fishermen stayed away, saying this inlet was haunted.

The fisherman's hook drifted down through the water, and caught, of all places, in the bones of Skeleton Woman's rib cage. The fisherman thought, "Oh, now I've really got a big one! Now I really have one!" In his mind he was thinking of how many people this great fish would feed, how long it would last, how long he might be free from the chore of hunting. And as he struggled with this great weight on the end of the hook, the sea was stirred to a thrashing froth, and his kayak bucked and shook, for she who was beneath struggled to disentangle herself. And the more she struggled, the more she tangled in the line. No matter what she did, she was inexorably dragged upward, tugged up by the bones of her own ribs.

The hunter had turned to scoop up his net, so he did not see her bald head rise above the waves, he did not see the little coral creatures glinting in the orbs of her skull, he did not see the crustaceans on her old ivory teeth. When he turned back with his net, her entire body, such as it was,

181

had come to the surface and was hanging from the tip of his kayak by her long front teeth.

"Agh!" cried the man, and his heart fell into his knees, his eyes hid in terror on the back of his head, and his ears blazed bright red. "Agh!" he screamed, and knocked her off the prow with his oar and began paddling like a demon toward shoreline. And not realizing she was tangled in his line, he was frightened all the more for she appeared to stand upon her toes while chasing him all the way to shore. No matter which way he zigged his kayak, she stayed right behind, and her breath rolled over the water in clouds of steam, and her arms flailed out as though to snatch him down into the depths.

"Aggggggghhhh!" he wailed as he ran aground. In one leap he was out of his kayak, clutching his fishing stick and running, and the coral-white corpse of Skeleton Woman, still snagged in the fishing line, bumpety-bumped behind right after him. Over the rocks he ran, and she followed. Over the frozen tundra he ran and she kept right up. Over the meat laid out to dry he ran, cracking it to pieces as his mukluks bore down.

Throughout it all she kept right up, in fact grabbed some of the frozen fish as she was dragged behind. This she began to eat, for she had not gorged in a long, long time. Finally, the man reached his snowhouse and dove right into the tunnel and on hands and knees scrabbled his way into the interior. Panting and sobbing he lay there in the dark, his heart a drum, a mighty drum. Safe at last, oh so safe, yes safe, thank the Gods, Raven, yes, thank Raven, yes, and all-bountiful Sedna, safe . . . at . . . last.

Imagine when he lit his whale oil lamp, there she—it—lay in a tumble upon his snow floor, one heel over her shoulder, one knee inside her rib cage, one foot over her elbow. He could not say later what it was, perhaps the firelight softened her features, or the fact that he was a lonely man. But a feeling of some kindness came into his breathing, and slowly he reached out his grimy hands and, using words softly like mother to child, began to untangle her from the fishing line.

"Oh, na, na, na." First he untangled the toes, then the ankles. "Oh, na, na, na." On and on he worked into the night, until dressing her in furs to keep her warm, Skeleton Woman's bones were all in the order a human's should be.

He felt into his leather cuffs for his flint, and used some of his hair to light a little more fire. He gazed at her from time to time as he oiled the precious wood of his fishing stick and rewound the gut line. And she in the furs uttered not a word—she did not dare—lest this hunter take her out and throw her down to the rocks and break her bones to pieces utterly.

The man became drowsy, slid under his sleeping skins, and soon was dreaming. And sometimes as humans sleep, you know, a tear escapes from the dreamer's eye; we never know what sort of dream causes this, but we know it is either a dream of sadness or longing. And this is what happened to the man.

The Skeleton Woman saw the tear glisten in the firelight, and she became suddenly soooo thirsty. She tinkled and clanked and crawled over to the sleeping man and put her mouth to his tear. The single tear was like a river and she drank and drank and drank until her many-years-long thirst was slaked.

While lying beside him, she reached inside the sleeping man and took out his heart, the mighty drum. She sat up and banged on both sides of it: *Bom, Bomm! . . . Bom, Bomm!*

As she drummed, she began to sing out "Flesh, flesh, flesh! Flesh, flesh, flesh!" And the more she sang, the more her body filled out with flesh. She sang for hair and good eyes and nice fat hands. She sang the divide between her legs, and breasts long enough to wrap for warmth, and all the things a woman needs.

And when she was all done, she also sang the sleeping man's clothes off and crept into his bed with him, skin against skin. She returned the great drum, his heart, to his body, and that is how they awakened, wrapped one around the other, tangled from their night, in another way now, a good and lasting way.

The people who cannot remember how she came to her first ill-fortune say she and the fisherman went away and were consistently well fed by the creatures she had known in her life under water. The people say that it is true and that is all they know.

From this man's tear and his beating heart, life was renewed. What can
you learn from the tears in your own dreams? Is there a way to use the
tears themselves, the sadness, to revive new life?

Clarissa Pinkola Estes, *Women Who Run With the Wolves* (New York: Ballantine Books, 1992), pp. 132-134.

Joseph Campbell

MYTHS AND DREAMS

Throughout his lifetime, Joseph Campbell studied, wrote, taught, and
spoke prolifically about world myth and religion.

... A DREAM IS A PERSONAL EXPERIENCE of that deep, dark ground that is the support of our conscious lives, and a myth is the society's dream. The myth is the public dream and the dream is the private myth. If your private myth, your dream, happens to coincide with that of the society, you are in good accord with your group. If it isn't, you've got an adventure in the dark forest ahead of you.

If you find a myth (or religious story or folk tale) that is similar to one
of your dreams, ask yourself if the story of the myth begins before that
of your dream. If so, does the myth provide any information about the
cause of the dream events relevant to your life? Similarly, if the mythic
story continues beyond the end of your dream, does the myth resolve
itself in a way applicable to your life?

Joseph Campbell, *The Power of Myth* (New York: Doubleday, 1988), p. 40.

Ewa Wasilewska

DREAMING OF THE WORLD'S END

Ewa Wasilewska teaches anthropology at the University of Utah and has written about Middle Eastern creation stories. She reminds us that there are many ancient traditions in which a man is chosen to survive a flood because of his piety. In several of them, the chosen one receives a message from God during a dream.

THE HERO AND THE ARK

In the Sumerian story, it was Ziusudra, the king and priest from the city of Shuruppak. His name can be translated as "Long of Life," which is an obvious reference to the immortality bestowed on him after the flood. Utnapishtim of the Gilgamesh story is possibly a free variation of Ziusudra; his name translates as "he saw [everlasting] life" .... Xisouthros of Berossus' account is a Greek version of the Sumerian Ziusudra.

Atrahasis is the name of yet another hero and means "the Exceedingly Wise." In fact, Utnapishtim is called this once in the Gilgamesh Epic. He was very close to the god Enki, with whom he conversed frequently as a sort of messenger on behalf of humans. The biblical hero is known as Noah, meaning "rest."

Although the names of mythical heroes differ, it is quite possible that one person was meant and described by these various attributes and epithets. Each of the heroes was warned by the divine being about the flood: through a dream, in the case of Ziusudra and Xisouthros; by indirect address, when Ea (Enki) talks to Utnapishtim and Atrahasis' reed huts; or directly (Noah). Each hero is given instructions about what to do and whom to save.

What faith it must have taken to ignore the scoffing of neighbors and act on the message! If your dreams were visions from God, what would that mean to you? What would be their messages and how would you incorporate them in your life?

Ewa Wasilewska, "The Destruction of Mankind: Creation Myths of the Middle East: Part Four," *The World and I*, article no. 12274, (1994), http://www.worldandi.com.

Thomas Bulfinch

HALCYONE'S DREAM OF DEATH AND RELEASE

A Boston bank clerk by day, Thomas Bulfinch studied and wrote by night. He first published his compilation of myths in 1855. In this myth we see how the Greek Gods brought dreams to inform and assist us.

CEYX WAS KING OF THESSALY, where he reigned in peace without violence or wrong. . . . Halcyone, the daughter of Aeolus, was his wife, and devotedly attached to him. Now Ceyx was in deep affliction for the loss of his brother, and direful prodigies following his brother's death made him feel as if the gods were hostile to him. He thought best, therefore, to make a voyage to Carlos in Ionia, to consult the oracle of Apollo. . . .

[*Ceyx said to Halcyone*] "I promise, by the rays of my father the Daystar, that if fate permits I will return before the moon shall have twice rounded her orb." When he had thus spoken he ordered the vessel to be drawn out of the shiphouse, and the oars and sails to be put aboard. When Halcyone saw these preparations she shuddered, as if with a presentiment of evil. With tears and sobs she said farewell, and then fell senseless to the ground.

Ceyx would still have lingered, but now the young men grasped their oars and pulled vigorously through the waves, with long and measured strokes. Halcyone raised her streaming eyes, and saw her husband standing on the deck, waving his hand to her. She answered his signal till the vessel had receded so far that she could no longer distinguish his form from the rest. When the vessel itself could no more be seen, she strained her eyes to catch the last glimmer of the sail, till that too disappeared. Then, retiring to her chamber, she threw herself on her solitary couch.

Meanwhile they glide out of the harbor, and the breeze plays among the ropes. The seamen draw in their oars, and hoist their sails. When half or less of their course was passed, as night drew on, the sea began to whiten with swelling waves, and the east wind to blow a gale. The master gave the word to take in sail, but the storm forbade obedience, for such is the roar of the winds and waves his orders are unheard. The men, of their own accord, busy themselves to secure the oars, to strengthen the ship, to reef the sail. While they thus do what to each one seems best, the storm increases. The shouting of the men, the rattling of the shrouds, and the dashing of the waves, mingle with the roar of the thunder. The swelling sea seems lifted up to the heavens, to scatter its foam among the clouds; then sinking away to the bottom assumes the color of the shoal—a Stygian blackness.

The vessel shares all these changes. It seems like a wild beast that rushes on the spears of the hunters. Rain falls in torrents, as if the skies were coming down to unite with the sea. When the lightning ceases for a moment, the night seems to add its own darkness to that of the storm; then comes the flash, rending the darkness asunder, and lighting up all with a glare. Skill fails, courage sinks, and death seems to come on every wave. The men are stupefied with terror. The thought of parents, and kindred, and pledges left at home, comes over their minds. Ceyx thinks of Halcyone. No name but hers is on his lips, and while he yearns for her, he yet rejoices in her absence. Presently the mast is shattered by a stroke of lightning, the rudder broken, and the triumphant surge curling over looks down upon the wreck, then falls, and crushes it to fragments. Some of the seamen, stunned by the stroke, sink, and rise no more; others cling to fragments of the wreck. Ceyx, with the hand that used to grasp the sceptre, holds fast to a plank, calling for help,—alas, in vain,—upon his father and his father-in-law. But oftenest on his lips was the name of Halcyone. To her his thoughts cling. He prays that the waves may bear his body to her sight, and that it may receive burial at her hands. At length the waters overwhelm him, and he sinks. The Day-star looked dim that night. Since it could not leave the heavens, it shrouded its face with clouds.

In the meanwhile Halcyone, ignorant of all these horrors, counted the days till her husband's promised return. Now she gets ready the garments which he shall put on, and now what she shall wear when he arrives. To all the gods she offers frequent incense, but more than all to Juno.* For her husband, who was no more, she prayed incessantly: that he might be safe; that he might come home; that he might not, in his absence, see any one that he would love better than her. But of all these prayers, the last was the only one destined to be granted. The goddess, at length, could not bear any longer to be pleaded with for one already dead, and to have hands raised to her altars that ought rather to be offering funeral rites. So, calling Iris, she said, "Iris, my faithful messenger, go to the drowsy dwelling of Somnus, and tell him to send a vision to Halcyone, in the form of Ceyx, to make known to her the event."

Iris puts on her robe of many colors, and tingeing the sky with her bow, seeks the palace of the King of Sleep. Near the Cimmerian country, a mountain cave is the abode of the dull god, Somnus. Here Phoebus[†] dares not come, either rising, at midday, or setting. Clouds and shadows are exhaled from the ground, and the light glimmers faintly. The bird of dawn, with crested head, never there calls aloud to Aurora, nor watchful dog, nor more sagacious goose disturbs the silence. No wild beast, nor cattle, nor branch moved with the wind, nor sound of human conversation, breaks the stillness. Silence reigns there; but from the bottom of the rock the River Lethe flows, and by its murmur invites to sleep. Poppies grow abundantly before the door of the cave, and other herbs, from whose juices Night collects slumbers, which she scatters over the darkened earth. There is no gate to the mansion, to creak on its hinges, nor any watchman; but in the midst, a couch of black ebony, adorned with black plumes and black curtains. There the god reclines, his limbs relaxed with sleep. Around him lie dreams, resembling all various forms, as many as the harvest bears stalks, or the forest leaves, or the seashore sand grains.

As soon as the goddess entered and brushed away the dreams that hovered around her, her brightness lit up all the cave. The god, scarce

---

* [In Roman mythology, Juno is the wife of Jupiter, the goddess of birth, women and marriage.]
†[Phoebus is the Roman sun god, also called Apollo.]

opening his eyes, and ever and anon dropping his beard upon his breast, at last shook himself free from himself, and leaning on his arm, inquired her errand,—for he knew who she was. She answered, "Somnus, gentlest of the gods, tranquillizer of minds and soother of care-worn hearts, Juno sends you her commands that you dispatch a dream to Halcyone, in the city of Trachine, representing her lost husband and all the events of the wreck."

Having delivered her message, Iris hasted away, for she could not longer endure the stagnant air, and as she felt drowsiness creeping over her, she made her escape, and returned by her bow the way she came. Then Somnus called one of his numerous sons,—Morpheus,—the most expert at counterfeiting forms, and in imitating the walk, the countenance, and mode of speaking, even the clothes and attitudes most characteristic of each. But he only imitates men, leaving it to another to personate birds, beasts, and serpents. Him they call Icelos; and Phantasos is a third, who turns himself into rocks, waters, woods, and other things without life. These wait upon kings and great personages in their sleeping hours, while others move among the common people. Somnus chose, from all the brothers, Morpheus, to perform the command of Iris; then laid his head on his pillow and yielded himself to grateful repose.

Morpheus flew, making no noise with his wings, and soon came to the Haemonian city, where, laying aside his wings, he assumed the form of Ceyx. Under that form, but pale like a dead man, naked, he stood before the couch of the wretched wife. His beard seemed soaked with water, and water trickled from his drowned locks. Leaning over the bed, tears streaming from his eyes, he said, "Do you recognize your Ceyx, unhappy wife, or has death too much changed my visage? Behold me, know me, your husband's shade, instead of himself. Your prayers, Halcyone, availed me nothing. I am dead. No more deceive yourself with vain hopes of my return. The stormy winds sunk my ship in the Aegean Sea, waves filled my mouth while it called aloud on you. No uncertain messenger tells you this, no vague rumor brings it to your ears. I come in person, a shipwrecked man, to tell you my fate. Arise! Give me tears, give me lamentations, let me not go down to Tartarus unwept." To these words Morpheus added the voice, which seemed to be that of her husband; he seemed to pour forth genuine tears; his hands had the gestures of Ceyx.

Halcyone, weeping, groaned, and stretched out her arms in her sleep, striving to embrace his body, but grasping only the air. "Stay!" she cried; "whither do you fly? Let us go together." Her own voice awakened her. Starting up, she gazed eagerly around, to see if he was still present, for the servants, alarmed by her cries, had brought a light. When she found him not, she smote her breast and rent her garments. She cares not to unbind her hair, but tears it wildly. Her nurse asks what is the cause of her grief. "Halcyone is no more," she answers; "she perished with her Ceyx. Utter not words of comfort, he is shipwrecked and dead. I have seen him, I have recognized him. I stretched out my hands to seize him and detain him. His shade vanished, but it was the true shade of my husband. Not with the accustomed features, not with the beauty that was his, but pale, naked, and with his hair wet with sea-water, he appeared to wretched me. Here, in this very spot, the sad vision stood,"—and she looked to find the mark of his footsteps. "This it was, this that my presaging mind foreboded, when I implored him not to leave me to trust himself to the waves. Oh, how I wish, since thou wouldst go, thou hadst taken me with thee! It would have been far better. Then I should have had no remnant of life to spend without thee, nor a separate death to die. If I could bear to live and struggle to endure, I should be more cruel to myself than the sea has been to me. But I will not struggle, I will not be separated from thee, unhappy husband. This time, at least, I will keep thee company. In death, if one tomb may not include us, one epitaph shall; if I may not lay my ashes with thine, my name, at least, shall not be separated." Her grief forbade more words, and these were broken with tears and sobs.

It was now morning. She went to the seashore, and sought the spot where she last saw him, on his departure. "While he lingered here and cast off his tacklings, he gave me his last kiss." While she reviews every object, and strives to recall every incident, looking out over the sea, she descries an indistinct object floating in the water. At first she was in doubt what it was, but by degrees the waves bore it nearer, and it was plainly the body of a man. Though unknowing of whom, yet, as it was of some shipwrecked one, she was deeply moved, and gave it her tears, saying, "Alas! unhappy one, and unhappy, if such there be, thy wife!" Borne by the waves, it came nearer. As she more and more nearly views it, she trembles more and more. Now, now it approaches the shore. Now marks that she recognizes appear. It is her husband! Stretching out her trembling hands towards it, she exclaims, "O, dearest husband, is it thus you return to me?"

There was built out from the shore a mole, constructed to break the assaults of the sea, and stem its violent ingress. She leaped upon this barrier and (it was wonderful she could do so) she flew, and striking the air with wings produced on the instant, skimmed along the surface of the water, an unhappy bird. As she flew, her throat poured forth sounds full of grief, and like the voice of one lamenting. When she touched the mute and bloodless body, she enfolded its beloved limbs with her new-formed wings, and tried to give kisses with her horny beak. Whether Ceyx felt it, or whether it was only the action of the waves, those who looked on doubted, but the body seemed to raise its head. But indeed he did feel it, and by the pitying gods both of them were changed into birds. They mate and have their young ones. For seven placid days, in winter time, Halcyone broods over her nest, which floats upon the sea. Then the way is safe to seamen. Aeolus guards the winds and keeps them from disturbing the deep. The sea is given up, for the time, to his grandchildren.

> *Only through a dream is Halcyone able to see past fear of her husband's fate and acknowledge that he has indeed died. In the end Halcyone's name has come to be synonymous with calm and prosperity. There is a message here we can apply to our own nightmares. Is there something frightening but true within a nightmare of yours? Perhaps your acceptance of the truth can open the way to profound mourning, and ultimately to peace.*

Thomas Bulfinch, *The Age of Fable or Stories of Gods and Heroes* (New York: Thomas Y. Crowell Company Publishers, 1913), pp. 69-75.

The Brothers Grimm

Born in Germany, Jacob and Wilhelm Grimm spent years gathering folk tales, including "Cinderella," and "Hansel and Gretel, which they began publishing in 1812.

MASTER PFRIEM

MASTER PFRIEM was a short, thin, but lively man, who never rested a moment. His face, of which his turned-up nose was the only prominent feature, was marked with small-pox and pale as death, his hair was gray and shaggy, his eyes small, but they glanced perpetually about on all sides. He saw everything, criticized everything, knew everything best, and was always in the right. When he went into the streets, he moved his arms about as if he were rowing; and once he struck the pail of a girl, who was carrying water, so high in the air that he himself was wetted all over by it. "Stupid thing," cried he to her, while he was shaking himself, "couldst thou not see that I was coming behind thee?" By trade he was a shoemaker, and when he worked he pulled his thread out with such force that he drove his fist into every one who did not keep far enough off. No apprentice stayed more than a month with him, for he had always some fault to find with the very best work. At one time it was that the stitches were not even, at another that one shoe was too long, or one heel higher than the other, or the leather not cut large enough. "Wait," said he to his apprentice, "I will soon show thee how we make skins soft," and he brought a strap and gave him a couple of strokes across the back. He called them all sluggards. He himself did not turn much work out of his hands, for he never sat still for a quarter of an hour. If his wife got up very early in the morning and lighted the fire, he jumped out of bed, and ran bare-footed into the kitchen, crying, "Wilt thou burn my house down for me? That is a fire one could roast an ox by! Does wood cost nothing?" If the servants were standing by their wash-tubs and laughing, and telling each other all they knew, he scolded them, and said, "There stand the geese cackling, and forgetting their work, to gossip! And why fresh soap? Disgraceful extravagance and shameful idleness into the bargain! They want to save their hands, and not rub the things properly!" And out he would run and knock a pail full of soap and water over, so that the whole kitchen was flooded. Someone was building a new house, so he hurried to the window to look on. "There, they are using that red sand-stone again that never dries!" cried he. "No one will ever be healthy in that house! And just look how badly the fellows are laying the stones! Besides, the mortar is good for nothing! It ought to have gravel in it, not sand. I shall live to see that house tumble down on the people who are in it." He sat down, put a couple of stitches in, and then jumped up again, unfastened his leather-apron, and cried, "I will just go out, and appeal to those men's consciences." He stumbled on the carpenters. "What's this?" cried he, "You are not working by the line! Do you expect the beams to be straight?—one wrong will put all wrong." He snatched an axe out of a carpenter's hand and wanted to show him how he ought to cut; but as a cart loaded with clay came by, he threw the axe away, and hastened to the peasant who was walking by the side of it: "You are not in your right mind," said he, "who yokes young horses to a heavily-laden cart? The poor beasts will die on the spot." The peasant did not give him an answer, and Pfriem in a rage ran back into his workshop. When he was setting himself to work again, the apprentice reached him a shoe. "Well, what's that again?" screamed he, "Haven't I told you you ought not to cut shoes so broad? Who would buy a shoe like this, which is hardly anything else but a sole? I insist on my orders being followed exactly." "Master," answered the apprentice, "you may easily be quite right about the shoe being a bad one, but it is the one which you yourself cut out, and yourself set to work at. When you jumped up a while since, you knocked it off the table, and I have only just picked it up. An angel from heaven, however, would never make you believe that."

One night Master Pfriem dreamed he was dead, and on his way to heaven. When he got there, he knocked loudly at the door. "I wonder," said he to himself, "that they have no knocker on the door,—one knocks one's knuckles sore." The apostle Peter opened the door, and wanted to see who demanded admission so noisily. "Ah, it's you, Master Pfriem," said he, "Well, I'll let you in, but I warn you that you must give up that habit of yours, and find fault with nothing you see in heaven, or you may fare ill.""You might have spared your warning," answered Pfriem. "I know already what is seemly, and here, God be thanked, everything is perfect, and there is nothing to blame as there is on earth." So he went in, and walked up and down the wide expanses of heaven. He looked around him, to the left and to the right, but sometimes shook his head, or muttered something to himself. Then he saw two angels who were carrying away a beam. It was the beam which some one had had in his own eye whilst he was looking for the splinter in the eye of another. They did not, however, carry the beam lengthways, but obliquely. "Did any one ever see such a piece of stupidity?" thought Master Pfriem; but he said nothing, and seemed satisfied with it. "It comes to the same thing after all, whichever way they carry the beam, straight or crooked, if they only get along with it, and truly I do not see them knock against anything." Soon after this he saw two angels who were drawing water out of a well into a bucket, but at the same time he observed that the bucket was full of holes, and that the water was running out of it on every side. They were watering the earth with rain. "Hang it," he exclaimed; but happily recollected himself, and thought, "Perhaps it is only a pastime. If it is an amusement, then it seems they can do useless things of this kind even here in heaven, where people, as I have already noticed, do nothing but idle about." He went farther and saw a cart which had stuck fast in a deep hole. "It's no wonder," said he to the man who stood by it; "who would load so unreasonably? What have you there?" "Good wishes," replied the man, "I could not go along the right way with it, but still I have pushed it safely up here, and they won't leave me sticking here." In fact an angel did come and harnessed two horses to it. "That's quite right," thought Pfriem, "but two horses won't get that cart out, it must at least have four to it." Another angel came and brought two more horses; she did not, however, harness them in front of it, but behind. That was too much for Master Pfriem, "Clumsy creature," he burst out with, "what are you doing there? Has any one ever since the world began seen a cart drawn in that way? But you, in your conceited arrogance, think that you know everything best." He was going to say more, but one of the inhabitants of heaven seized him by the throat and pushed him forth with irresistible strength. Beneath the gateway Master Pfriem turned his head round to take one more look at the cart, and saw that it was being raised into the air by four winged horses.

At this moment Master Pfriem awoke. "Things are certainly arranged in heaven otherwise than they are on earth," said he to himself, "and that excuses much; but who can see horses harnessed both behind and before with patience; to be sure they had wings, but who could know that? It is, besides, great folly to fix a pair of wings to a horse that has four legs to run with already! But I must get up, or else they will make nothing but mistakes for me in my house. It is a lucky thing for me though, that I am not really dead."

> *In this fairy tale, the protagonist had a dream that illuminates the error of his attitude in his waking life, but he misses the point: he responds to the dream through the bias of his waking mind. A good warning for us all in examining our dreams or the dreams of others!*

JORINDA AND JORINGEL

THERE WAS ONCE AN OLD CASTLE in the midst of a large and dense forest, and in it an old woman who was a witch dwelt all alone. In the daytime she changed herself into a car or a screech-owl, but in the evening she took her proper shape again as a human being. She could lure wild beasts and birds to her, and then she killed and boiled and roasted them. If anyone came within one hundred paces of the castle he was obliged to stand still, and could not stir from the place until she bade him be free. But whenever an innocent maiden came within this circle, she changed her into a bird, and shut her up in a wicker-work cage, and carried the cage into a room in the castle. She had about seven thousand cages of rare birds in the castle. . . .

Now, there was once a maiden who was called Jorinda, who was fairer than all other girls. She and a handsome youth named Joringel had promised to marry each other. They were still in the days of betrothal, and their greatest happiness was being together. One day in order that they might be able to talk together in peace they went for a walk in the forest. . . . the sun shone brightly between the trunks of the trees into the dark green of the forest, and the turtle-doves sang mournfully upon the beech trees. . . . Then they looked around them, and were quite at a loss, for they did not know by which way they should go home. The sun was still half above the mountain and half under. Joringel looked through the bushes, and saw the old walls of the castle close at hand. He was horror-stricken and filled with deadly fear. . . .

Joringel looked for Jorinda. She was changed into a nightingale, and sang, "jug, jug, jug." A screech-owl with glowing eyes flew three times round about her, and three times cried, "to-whoo, to-whoo, to-whoo."

Joringel could not move: he stood there like a stone, and could neither weep nor speak, nor move hand or foot. The sun had now set. The owl flew into the thicket, and directly afterwards there came out of it a crooked old woman, yellow and lean, with large red eyes and a hooked nose, the point of which reached to her chin. She muttered to herself, caught the nightingale, and took it away in her hand. Joringel could neither speak nor move from the spot. The nightingale was gone. At last the woman came back, and said in a hollow voice, "Greet you, Zachiel. If the moon shines on the cage, Zachiel, let him loose at once." Then Joringel was freed. He fell on his knees before the woman and begged that she would give him back his Jorinda, but she said that he should never have her again, and went away. He called, he wept, he lamented, but all in vain, "Ah, what is to become of me?"

Joringel went away, and at last came to a strange village, where he kept sheep for a long time. He often walked round and round the castle, but not too near to it. At last he dreamt one night that he found a blood-red flower . . . that he picked the flower and went with it to the castle, and that everything he touched with the flower was freed from enchantment. He also dreamt that by means of it he recovered his Jorinda.

In the morning, when he awoke, he began to seek over hill and dale for such a flower. He sought until the ninth day, and then, early in the morning, he found the blood-red flower. In the middle of it there was a large dew-drop, as big as the finest pearl.

Day and night he journeyed with this flower to the castle. When he was within a hundred paces of it he was not held fast, but walked on to the door. Joringel was full of joy. He touched the door with the flower, and it sprang open. He walked in through the courtyard, and listened for the sound of the birds. At last he heard it. He went on and found the room from whence it came, and there the witch was feeding the birds in the seven thousand cages.

When she saw Joringel she was angry, very angry, and scolded and spat poison and gall at him, but she could not come within two paces of him. He did not take any notice of her, but went and looked at the cages with the birds. But there were many hundred nightingales, how was he to find his Jorinda again. Just then he saw the old woman quietly take away a cage with a bird in it, and go towards the door.

Swiftly he sprang towards her, touched the cage with the flower, and also the old woman. She could now no longer bewitch anyone. And Jorinda was standing there, clasping him round the neck, and she was as beautiful as ever. Then all the other birds were turned into maidens again, and he went home with his Jorinda, and they lived happily together for a long time.

What benefit might accrue if you responded to your own dreamed solution with the commitment shown by Joringel?

Jacob and Wilhelm Grimm, *Fairy Tales of the Brothers Grimm* (*Household Tales*), trans. Margaret Hunt, (1884).

The Hebrew Bible

JOSEPH'S CELLMATES

*In an Egyptian prison, Joseph interprets the dreams of two cellmates,
telling them first that the art of dream interpretation comes from God,
who has given him the keys to decipher the symbols. The implication of
the story is that everyone, even a criminal in jail, has a connection to
the voice of God through his or her dreams. How else would the dreams
of common people and (as in the next story) Pharaoh alike foretell the
future?*

*If you think of your dreams as messages from God, does that
change your attitude toward them?*

AND IT CAME TO PASS AFTER THESE THINGS, that the butler of the king
of Egypt and his baker offended their lord the king of Egypt. And Pharaoh was wroth against his two officers, against the chief of the butlers,
and against the chief of the bakers. And he put them in ward in the house
of the captain of the guard, into the prison, the place where Joseph was
bound. And the captain of the guard charged Joseph to be with them, and
he ministered unto them; and they continued a season in ward. And they
dreamed a dream both of them, each man his dream, in one night, each
man according to the interpretation of his dream, the butler and the baker
of the king of Egypt, who were bound in the prison. And Joseph came in
unto them in the morning, and saw them, and, behold, they were sad. And
he asked Pharaoh's officers that were with him in the ward of his master's
house, saying: "Wherefore look ye so sad today?" And they said unto him:
"We have dreamed a dream, and there is none that can interpret it." And
Joseph said unto them: "Do not interpretations belong to God? tell it me,
I pray you." And the chief butler told his dream to Joseph, and said unto
him: "In my dream, behold, a vine was before me; and in the vine were
three branches; and as it was budding, its blossoms shot forth, and the
clusters thereof brought forth ripe grapes, and Pharaoh's cup was in my
hand; and I took the grapes and pressed them into Pharaoh's cup, and I
gave the cup into Pharaoh's hand." And Joseph said unto him: "This is the

interpretation of it: the three branches are three days; within yet three days shall Pharaoh lift up thy head, and restore thee unto thine office; and thou shalt give Pharaoh's cup into his hand, after the former manner when thou wast his butler. But have me in thy remembrance when it shall be well with thee, and show kindness, I pray thee, unto me, and make mention of me unto Pharaoh, and bring me out of this house." . . .

When the chief baker saw that the interpretation was good, he said unto Joseph: "I also saw in my dream, and, behold, three baskets of white bread were on my head; and in the uppermost basket there was all manner of baked food for Pharaoh; and the birds did eat them out of the basket upon my head." And Joseph answered and said: "This is the interpretation thereof: the three baskets are three days; within yet three days shall Pharaoh lift up thy head from off thee, and shall hang thee on a tree; and the birds shall eat thy flesh from off thee." And it came to pass the third day, which was Pharaoh's birthday, that he made a feast unto all his servants; and he lifted up the head of the chief butler and the head of the chief baker among his servants. And he restored the chief butler back unto his butlership; and he gave the cup into Pharaoh's hand. But he hanged the chief baker, as Joseph had interpreted to them. Yet did not the chief butler remember Joseph, but forgot him.

PHARAOH'S DREAMS

Continuing the story from the previous selection, Joseph is eventually remembered, taken from prison, and asked to interpret a dream of Pharaoh's. Again Joseph credits God with the ability to interpret dreams, and again finds the key to the predictive symbols of the dream given to him. Through his gift of dream interpretation Joseph is given a place of honor. To whom do you credit your interpretations?

AND IT CAME TO PASS AT THE END OF TWO FULL YEARS, that Pharaoh dreamed . . . . And Pharaoh awoke, and, behold, it was a dream. And it came to pass in the morning that his spirit was troubled; and he sent and called for all the magicians of Egypt, and all the wise men thereof; and Pharaoh told them his dream; but there was none that could interpret them unto Pharaoh. Then spoke the chief butler unto Pharaoh, saying: "I make mention of my faults this day: Pharaoh was wroth with his servants, and put me in the ward of the house of the captain of the guard, me and the chief baker. And we dreamed a dream in one night, I and he; we dreamed each man according to the interpretation of his dream. And there was with us there a young man, a Hebrew, servant to the captain of the guard; and we told him, and he interpreted to us our dreams; to each man according to his dream he did interpret. And it came to pass, as he interpreted to us, so it was: I was restored unto mine office, and he was hanged." Then Pharaoh sent and called Joseph, and they brought him hastily out of the dungeon. And he shaved himself, and changed his raiment, and came in unto Pharaoh. And Pharaoh said unto Joseph: "I have dreamed a dream, and there is none that can interpret it; and I have heard say of thee, that when thou hearest a dream thou canst interpret it." And Joseph answered Pharaoh, saying: "It is not in me; God will give Pharaoh an answer of peace." And Pharaoh spoke unto Joseph: "In my dream, behold, I stood upon the brink of the river. And, behold, there came up out of the river seven kine, fat-fleshed and well-favoured; and they fed in the reed-grass. And, behold, seven other kine came up after them, poor and very ill-favoured and lean-fleshed, such as I never saw in all the land of Egypt for badness. And the lean and ill-favoured kine did eat up the first seven fat kine. And when they had eaten them up, it could not be known that they had eaten them; but they were still ill-favoured as at the beginning. So I awoke. And I saw in my dream, and, behold, seven ears came up upon one stalk, full and good. And, behold, seven ears, withered, thin, and blasted with the east wind, sprung up after them. And the thin ears swallowed up the seven good ears. And I told it unto the magicians; but there was none that could declare it to me." And Joseph said unto Pharaoh: "The dream of Pharaoh is one; what God is about to do He hath declared unto Pharaoh. The seven good kine are seven years; and the seven good ears are seven years: the dream is one. And the seven lean and ill-favoured kine that came up after them are seven years, and also the seven empty ears blasted with the east wind; they shall be seven years of famine. That is the thing which I spoke unto Pharaoh: what God is about to do He hath shown unto Pharaoh. Behold, there come seven years of great plenty throughout all the land of Egypt. And there shall arise after them seven years of famine; and all the plenty shall be forgotten in the land of Egypt; and the famine shall consume the land; and the plenty shall not be known in the land by reason of that famine which followeth; for it shall be very grievous. And for that the dream was doubled unto Pharaoh twice, it is because the thing is established by God, and God will shortly bring it to pass. Now therefore let Pharaoh look out a man discreet and wise, and set him over the land of Egypt. Let Pharaoh do this, and let him appoint overseers over the land, and take up the fifth part of the land of Egypt in the seven years of plenty. And let them gather all the food of these good years that come, and lay up corn under the hand of Pharaoh for food in the cities, and let them keep it. And the food shall be for a store to the land against the seven years of famine, which shall be in the land of Egypt; that the land perish not through the famine." And the thing was good in the eyes of Pharaoh, and in the eyes of all his servants. And Pharaoh said unto his servants: "Can we find such a one as this, a man in whom the spirit of God is?" And Pharaoh said unto Joseph: "Forasmuch as God hath shown thee all this, there is none so discreet and wise as thou. Thou shalt be over my house, and according unto thy word shall all my people be ruled; only in the throne will I be greater than thou." And Pharaoh said unto Joseph: "See, I have set thee over all the land of Egypt." And Pharaoh took off his signet ring from his hand, and put it upon Joseph's hand, and arrayed him in vestures of fine linen, and put a gold chain about his neck. And he made him to ride in the second chariot which he had; and they cried before him: "Abrech"; and he set him over all the land of Egypt. And Pharaoh said unto Joseph: "I am Pharaoh, and without thee shall no man lift up his hand or his foot in all the land of Egypt." And Pharaoh called Joseph's name Zaphenath-paneah; and he gave him to wife Asenath the daughter of Poti-phera priest of On.

The Holy Scriptures, Genesis 40-41 (Philadelphia: The Jewish Publication Society of America, 1960).

The Talmud

Several excerpts are taken from the Babylonian Talmud, a collection of ancient rabbinic writings and stories. Transmitted orally for centuries, Talmudic teachings and commentary were written down in about 400 CE. In the original text, the margins were filled with commentary and clarifications that appear as footnotes in modern published versions. The Talmud is similar to the hadith in Islamic tradition. (See p. 220 for an excerpt from the hadith.)

DREAM WISDOM

R. HISDA SAID: Any dream rather than one of a fast.[1] R. Hisda also said: A dream which is not interpreted is like a letter which is not read.[2] R. Hisda also said: Neither a good dream nor a bad dream is ever wholly fulfilled. R. Hisda also said: A bad dream is better than a good dream.[3] R. Hisda also said: The sadness caused by a bad dream is sufficient for it and the joy which a good dream gives is sufficient for it.[4] R. Joseph said: Even for me[5] the joy caused by a good dream nullifies it. R. Hisda also said: A bad dream is worse than scourging, since it says, God hath so made it that men should fear before Him,[6] and Rabbah b. Bar Hanah said in the name of R. Johanan: This refers to a bad dream.

A prophet that hath a dream let him tell a dream: and he that hath My word let him speak My word faithfully. What hath the straw to do with the wheat, saith the Lord.[7] What is the connection of straw and wheat with a dream? The truth is, said R. Johanan in the name of R. Simeon b. Yohai,

---

[1] I.e., to dream oneself fasting. So Rashi. The Aruch, however, explains: There is reality in every dream save one that comes in a fast.

[2] Compare the dictum *infra*, 'A dream follows its interpretation'.

[3] Because it incites one to repentance.

[4] I.e., there is no need for them to be fulfilled.

[5] R. Joseph was blind, and consequently could not derive so much pleasure from a dream.

[6] Eccl. III, 14.

that just as wheat cannot be without straw, so there cannot be a dream without some nonsense. R. Berekiah said: While a part of a dream may be fulfilled, the whole of it is never fulfilled. Whence do we know this? From Joseph, as it is written, *And behold the sun and the moon [and eleven stars bowed down to me,]*[8] and [55b] at that time his mother was not living. R. Levi said: A man should await the fulfillment of a good dream for as much as twenty-two years. Whence do we know this? From Joseph. For it is written: *These are the generations of Jacob. Joseph being seventeen years old, etc.;*[9] and it is further written, *And Joseph was thirty years old when he stood before Pharaoh.*[10] How many years is it from seventeen to thirty? Thirteen. Add the seven years of plenty and two of famine,[11] and you have twenty-two.

R. Huna said: A good man is not shown a good dream, and a bad man is not shown a bad dream.[12] It has been taught similarly; David, during the whole of his lifetime, never saw a good dream and Ahitophel, during the whole of his lifetime, never saw a bad dream. . . .

R. Huna b. Ammi said in the name of R. Pedath who had it from R. Johanan: If one has a dream which makes him sad he should go and have it interpreted in the presence of three. He should have it interpreted! Has not R. Hisda said: A dream which is not interpreted is like a letter which is not read?[13] —Say rather then, he should have a good turn given to it in the presence of three. Let him bring three and say to them: I have seen a good dream; and they should say to him, Good it is and good may it be. May the All-Merciful turn it to good; seven times may it be decreed from heaven that it should be good and may it be good. They should say three verses with the word *hapak* [turn], and three with *the word padah* [redeem] and three with the word shalom [peace]. . . .

---

[7] Jer. XXIII, 28.
[8] Gen. XXXVII, 9.
[9] Ibid. 2.
[10] Gen. XLI, 46.
[11] After which Joseph saw his brothers.
[12] Rashi reads: A good man is shown a bad dream and a bad man is shown a good dream. The purpose is to turn the good man to repentance and to give the bad man his reward in this world.
[13] And therefore what harm can it do?

When Samuel had a bad dream, he used to say, *The dreams speak falsely.*[14] When he had a good dream, he used to say, Do the dreams speak falsely, seeing that it is written, *I [God] do speak with him in a dream?*[15] Raba pointed out a contradiction. It is written, "I *do speak with him in a dream,*" and it is written, "*the dreams speak falsely.*"— There is no contradiction; in the one case it is through an angel, in the other through a demon.

... R. Bana'ah [*said*] ... There were twenty-four interpreters of dreams in Jerusalem. Once I dreamt a dream and I went round to all of them and they all gave different interpretations, and all were fulfilled, thus confirming that which is said: All dreams follow the mouth.[16] ...

R. Johanan ... said: Three kinds of dream are fulfilled: an early morning dream, a dream which a friend has about one, and a dream which is interpreted in the midst of a dream. Some add also, a dream which is repeated, as it says, *and for that the dream was doubled unto Pharaoh twice,* etc.[17]

R. Samuel b. Nahmani said in the name of R. Jonathan: A man is shown in a dream only what is suggested by his own thoughts, as it says, *As for thee, Oh King, thy thoughts came into thy mind upon thy bed.*[18] Or if you like, I can derive it from here: *That thou mayest know the thoughts of thy heart.*[19] ...

> *In the excerpt above, there are many concise ideas you can try on your own dreams. For example, the passage about twenty-four different and correct interpretations of a single dream confirms the multiplicity of meanings to be gleaned from a single dream. (Jung expresses a similar idea.) Once you find a meaning that fits for your dream, turn it around, and look at it from the other side: What does the dream mean from the point of view of another of the characters or scenes in it?*

---

[14] Zech. X, 2.
[15] Num. XII, 6.
[16] "Mouth" here seems to have the sense of interpretation.
[17] Gen. XLI, 32.
[18] Dan. II, 29.
[19] Ibid. 30.

SHOCKING IMAGES

Occasionally, we all have shocking and embarrassing dreams with images far beyond normal or even moral behavior. Addressing such images, the writers of the Talmud remind us to suspend our judgment and consider meanings that may be vastly different than the preconceptions of our waking minds. On page 3, Freud also encouraged us to suspend judgment when seeking associations for our dream images.

IF ONE DREAMS that he has intercourse with his mother, he may expect to obtain understanding, since it says, *Yea, thou wilt call understanding "mother."*[20] If one dreams he has intercourse with a betrothed maiden, he may expect to obtain knowledge of Torah, since it says, *Moses commanded us a law [Torah], an inheritance of the congregation of Jacob.*[21] Read not *morashah* [inheritance], but *me'orasah* [betrothed]. If one dreams he has had intercourse with his sister, he may expect to obtain wisdom, since it says, *Say to wisdom, thou art my sister.*[22] If one dreams he has intercourse with a married woman, he can be confident that he is destined for the future world,[23] provided, that is, that he does not know her and did not think of her in the evening.

---

[20] Prov. II, ₃ with a slight change of reading. E.V. *Yea, if thou wilt call for understanding.*
[21] Deut. XXXIII, 4.
[22] Prov. VII, 4.
[23] The signification being that he obtains his own share and that of his neighbour (Rashi).

DREAMING OF THE BIBLE

Just as Gerhard Adler provided mythological associations with animals
(p. 34), and Hippocrates provided associations with celestial images
(p. 97), the Talmud contains associations with some of the most
outstanding images in the Hebrew Bible.

OUR RABBIS TAUGHT there are three kings [who are important for dreams]. If one sees David in a dream, he may hope for piety; if Solomon, he may hope for wisdom; if Ahab, let him fear for punishment. There are three prophets [of significance for dreams]. If one sees the Book of Kings, he may look forward to greatness; if Ezekiel, he may look forward to wisdom; if Isaiah he may look forward to consolation; if Jeremiah, let him fear for punishment. There are three larger books of the Hagiographa* [which are significant for dreams]. If one sees the Book of Psalms, he may hope for piety; if the Book of Proverbs, he may hope for wisdom; if the Book of Job, let him fear for punishment. There are three smaller books of the Hagiographa [significant for dreams]. If one sees the Songs of Songs in a dream, he may hope for piety;[24] if Ecclesiastes, he may hope for wisdom; if Lamentations, let him fear for punishment; and one who sees the Scroll of Esther will have a miracle wrought for him. . . .

The writers of the Talmud chose examples that show us how to find
associations for any image in our dreams. For example, if Solomon
showed up in your dream and you hadn't read this excerpt, you might
still think he was best known for his wisdom. Does your dream Solomon
appear to bring you wisdom?

The Babylonian Talmud: Seder Zera'im, ed. Isodore Epstein, trans. Maurice Simon (London: Soncino Press, 1948), Berakoth 55a-55b, 56a, 57a-57b.

---

* [A reference to specific books of the Hebrew Bible, including Psalms, Proverbs, Job, Song of Solomon, Ruth, Lamentations of Jeremiah, Ecclesiastes, Esther, Daniel, Ezra, Nehemiah, and I and II Chronicles.]
[24] The Song of Songs being calculated to implant in the reader the love of God.

Yosef Marcus

KABBALAH AND PHARAOH'S DREAM

The American rabbi Yosef Marcus is a translator of Chasidic discourses. Here he uses principles from Jewish mysticism to understand the coexistence of opposites in dreams. Are there ways you constrain the interpretation of your dreams by disallowing concepts that would be contradictory in waking life?

IN MIKETZ AND VAYEISHEV the Torah tells us of a number of dreams: the dreams of Joseph that incited his brothers' jealousy, which led to his descent to Egypt, and the dreams of Joseph's prison mates and those of Pharaoh, which led to Joseph's elevation to viceroy of Egypt, which eventually brought about the descent of Jacob and his sons to Egypt, the beginning of the Egyptian exile. . . .

Dreams accommodate impossibilities. They allow opposites to coexist as one. This is because the part of the brain that discriminates between what can and cannot be does not function when one is asleep. All that remains is the power of imagination and fantasy, which allows for such imagery as a boat flying through the air . . . or an elephant going through the eye of a needle . . . . In a dream one can imagine oneself killed or dead while at the same time alive, or present in two places at once; the logical absurdity is lost on the dreamer. . . .

This explains a perplexing matter in the story of Joseph's interpretation of Pharaoh's dream. Firstly, what was the great genius of Joseph's interpretation of Pharaoh's dream, and why were the Egyptian wizards incapable of such a simple interpretation?

Secondly, after interpreting the dream, Joseph tells Pharaoh to appoint someone to oversee the stockpiling of food; why is Joseph giving advice to Pharaoh on how to run his country? He was asked to interpret a dream, not to dictate domestic policy. And finally, Pharaoh reacts only to Joseph's suggestion—"and the matter was good in his eyes" (Gen. 41:37)—not to his interpretation *per se*; why is this?

The main problem with Pharaoh's dream was the fact that it contained opposites. The seven fat cows and the seven lean cows existed together at the same time, before the lean cows ate the fat cows. Thus, the Egyptian wizards were thrown off. If the dream meant that seven years of plenty would be followed by seven years of famine, why was there a time when both cows existed together, implying that there would be plenty and famine simultaneously?

As a result, they came up with other interpretations (such as the one cited by Rashi) that sought to account for this contradiction. They said that seven daughters would be born to Pharaoh and seven of his *other* daughters would die, *at the same time*. (It is not implausible that Pharaoh would have 14 daughters at the same time, since he presumably had many wives and concubines.)

Joseph, however, saw the contradiction as the key to preparing for the upcoming famine. The simultaneous presence of both types of cows meant to say that during the years of plenty, Egypt should be *conscious* of the upcoming famine and prepare for it. Conversely, when the years of famine would arrive, they would *simultaneously* experience the years of plenty by drawing on what had been saved during those years.

So Pharaoh's dream, which ultimately led to all of the Jewish exiles, contains within it the motif of contradiction, the symbol of exile, when the "years of plenty," i.e. love for G-d, stand side by side with the "years of famine," i.e. spiritual lethargy. And it is Joseph, who stems from the level of *Igulim*,* that sees beyond the immediate contradiction of the dream and sees its source, the level of *Igulim*, where it is not a contradiction at all.

Yosef Marcus, "Dreams and Circles" (KabbalaOnline.org: 2003). Adapted from discourses of Rabbi Dovber Shneerson, "Maamorei Admur Haemtzai, Miketz and Vayigash 5670 (Genesis 41:1-44:17)." http://www.kabbalaonline.org/WeeklyTorah/ChabadDiscourses/Dreams_and_Circles.asp.

* [According to the author, "The level of Igulim is a nebulous "place" of latent potential that is beyond division. Like a circle, which has no beginning or end, the level of Igulim does not contain higher and lower levels, nor right and left, kindness and restraint; all is one and equal."]

Yakov Leib HaKohain

KABBALAH AND
THE INTERPRETATION OF DREAMS

American Reb Yakov Leib HaKohain combines Jungian psychology and Kabbalah in his writing. In this case study he uses the dreamer's familiarity with Kabbalah to interpret the meaning for the dreamer. To the degree the images are truly archetypal–part of the shared (collective) consciousness of us all–they have application for others as well. HaKohain's approach also shows how we can use the images most central to our beliefs and experience to interpret our own dreams.

I now [*present*] a Kabbalistic analysis of [*a dream*] . . . brought to me by [*a man*] . . . during the course of our spiritual work together. . . . The dreamer is a 50-year-old Jewish man who had been in Jungian counseling with me for over four years. He is divorced, intensely spiritual with a mystical bent, and is employed in a healing profession, although also artistic by nature. He is, in Jung's terms, an extroverted intuitive-thinking type. He is well educated, holds advanced degrees and possesses a considerable knowledge of esoteric religions, including Kabbalah. Although his dreams up to this point frequently reflected that knowledge, they were not, until he had this particular series, as deeply archetypal and Kabbalistic in content. In other words, this series represents something of a breakthrough in his life at a time of considerable inner crisis. . . .

With these considerations in mind, we now turn to the [the dream] . . . .

"I hear a voice in my sleep saying, 'The letter H-H is coming like a blazing flame.'"

The dreamer's immediate association to "the letter H-H" was the Tetragrammaton YHVH, or "Yahweh." This would translate, then, to mean, "Yahweh is coming like a blazing flame." This symbolic association between God and "fire" is not unusual. For example, we read in Deuteronomy, "Yahweh your God is a consuming Fire" (Deut. 4:24) and the *Zohar* states: "In the beginning . . . within the most hidden recess, a dark flame issued from the mystery of En-Sof, the Infinite, like a fog forming in the unformed . . . Only after this flame began to assume size and dimension, did it produce radiant colors. From the innermost center of the flame sprang forth a well out of which colors issued and spread upon everything beneath, hidden in the mysterious hidden-ness of En Sof . . . Beyond this point nothing can be known." (Zohar 1:15a-15b)

So in his dream, the image of the "H-H" appears to symbolize the emerging Self "coming like a blazing flame" (as the dreamer puts it), "from the mystery of En-Sof" (as the Zohar describes it). Thus, the symbol of the flame "coming" appears to represent an impending differentiation of numinosity in the dreamer's consciousness.

But a question still remains about "the letter H-H." If it represents Yahweh, then what is its meaning? The following quotation from [Gershom] Scholem removes all question about the "H-H" and clearly defines its intent as an archetypal symbol of Tikkun: "Tikkun restores the unity of God's name which was destroyed by the original defect [of creation]— Luria speaks of the letters YH as being 'torn away' from the VH in the name YHVH—and every true religious act is directed towards the same aim [of reunifying the two parts]." (Gershom Scholem, *Major Trends in Jewish Mysticism*, fn. 4, p. 275)

Thus, the relationship between Lurianic Kabbalah, the dreamer's practice of Neo-Sabbatian Tikkun . . . and this quotation from Scholem all point the way to his emerging process of individuation, of "encountering God." Moreover, there is an implication here of his having *restored the unity of God's name* through his practice of Neo-Sabbatian Tikkun; that is, "the letter H-H" (and note the use of the singular "letter" rather than the plural "letters") suggests that the two halves of the Holy Name that were torn away from each other at the "Breaking of the Vessels" are being *rejoined* in the dreamer's Psyche. The flaw in the God-Imago, in the "Face of God," the split into duality it suffered at the birth of consciousness, is undergoing repair: It is moving once again towards wholeness.

Reb Yakov Leib HaKohain, ed. J. Marvin Spiegelman, "Kabbalah and the Interpretation of Dreams," in *Modern Jew in Search of a Soul* (Tempe, AZ: New Falcon Press, 1986). Updated version at http://www.donmeh-west.com/intrpdrms.shtml.

Gospel of Matthew

JOSEPH'S DREAM OF THE VIRGIN BIRTH

In another famous example of a dream as the vehicle of God, the Gospel of Matthew tells the story of the angel of God visiting Joseph to reassure him about the chaste conception of Jesus.

NOW THE BIRTH OF JESUS CHRIST was on this wise: When as his mother Mary was espoused to Joseph, before they came together, she was found with child of the Holy Ghost.

Then Joseph her husband, being a just man, and not willing to make her a publick example, was minded to put her away privily. But while he thought on these things, behold, the angel of the LORD appeared unto him in a dream, saying, Joseph, thou son of David, fear not to take unto thee Mary thy wife: for that which is conceived in her is of the Holy Ghost. And she shall bring forth a son, and thou shalt call his name JESUS: for he shall save his people from their sins. Now all this was done, that it might be fulfilled which was spoken of the Lord by the prophet, saying, Behold, a virgin shall be with child, and shall bring forth a son, and they shall call his name Emmanuel, which being interpreted is, God with us. Then Joseph being raised from sleep did as the angel of the Lord had bidden him, and took unto him his wife: And knew her not till she had brought forth her firstborn son: and he called his name JESUS.

The Bible, Matthew, 1:18-1:25, King James Version.

Thomas Aquinas

INTERNAL AND EXTERNAL INSPIRATION

The 13th-century Christian philosopher and theologian, Thomas Aquinas, joined many others in asserting that God speaks to us in our dreams. But Aquinas tells us that dreams may originate from other sources as well.

WHATEVER IS HIDDEN, is known to God, wherefore hidden sins are to the judgment of God, just what public sins are to the judgment of man. Nevertheless God does rebuke sinners sometimes by secretly admonishing them, so to speak, with an inward inspiration, either while they wake or while they sleep, according to Job 33:15-17: "By a dream in a vision by night, when deep sleep falleth upon men ... then He openeth the ears of men, and teaching instructeth them in what they are to learn, that He may withdraw a man from the things he is doing." . . .

We must, then, consider what is the cause of dreams, and whether it can be the cause of future occurrences, or be cognizant of them.

Accordingly it is to be observed that the cause of dreams is sometimes in us and sometimes outside us. The inward cause of dreams is twofold: one regards the soul, in so far as those things which have occupied a man's thoughts and affections while awake recur to his imagination while asleep. As such like cause of dreams is not a cause of future occurrences, so that dreams of this kind are related accidentally to future occurrences, and if at any time they concur it will be by chance. But sometimes the inward cause of dreams regards the body: because the inward disposition of the body leads to the formation of a movement in the imagination consistent with that disposition; thus a man in whom there is abundance of cold humors dreams that he is in the water or snow: and for this reason physicians say that we should take note of dreams in order to discover internal dispositions.

In like manner the outward cause of dreams is twofold, corporal and spiritual. It is corporal in so far as the sleeper's imagination is affected either by the surrounding air, or through an impression of a heavenly body, so that certain images appear to the sleeper, in keeping with the disposition of the heavenly bodies. The spiritual cause is sometimes referable to God, Who reveals certain things to men in their dreams by the ministry of the angels, according to Num. 12:6, "If there be among you a prophet of the Lord, I will appear to him in a vision, or I will speak to him in a dream." Sometimes, however, it is due to the action of the demons that certain images appear to persons in their sleep, and by this means they, at times, reveal certain future things to those who have entered into an unlawful compact with them.

Accordingly we must say that there is no unlawful divination in making use of dreams for the foreknowledge of the future, so long as those dreams are due to divine revelation, or to some natural cause inward or outward, and so far as the efficacy of that cause extends. But it will be an unlawful and superstitious divination if it be caused by a revelation of the demons, with whom a compact has been made, whether explicit, through their being invoked for the purpose, or implicit, through the divination extending beyond its possible limits.

Thomas Aquinas, trans. by Fathers of the English Dominican Province, *Summa Theologica* (New York: Benziger Brothers, 1947), Second part of Part II, Question 33, article 7, and . Question 95, article 6.

Mark and Patti Virkler

CHRISTIAN DREAM INTERPRETATION

American Christian writers Mark and Patti Virkler offer a series of questions that you can apply to a current dream of yours.

SEVEN FOUNDATIONAL PRINCIPLES FOR INTERPRETING DREAMS
1. Most dreams are symbolic (including biblical dreams), so view them the same way you would view a political cartoon. Throw the switch in your brain that says, "Look at this symbolically."

You can learn the art of communicating symbolically by playing the game "Pictionary" or "Bible Pictionary."

2. The symbols will come from the dreamer's life, so ask, "What does this symbol mean to me?" or, if working on another's dream, ask, "What does this symbol mean to you?"

    For example, Joseph was a shepherd, and he dreamed of sheaves and sun, moon and stars bowing down (Gen. 37:1-11). These images surround a shepherd boy who lives in the fields. Nebuchadnezzar, a king, dreamed of statues of gold (Dan 2:31ff), which surround kings who live in palaces.

3. The dream generally speaks of the concerns which your heart is currently facing. So ask, "What issues was I processing the day before I had the dream?"

    For example, Paul was wondering where to go next on his missionary journey and had a dream of a Macedonian man motioning for him to come on over (Acts 16:6-11). Nebuchadnezzar was thinking his kingdom would go on forever (Dan. 4:28-33) and he had a dream of a tree being chopped off at the roots (Dan. 4:9-27). Once you know the thoughts that were on the dreamer's heart when he fell asleep, it is much easier to draw out the meaning of the dream.

4. The meaning of the dream must be drawn from the dreamer. Realize you know nothing about the dream, but through dependence upon the Holy Spirit and the skillful use of questions, you can draw the meaning of the dream out from the heart of the dreamer.

    As for these four children, God gave them knowledge and skill in all learning and wisdom: and Daniel had understanding in all visions and dreams (Dan. 1:17). Counsel in the heart of man is like deep water; but a man of understanding will draw it out (Prov. 20:5).

5. The dreamer's heart will leap and "witness" and say, "Aha!" when it hears the right interpretation, so never accept an interpretation that does not bear witness in the dreamer's heart.

6. Dreams reveal but do not condemn. Their goal is to preserve life, not to destroy it (Job 33:13-18).

7. Never make a major decision in your life based only on a dream without receiving additional confirmation from the other ways that God speaks to us and guides us (peace in our hearts, the counsel of others, illumined Scriptures, God's still small voice, prophecy, anointed reasoning, etc.).

Mark and Patti Virkler, "Principles of Christian Dream Interpretation," (New York: Communion with God Ministries, 2004), http://www.cwgministries.org/books/Christian-Dream-Interpretation.pdf.

Kelly Bulkeley

Kelly Bulkeley writes about dreams and religion and is a visiting scholar at the Graduate Theological Union at the University of California at Berkeley.

THE QUR'AN AND ISLAMIC DREAM TRADITIONS

FEW WESTERN DREAM RESEARCHERS have any familiarity with the rich dream traditions of Islam. The Muslim faith first emerged in seventh century B.C.E. Arabia as a profound revisioning of early Jewish and Christian beliefs and practices. One theme the Prophet Muhammed (pbuh) *[peace be upon him]* drew from the scriptures of those two religions was a reverence for dreaming. In the Qur'an, as in the Jewish Torah and the Christian New Testament, dreams serve as a vital medium by which God communicates with humans. Dreams offer divine guidance and comfort, warn people of impending danger, and offer prophetic glimpses of the future. Although the three religions drastically differ on many other topics, they find substantial agreement on this particular point: dreaming is a valuable source of wisdom, understanding, and inspiration. Indeed, as I will propose in this brief essay, Islam has historically shown greater interest in dreams than either of the other two traditions, and has done more to

weave dreaming into the daily lives of its members. From the first revelatory visions of Muhammed to the myriad dream practices of present-day
Muslims, Islam has developed and sustained a complex, multi-faceted
tradition of active engagement with the dreaming imagination....

DREAMS IN THE QUR'AN

Muhammed recorded the Qur'an between the years 610 and 632
C.E. Tradition has it that the first revelation of the Qur'an was given to
Muhammed by the angel Gabriel in a dream.[1] The text of the Qur'an
contains 114 chapters (suras) of varying length and content. Unlike Jewish and Christian scriptures, which were produced by multiple authors
from different historical times and cultural backgrounds, the Qur'an is
the work of a single man, in a single lifetime. The text thus bears a strong
stamp of that man's personality—Muhammed is the Prophet of Allah,
the human medium of God's ultimate revelation. To learn about Islam is
inevitably to learn about the Prophet Muhammed.

Several passages of the Qur'an contain discussions of dreams and
dreaming, and because of the absolute centrality of the Qur'an to Muslim
faith these passages have become fundamental to all later Islamic dream
traditions. What follows are brief synopses of four suras in which dreams
play a significant role.

12: Joseph. In this chapter Muhammed gives a condensed version of
the story of Joseph (following the essential outline found in the Torah's
[Book of] Genesis 37-50). While much of the material from the Genesis
version has been removed, the three major dream episodes in Joseph's life
all remain, and these episodes combine to make a clear point: dreams,
and the ability to interpret them, are an important sign of God's favor.
Muhammed starts sura 12 with the young Joseph telling his father he had
a dream in which "eleven stars and the sun and the moon were prostrat-
ing themselves before me."[2] Joseph's father warns the boy not to tell the

---

[1] Marcia Hermansen, "Dreams and Dreaming in Islam," in Dreams: A Reader in the Religious, Cultural, and
Psychological Dimensions of Dreaming (edited by Kelly Bulkeley) (New York: Palgrave, 2001), p. 74.
[2] All quotes from the Qur'an are from the translation of N.J.Dawood (New York: Penguin Books,
1956).

dream to his older brothers, who jealously harbor murderous intentions toward him (in Genesis the dream is interpreted to mean that one day Joseph's eleven brothers, mother, and father will all bow down to him—a prospect that enrages his brothers). Joseph's father prophesizes [*sic*] that his youngest son "shall be chosen by your Lord. He will teach you to interpret visions." The prophecy is borne out later in the sura when Joseph, unjustly imprisoned in Egypt, is asked to interpret the dreams of two fellow prisoners:

"One of them said: 'I dreamt that I was pressing grapes.' And the other said: 'I dreamt that I was carrying a loaf upon my head, and that the birds came and ate of it. Tell us the meaning of these dreams, for we can see you are a man of learning.' Joseph replied: 'I can interpret them long before they are fulfilled. This knowledge my lord has given me, for I have left the faith of those that disbelieve in Allah and deny the life to come. I follow the faith of my forefathers, Abraham, Isaac, and Jacob.'"

Joseph tells the first man his dream means he will be released and serve the king wine, while the second man's dream means he will be crucified, and the birds will peck at his head. When these predictions come true, Joseph's skill as a dream interpreter comes to the attention of Egypt's king, who has been troubled by two dreams of his own, one in which seven fatted cows devour seven lean ones, and the other in which seven green ears of corn devour seven dry ones. The king asks his royal advisors to tell him the meaning of these dreams, but they cannot do so, saying "It is but an idle dream; nor can we interpret dreams." Joseph, however, is able to interpret the dreams accurately as anticipations of the future welfare of the land and its people, when seven years of plenty will be followed by seven years of famine. The king is pleased with this interpretation, and as a reward makes Joseph his personal servant.

Very much like the Genesis version, the Qur'an portrays Joseph as an exemplary man of faith and piety, and one clear sign of his close relationship with God is his ability to have and interpret revelatory dreams.

37. The Ranks. Like sura 12, this one also retells a story found in the book of Genesis. Here the main subject is Abraham, whose life is recounted in Genesis 12-25. The Qur'anic version focuses specifically on

God's command to Abraham to sacrifice his only son, Isaac (cf. Genesis 22):

"[Abraham said] 'Grant me a son, Lord, and let him be a righteous man.' We [Allah] gave him news of a gentle son. And when he reached the age when he could work with him his father said to him: 'My son, I dreamt that I was sacrificing you. Tell me what you think.' He replied: 'Father, do as you are bidden. Allah willing, you shall find me faithful.' And when they had both surrendered themselves to Allah's will, and Abraham had laid down his son prostrate upon his face, We called out to him, saying: 'Abraham, you have fulfilled your vision.' Thus did We reward the righteous. That was indeed a bitter test."

Several points are worth noting here. First is the explicit reference to a dream as the means by which Abraham receives this command; the Genesis version does not emphasize the dream provenance as clearly. Second is the unquestioned assumption by both Abraham and his son that the dream is a command from Allah. The dream as Abraham describes it has no special markers of divine origin, and yet he and his son immediately agree that what Abraham has envisioned is ordained by God and must be done. This leads to the third and theologically most important point: the dream and their interpretation of it lead Abraham and his son to "surrender themselves to Allah's will." This humble obedience is the very heart of the Muslim faith—the absolute trust in God, even to the point of sacrificing one's most cherished human attachments ("That was indeed a bitter test"). Muhammed's retelling of the story of Abraham and Isaac in many ways encapsulates the whole of the Qur'an. A fourth and final point to note here is the interesting twist at the end of the story, which differs quite dramatically from the Genesis version. In sura 37, Abraham is stopped in the sacrifice of his son by God's sudden words, "Abraham, you have fulfilled your vision." Abraham is true to his dream not by literally enacting it in the physical sacrifice of his son; rather, he "fulfills his vision" by a symbolic demonstration of his absolute obedience to God. As I will discuss later, this emphasis on the symbolic rather than the literal will pave the way for later Muslim philosophical and theological thinking about what kinds of truth can be discerned via the dreaming imagination.[3]

8: The Spoils. This sura describes two of Muhammed's own dream experiences. He mentions them in the context of telling how in the early years of his mission he struggled to lead his followers in battle against their opponents—"some of the faithful were reluctant. They argued with you [Muhammed] about the truth that had been revealed, as though they were being led to certain death." Muhammed says he prayed to God for help, and God responded as follows:

"You [Muhammed] were overcome by sleep, a token of His [Allah's] protection. He sent down water from the sky to cleanse you and to purify you of Satan's filth, to strengthen your hearts and to steady your footsteps. Allah revealed His will to the angels, saying: 'I shall be with you. Give courage to the believers. I shall cast terror into the hearts of the infidels. Strike off their heads, maim them in every limb!'"

A little further on, Muhammed describes his experience the night before a particular battle, when he and his army were encamped across a valley from a gathering of hostile warriors:

"Allah made them appear to you in a dream as a small band. Had He showed them to you as a great army, your courage would have failed you and discord would have triumphed in your ranks. But this Allah spared you. He knows your inmost thoughts."

The two dreams reflect the warlike environment in which Muhammed and his followers first established the Muslim faith. Although Muhammed spent much time alone in desert caves praying and meditating, he was also a charismatic warrior who led his troops through several harrowing battles. The dream experiences reported in this sura express Muhammed's faith in God's rousing presence during times of violent struggle. In this way the two dreams are similar to many passages in the Torah and the New Testament, where God appears to the faithful in times

---

[3] For example, see Henri Corbin, "The Visionary Dream in Islamic Spirituality," in *The Dream and Human Societies* (edited by G. E. von Grunebaum and Roger Callois) (Berkeley: University of California Press, 1966).

of danger, violence, and despair to offer reassurance and heavenly comfort (e.g., Genesis 28; Matthew 1, 2; Acts 16, 27). An unusual feature in this sura is the frank acknowledgment that God may use dreams to deceive the faithful for their own good. Muhammed is grateful that Allah knew his "inmost thoughts," i.e., his secret fear that his army would be defeated, and sent a dream that reassured him. The value of the dream is clearly not in the accuracy of its representation of physical reality, but rather in its inspiring emotional effect on Muhammed—the dream emboldens him to ignore any "realistic" appraisal of his chances and to continue fighting in total confidence of ultimate victory.

Perhaps one of the more interesting points he makes about the Islamic use of dreams is the insight that even the messages from God can be symbolic. That is, Abraham was able to symbolically satisfy God's dream command to sacrifice his son without shedding his blood.

DREAMS IN THE HADITH

Bulkeley continues by telling us of Muhammed's approaches to dream work as recorded by others in the hadith. In one example we are told to share our dreams with a loved one or someone knowledgeable. In another, we are told not to talk about nightmares, but instead to pray and seek refuge in God.

(The hadith were originally oral accounts of Muhammed's life and clarification of Islamic tradition. Later written down, the hadith are still a source of Islamic history, biography, and inspiration.)

BOTH DURING AND AFTER MUHAMMED'S DEATH a number of accounts were written of his words and deeds, and these accounts are gathered in the hadith. Among the various sayings of the hadith are several detailed discussions of dreams and dreaming. Although secondary in theological importance to the passages from the Qur'an, the references to dreaming in the hadith are extremely significant historically, and they have added important conceptual and technical elements to the dream traditions of Islam. In particular, the hadith contain abundant references to the practice of dream interpretation, and many of the interpretive principles enunciated in these passages continue to guide the dream practices of present-day Muslims in countries around the world.

The legitimacy of dream interpretation as a religious activity receives strong endorsement from the hadith, most directly in the verses that state: "When the companions of the Messenger of God [Muhammed] saw dreams while he was still alive they would tell him of their dreams and he, for his part, would interpret them as God willed."[4] Many hadith describe Muhammed's interpretations of particular images and symbols in the dreams of his followers, while other verses tell of Muhammed's own dreams and his interpretations of them. For example, the hadith report several dreams Muhammed had of his friend 'Umar, who later became one of his successors. The dreams express Muhammed's respect and admiration for the power of 'Umar's faith, and this provided 'Umar with a kind of divine sanction for the day when he assumed religious authority following the death of Muhammed.[5]

According to these texts, Muhammed was sensitive to the practical difficulties encountered by many of his followers who were trying to interpret their own dreams. The first suggestion Muhammed makes is to tell the dream to someone else: "A dream rests on the feathers of a bird and will not take effect unless it is related to someone." However, people should be careful not to reveal too much in public; "tell your dreams only to knowledgeable persons and loved ones," and beware those who will use your dreams against you (like Joseph's brothers did against him). Muhammed gives a colorful warning to those who abuse the practice of dream interpretation: "Whoever claims to have had a dream in which he says he saw something he did not shall be ordered [in Hell] to tie a knot between two barley grains and will not be able to do so." To help people increase their chances of having a good dream, Muhammed offers suggestions about how to approach sleep in a state of ritual purity, with the

---

[4] Hermansen, "Dreams and Dreaming in Islam," p. 75.
[5] Ibid., p. 75.

specific instruction to try sleeping on the right side.[6] Bad dreams come from Satan, and he says people should refrain from talking about these dreams and instead "offer a prayer" and "seek refuge with Allah from [the dream's] evil."

The hadith that reads, "Whoever sees me [the Prophet] in dreams will see me in wakefulness [the Hereafter] for Satan cannot take my shape" has long been understood to mean that a dream in which Muhammed appears as a character is unquestionably a true dream. Every other kind of dream could be a malevolent deception sent by Satan, but a dream of Muhammed can be accepted with complete confidence as an authentic revelation because Satan does not have the power to assume the shape of God's Prophet. Perhaps the most oft quoted hadith on the subject of dreams reads, "The good dream is 1/46th of prophecy." While commentators have long debated the significance of this exact number,[7] the general sense of the passage is clear: dreams are a legitimate source of divine knowledge.[8] This basic attitude in the hadith—dreams are not the only source of religious revelation, but nevertheless a real and important one available to a wide spectrum of people—builds on the positive evaluation of dreams in the Qur'anic verses discussed above and gives a more definitive shaping to the beliefs and practices of later Muslims.

---

[6] The Muslim practice of religiously-oriented dream incubation, istikhara, is itself a topic worthy of greater investigation. See, for example, J. Spencer Trimmingham, Islam in West Africa (Oxford: Clarendon Press, 1959).

[7] One common explanation is that the number 1/46th involves a doubling of the number of years (23) between the beginning of Muhammed's revelation and his death.

[8] All quotes in this paragraph are from Hermansen, "Dreams and Dreaming in Islam," pp. 75-76.

ISLAM AND LATER DEVELOPMENTS IN DREAM INTERPRETATION

INSPIRED BY THESE TEACHINGS from the Qur'an and the hadith, Muslim philosophers and theologians in subsequent years continued the process of developing new techniques and conceptual frameworks for the practice of dream interpretation. The most famous of the early dream interpreters was Ibn Sirin, whose name was reverently attached to dream interpretation manuals for many centuries after his death in 728 C.E. One of Ibn Sirin's key teachings was to pay close attention to the personal characteristics of the dreamer. The following anecdote about his interpretive method appears in several texts:

"Two dreamers came to Ibn Sirin within an hour of each other and each had dreamed of being the caller to prayer (muezzin). The first person was told that his dream foretold that he would perform the Muslim pilgrimage to Mecca. The second man, who seemed to be of a baser character, was told that he would be accused of a theft. [His] pupils then questioned how Ibn Sirin could come up with such radically different interpretations for the same dream. His response was that the character of each dreamer was evident from his appearance and demeanor. Therefore, the first one's dream evoked the Qur'anic verse 'Proclaim to the people a solemn pilgrimage' (20:28) since he was clearly pious. The second man's dream evoked the verse 'Then a crier called after them, O company of travelers [Joseph's brothers], you are surely thieves' (12:70)."[9]

Ibn Sirin's reference to specific scriptural passages reflects the fact that Muslims are thoroughly steeped from an early age in the text of the Qur'an. Memorization of Qur'anic verses has long been a central feature of Muslim education, and Ibn Sirin's interpretive strategy relies heavily on people's intimate familiarity with the language, characters, and themes of the Qur'an. Perhaps of most interest to Western psychological researchers, Ibn Sirin explicitly teaches that a given dream's meaning cannot be determined without reference to the personality characteristics of the

---

[9] Ibid., p. 78.

dreamer. There is, in other words, no "one size fits all" interpretation for any particular dream symbol; the meaning depends on the personality and life circumstances of the dreamer. . . .

Looking in more detail at the Muslim teachings, the first example to consider comes from the philosopher Ibn Arabi (1164-1240), who devised a grand metaphysical system merging Islamic theology with Greek philosophy.[10] His typology of dreaming establishes the basic framework used throughout later Muslim history. According [to] Ibn Arabi, there are three basic types of dream. The first is an "ordinary" dream, produced by the imagination when it takes experiences from daily life and magnifies them as in a mirror, reflecting in a distorted symbolic fashion our wishes and desires. The second and much more significant type of dream draws its material not from daily life but from the "Universal Soul," a source of knowledge closely associated with the faculty of abstract reasoning. "Universal Soul" dreams reveal fundamental truths about reality, although like the first type of dream these ones are distorted by the imperfect mirror of the human imagination. Interpretation is therefore required to discover what the symbolic images mean. The third and final type of dream involves a direct revelation of reality, with no distortion or symbolic mediation—a clear vision of divine truth.

Kelly Bulkeley, "Reflections on the Dream Traditions of Islam," *Sleep and Hypnosis*, 4:1 (2002).

---

[10] Rom Landau, "The Philosophy of Ibn Arabi," *The Muslim World* (1957), vol. 47, pp. 46-61.

Refik Algan

THE DREAM AND THE SLEEPER
IN SUFI TRADITION

Refik Algan is a Turkish writer, translator, and Sufi teacher. Here,
his description of dream work includes aspects unique to Sufi tradition
and others that strike familiar themes. He reiterates, for instance, that
dreams are a window into the state of our psyche and allow us to see the
nature of our concerns and preoccupations. He also stresses the need to
work with someone who has direct experience with the subtler states of
mind who can inspire our exploration and help us on the path.

Other readings in this book emphasize suspending judgment to find
the unfiltered messages of our dreams (Freud, p. 3; Gendlin, p. 72).
Algan makes a similar point using the Sufi vocabulary of "subjective"
and "objective" perspectives.

ALTHOUGH DREAMS AND THEIR INTERPRETATIONS are not the primary
focus of Sufism, they are still of vital importance. It is generally accepted
that the prophets of the Old and New Testaments and the Holy Qur'an
all completed the path with the help of dreams. The Prophet Muhammad, peace and blessings be upon him, taught a method by which certain
information can be received through dreams. He always recommended
this method as an aid to making important decisions in life.

Before we start talking about dreams, we have to remind ourselves
that each traditional teaching has its own policies, etiquette, principles,
puzzles and style of sharing knowledge. Muhammad also advised that one
speak to others according to their capacity. Therefore what and how much
can be spoken of, the quantity and the quality of information conveyed
through words, is limited. And these words can only be small hints of
direct experiences of one's own in the future.

Everyone dreams, either frequently or rarely, and we are all familiar
with the concept of a dream. But serious seekers have learned that what
Sufi teachers mean by "dreams" is broader and more flexible than what

we understand as dreams in the everyday sense. Under the category of dreams are included a complex network of experiences and various levels of dreamlike states. For this reason, according to Sufism, the help of someone who has passed through all these states and levels is absolutely necessary for the teaching and purification process.

One could say that coming to understand dreams and their interpretation is a dynamic process that parallels the seeker's progress in general. So a certain kind of development is required of the seeker as he or she proceeds, and this involves a positive feedback mechanism with a mature guide until a certain stage is reached. At every stage, the dreams of the seeker change their symbols, color, brightness and intensity. At every stage the seeker understands something different by the word "dream." This transformation has to be experienced and understood directly by the seeker, and his or her understanding has to be verified by the guide. The seeker has to discover his own way and verify its validity with the help of the teacher.

In Sufism, a mature teacher provides a stimulus that may come in many forms, conscious and unconscious, intellectual, emotional, psychic, and spiritual. From these stimuli something is expected to grow in the seeker, pass through certain stages, and bear its fruits. Great misunderstandings and loss of one's way are almost inevitable if one tries to interpret the dream alone or from a book, or with someone who is not licensed within the teaching.

Classical Sufi teachers have classified dreams according to their origins: they may come from the ego, worldly influences, angels, dark forces, and so on. Other classifications proceed according to the developmental levels of the self (the seven stages between the compulsive self and the enlightened self), or according to symbols, dominating colors, and brightness. But such classifications refer to the stage of the seeker after meeting the teacher. It is generally accepted that until one reaches a true teacher, a person's dreams are mostly related to the same dimension of the psyche that conventional psychology deals with. But after meeting the teacher and receiving the first exercises, the characteristics of one's dreams start changing. This is due to the energy radiated by the teacher and the exercise he has given. Besides these exercises, certain precautions are also necessary for remembering the dreams after one wakes up, or even for being aware of dreams during sleep.

So one may say that dreams that show up in the beginning are mostly indicators of the receptivity of the unconscious of the seeker, and they reveal the stage of the purification process. These signs are specific to each teaching method. This is very important to know because the same symbols and signs may have totally different meanings in an Eastern religion, in a different order, or even among different teachers of the same order.

This brings us face to face with a different question: Are all dream systems relativistic, or can there be a single, absolute dream system in which no symbolism is presumed? One of the main characteristics of an operating dream system, even if it be mostly relativistic, is its accordance with the function and structure of the brain itself. Therefore, even a relativistic dream system (such as that of a particular Sufi order) sooner or later has to pass from relativistic imagery to certain points of contact with the objective world, and finally one has to end at an absolute destination which is the brain's naked structure itself, i.e., the "hardware." At a certain stage dreams will begin to reflect certain objective features of the nervous system. As the Turkish poet Yunus Emre said, "We found it all in the body." . . .

. . . the frequency of the appearance of absolute themes (i.e., those relating to the divine) within the seeker's dreams indicates his or her closeness to the objective world. Here is where the interval between the subjective and objective begins to diminish. At last, being freed from relativistic and personal dreams, the brain can see the outside world as it is. Then the inside and outside have become one and there is no veil of ignorance between them. From then on, as it has been traditionally expressed, "the mirror has been polished" or cleaned of dreams. In modern terms, one has reached objective consciousness. This is the state where the outside is reflected onto the inside without distortion.

Do dreams come to an end here? Is there also a symbolism, perhaps even an absolute one, for the objective world? Mevlâna Jalâluddîn Rumi, the great Sufi teacher, says:

> When it is said, "the vision He granted to His messenger," now this vision is the dreams of lovers and true men of God, and the interpretation of that vision is revealed in the other world. When you see in a dream that you are riding a horse, you will gain your goal; yet what connection has the horse with the goal? If you dream you have been given coins of good currency, the meaning is that you will hear true and wise words spoken by a learned man; in what respect does a coin resemble a word? If you dream that you have been hanged on the gallows, you will become the leader of a people; how do the gallows resemble a position of leadership? So it is that the affairs of the world are a dream. "This world is the dream of a sleeper;" their interpretation in the other world will be quite different, not resembling this. That will be interpreted by a Divine Interpreter, for to Him all things are revealed.

On the one hand, the outward world and its events may be grossly distorted by our subjectivity. As we undergo the process of clearing the mirror of the heart, we move from subjectivity to objectivity. We free ourselves from the gross distortions of our egoism. Eventually we may begin to approach the seeing of that Divine Interpreter to whom the real meaning of all things is clear. . . .

In our egoism and subjectivity we look to this world for our satisfaction. As Muhammad said, "The world is like a dream that a sleeping man sees." But everything we desire in this dream and every satisfaction we have is, from the vantage point of the Divine Interpreter, like a sleeping man enjoying aperitifs and delicacies: when he wakes up, he will find that neither his hunger nor this thirst were satisfied. What we ask for in the dream may be given in the dream, but is it possible to awaken and to know we have been dreaming and to break the vicious cycle?

Again Rumi says:

> All things in this world, wealth, wife, and clothing, are sought after for the sake of something else, they are not sought for themselves. Do you not see that even if you had a hundred thousand dirhams and were hungry and could not find any bread, you would not be able to eat and feed yourself on those dirhams? A wife may be for the sake of children, and to satisfy passion. Clothes are to ward off the cold. In the same way, all things are concatenated with God, the most Glorious: He is sought and desired for His own sake, not for anything else. In so far as He is beyond all and better, subtler than all, how should He be desired for something less than Himself? "Unto Him is the final end." When they have reached Him they have reached their final goal, beyond which nothing can go . . .

Refik Algan, "The Dream of the Sleeper—Dream Interpretation and Meaning in Sufism," *Gnosis* #22 (Winter 1992).

The Dalai Lama

His Holiness the Dalai Lama, head of state and spiritual leader of Tibet, engaged in dialogue with Western scientists on the nature of consciousness. The dialogues were made into the book Sleeping, Dreaming and Dying, *edited by the Chilean neuroscientist Francesco Varela.*

THE UNCONSCIOUS AND DREAMS

In one section of Sleeping, Dreaming, and Dying, *Joyce McDougall, a Parisian psychoanalyst, asks the Dalai Lama about dreams and the unconscious.*

[AT THE END OF JOYCE MCDOUGALL'S PRESENTATION *on psychoanalytic theories of consciousness*] . . . His Holiness acknowledged Joyce's effort with a big smile. She did not lose a moment in launching a question that was clearly burning for her, and for many of us: "I would like to ask Your Holiness if the Freudian concept of the unconscious has any corresponding ideas in Tibetan philosophy?"

He answered immediately. "First of all, within Tibetan Buddhism, you can speak of manifest versus latent states of consciousness. Beyond that, you can speak of latent propensities, or imprints (Skt. *vāsanā*; Tib. *bag chags*, pronounced *bakchak*). These are stored in the mind as a result of one's previous behavior and experience. Within the category of latent states of consciousness, there are states that can be aroused by conditions and others that are not aroused by conditions. Finally, it is said in Buddhist scriptures that during the daytime one accumulates some of these latent propensities through one's behavior and experiences, and these imprints that are stored in the mental continuum can be aroused, or made manifest, in dreams. This provides a relationship between daytime experience and dreams. There are certain types of latent propensities that can manifest in different ways, for example by affecting one's behavior, but they cannot be consciously recalled.

"However, there are divergent views within Tibetan Buddhism, and some schools maintain that these types of latent propensities can be recalled...."

> If, as Tibetan Buddhists believe, dreams arise from imprints of daytime behavior and experience, then it would be appropriate to seek the waking experiences or behaviors that are associated with a dream.

SLEEP, ORGASM, AND DEATH

JOYCE MCDOUGALL added an interesting remark from her own profession. "Psychoanalysis may offer a comment on the relation between sleep and orgasm, which can both be linked imaginatively to the idea of dying. People who suffer from insomnia and people who cannot achieve orgasm may discover in the course of analysis that their inability to fall asleep or to fuse with someone they love in an erotic union derives from a terror of losing the sense of self. It's interesting, too, that in France, orgasm is called *la petite mort*, the little death. In Greek mythology, sleep and death are brothers, Morpheus and Thanatos. To let yourself sink into sleep you have to let go of your personal idea of self and dissolve into the primal fusion with the world, or with the mother or the womb. Losing the everyday self is experienced as a loss instead of an enrichment. This can also apply to people who cannot enjoy orgasm.... The willingness to lose our sense of self that allows us to sink into sleep or orgasmic fusion can also allow us to be unafraid of dying. We might say that sleeping and orgasm are sublimated forms of dying."

Laughing, His Holiness said that in Tibet the best solution for those who have such fears was to take ordination. On a more serious note he added, "In the Tibetan Buddhist literature, it is said that one experiences a glimpse of clear light on various occasions, including sneezing, fainting, dying, sexual intercourse, and sleep. Normally, our sense of self, or ego, is quite strong and we tend to relate to the world with that subjectivity. But on these particular occasions, this strong sense of self is slightly relaxed.

> *If sleep is a period in which the sense of self is somewhat relaxed, wouldn't it be understandable that our psyches allow us to be, think, or act in dreams in ways we cannot allow ourselves when awake? In a dream of yours, do you behave in ways that would be embarrassing or unacceptable while awake? Are there flattering or unflattering dream images that you would censor in your waking world?*

DREAMING, SLEEPING, AND DEATH

In this dialogue with American psychologist Jayne Gackenback, The Dalai Lama draws parallels between the "clear light" states of death, bardo (transition after death), and rebirth with the states of sleep, dream, and waking. In doing so, he identifies the dream state as an alternate form of consciousness.

"To CONCLUDE, let me [*Jayne Gackenback*] summarize these tentative observations . . . . [*psychology and meditation researcher Fred Travis*] suggests that waking, sleeping, and REM dreaming emerge out of a pure consciousness, a silent void. Where each state meets the next there's a little gap, in which Travis postulates that everybody very briefly experiences transcendental consciousness. When we go from sleeping to dreaming, or from dreaming to waking, these little gaps or junction points occur, and so he calls this the *junction point model of mind.*"

"This is quite similar to a Buddhist explanation of these little interludes of the clear light of sleep," said His Holiness. "This is precisely the continuity of the very subtle mind. The major occasions are the times of dying, the *bardo,* and then conception. These are junctures, if you like. The subtlest clear light manifests at the time of death, which is one of these junctures. These three occasions of death, *bardo*, and conception are analogous to the states of falling asleep, the dream state, and then waking. There's also a facsimile of the clear light of death in the clear light of sleep. It's not the same as the clear light of death, but it is analogous to it, though less subtle."

Francisco Varela (ed.), *Sleeping, Dreaming, and Dying: An Exploration of Consciousness with the Dalai Lama* (Boston: Wisdom Publications, 1997), p. 49, p. 79, and pp. 109-110.

Pema Chödrön

MONSTERS IN THE NIGHT

Pema Chödrön is an American-born Buddhist nun ordained in the Tibetan tradition, and author of many books. In this excerpt she tells a wonderful childhood story about the way her friend resolved a recurring nightmare with curiosity and courage. Just bringing the light of awareness to the monsters reduced their power, as happens with bullies when they're finally challenged. This approach to facing the bullies of the night sounds a lot like the advice Kilton Stewart attributes to the Senoi on page 255.

WHEN I WAS ABOUT TEN, my best friend started having nightmares: she'd be running through a huge dark building pursued by hideous monsters. She'd get to a door, struggle to open it, and no sooner had she closed it behind her than she'd hear it opened by the rapidly approaching monsters. Finally she'd wake up screaming and crying for help.

One day we were sitting in her kitchen talking about her nightmares. When I asked her what the demons looked like, she said she didn't know because she was always running away. After I asked her that question, she began to wonder about the monsters. She wondered if any of them looked like witches and if any of them had knives. So on the next occurrence of the nightmare, just as the demons began to pursue her, she stopped running and turned around. It took tremendous courage, and her heart was pounding, but she put her back up against the wall and looked at them. They all stopped right in front of her and began jumping up and down, but none of them came closer. There were five in all, each looking something like an animal. One of them was a gray bear, but instead of claws, it had long red fingernails. One had four eyes. Another had a wound on its cheek. Once she looked closely, they appeared less like monsters and more like the two-dimensional drawings in comic books. Then slowly they began to fade. After that she woke up, and that was the end of her nightmares.

There is a teaching on the three kinds of awakening: awakening from the dream of ordinary sleep, awakening at death from the dream of life, and awakening into full enlightenment from the dream of delusion. These teachings say that when we die, we experience it as waking up from a very long dream. When I heard this teaching, I remembered my friend's nightmares. It struck me right then that if all this is really a dream, I might as well spend it trying to look at what scares me instead of running away. I haven't always found this all that easy to do, but in the process I've learned a lot about maitri [*loving-kindness and compassion*].

Our personal demons come in many guises. We experience them as shame, as jealousy, as abandonment, as rage. They are anything that makes us so uncomfortable that we continually run away.

We do the big escape: we act out, say something, slam a door, hit someone, or throw a pot as a way of not facing what's happening in our hearts. Or we shove the feelings under and somehow deaden the pain. We can spend our whole lives escaping from the monsters of our minds.

All over the world, people are so caught in running that they forget to take advantage of the beauty around them. We become so accustomed to speeding ahead that we rob ourselves of joy.

Once I dreamt that I was getting a house ready for Khandro Rinpoche. I was rushing around cleaning and cooking. Suddenly her car drove up, and there she was with her attendant. As I ran up and greeted them, Rinpoche smiled at me and asked, "Did you see the sun come up this morning?" I answered, "No, Rinpoche, I didn't. I was much too busy to see the sun." She laughed and said, "Too busy to live life!"

Sometimes it seems we have a preference for darkness and speed. We can protest and complain and hold a grudge for a thousand years. But in the midst of the bitterness and resentment, we have a glimpse of the possibility of maitri. We hear a child crying or smell that someone is baking bread. We feel the coolness of the air or see the first crocus of spring. Despite ourselves we are drawn out by the beauty in our own backyard.

The way to dissolve our resistance to life is to meet it face to face. When we feel resentment because the room is too hot, we could meet the heat and feel its fieriness and its heaviness. When we feel resentment because the room is too cold, we could meet the cold and feel its iciness and its bite. When we want to complain about the rain, we could feel its wetness instead. When we worry because the wind is shaking our windows, we could meet the wind and hear its sound. Cutting our expectations for a cure is a gift we can give ourselves. There is no cure for hot and cold. They will go on forever. After we have died, the ebb and flow will still continue. Like the tides of the sea, like day and night—this is the nature of things. Being able to appreciate, being able to look closely, being able to open our minds—this is the core of maitri.

Chödrön presents the Buddhist understanding of a correspondence between the dreams we have at night and the dream that is our life. It is another example among many, across time and across the world, that link our dream life and our waking life. For example, Mohammed said, "The world is like a dream that a sleeping man sees" (p. 228).

Pema Chödrön, *When Things Fall Apart* (Boston: Shambhala Publications, Inc., 1997), pp. 28-30.

Joseph Campbell

Joseph Campbell's work also appears on page 184 and page 261.

OM

In this selection, Campbell recounts Hindu teaching on the four states of consciousness. The first state is associated with waking life and the external world, the second to dreaming and an internal world, and the two others go beyond such distinctions. Campbell implies that the third and fourth states require an engagement so intimate that there is no room for the intellectual separation created by labels of objective and subjective, real or dreaming. There is only the present experience, without judgment. To use these concepts in working with your dreams, try fully engaging in the dream story, not as the truth, but as a truth. What thoughts and feelings now arise?

THIS SACRED INDIAN SYLLABLE [*OM or AUM*] of prayer and meditation is said to be composed of four symbolic elements. First, since the O, in Sanskrit, is regarded as an amalgam of the two sounds A and U, the sacred syllable can be written and heard as AUM, and when it is so displayed, three of its four elements are made visible. The fourth, then, is the Silence that surrounds the syllable, so viewed, out of which it rises, back into which it falls, and which supports it as the ground of its appearance.

Now when pronounced, the A of AUM is heard proceeding from the back of the mouth. Coming forward with U, the sounding air mass fills the whole mouth cavity; and with M it is closed at the lips. When thus pronounced, they say, the syllable contains the sounds of all the vowels of speech. And since the consonants are but interruptions of these sounds, the holy syllable contains in itself—when properly pronounced—the seed sounds of all words and thus the names of all things and relationships.

There is an extremely interesting and important Upanishad, the *Manduka*, in which the four symbolic elements of the syllable—the A, the U, the M, and the Silence—are interpreted allegorically as referring to four planes, degrees, or modes of consciousness. The A, resounding from the back of the mouth, is said to represent waking consciousness. Here the subject and the objects of its knowledge are experienced as separate from each other. Bodies are of gross matter; they are not self-luminous and they change their forms slowly. An Aristotelian logic prevails: *a* is not *not-a*. The nature of thought on this level is that of mechanistic science, positivistic reasoning, and the aims of its life are as envisioned at *chakras* 1, 2, and 3.

Next, with U, where the sound mass, moving forward, fills the whole head as it were, the Upanishad associates dream consciousness; and here the subject and object, the dreamer and his dream, though they may seem to be separate, are actually one, since the images are of the dreamer's own will. Further, they are of a subtle matter, self-luminous, and of rapidly changing form. They are of the nature of divinities: and indeed all the gods and demons, Heavens and Hells, are in fact the cosmic counterparts of dream. Moreover, since on this subtle plane the seer and the seen are one and the same, all the gods and demons, Heavens and Hells are within us; are ourselves. Turn within, therefore, if you seek your model for the image of a god. Accordingly, it is experiences of this plane of consciousness that are rendered visible in the Oriental arts.

Next, M, third element of the syllable, where the intonation of this holy sound terminates forward, at the closed lips, the Upanishad associates with deep dreamless sleep. There is here neither object seen nor seeing subject, but unconsciousness—or rather, latent, potential consciousness, undifferentiated, covered with darkness. Mythologically this state is identified with that of the universe between cycles, when all has returned to the cosmic night, the womb of the cosmic mother: "chaos," in the language of the Greeks, or in Genesis, the first "formless waste, with darkness over the seas." There is no consciousness of any objects either of waking or of dream, but only uninflected consciousness in its pristine, uncommitted state—lost, however, in darkness.

The ultimate aim of yoga, then, can be only to enter that zone awake: which is to say, to "join" or to "yoke" (Sanskrit verbal root *yuj*, whence the noun *yoga*) one's waking consciousness to its source in consciousness *per se*, not focused on any object or enclosed in any subject, whether of the waking world or of sleep, but sheer, unspecified and unbounded. And since all words refer to objects or to object-related thoughts or ideas, we have no word or words for the experience of this fourth state. Even such words as "silence" or "void" can be understood only with reference to sound or to things—as of no sound, or as of no thing. Whereas here we have come to the primal Silence antecedent to sound, containing sound as potential, and to the Void antecedent to things, containing as potential the whole of space-time and its galaxies. No word can say what the Silence tells that is all around and within us, this Silence that is no silence but to be heard resounding through all things, whether of waking, dream, or dreamless night—as surrounding, supporting, and suffusing the syllable AUM.

Listen to the sound of the city. Listen to the sound of your neighbor's voice, or of the wild geese honking skyward. Listen to any sound or silence at all without interpreting it, and the Anahata will be heard of the Void that is the ground of being, and the world that is the body of being, the Silence and the Syllable. Moreover, when once this sound has been "heard," as it were, as the sound and being of one's own heart and of all life, one is stilled and brought to peace; there is no need to quest any more, for it is here, it is there, it is everywhere.

Joseph Campbell, *Myths to Live By* (New York: Bantam Books, 1972), pp. 112-114.

VISHNU, THE HINDU GOD
THAT DREAMS THE WORLD

Here Campbell says that all we know of the world is but a part of Vishnu's dream, and when Vishnu awakes, the dream ceases and all is gone.

... VISHNU SLEEPS IN THE COSMIC OCEAN, and the lotus of the universe grows from his navel. On the lotus sits Brahma, the creator. Brahma opens his eyes, and a world comes into being, governed by an Indra. Brahma closes his eyes, and a world goes out of being. The life of a Brahma is four-hundred-and-thirty-two-thousand years. When he dies, the lotus goes back, and another lotus is formed, and another Brahma. Then think of the galaxies beyond galaxies in infinite space, each a lotus with a Brahma, sitting on it, opening his eyes, closing his eyes. ...

Joseph Campbell, *Power of Myth* (New York: Doubleday, 1988), p. 63.

Janice Hinshaw Baylis

YIN, YANG, AND THE BALANCE OF OPPOSITES

The Taoists conceive of yin and yang as feminine and masculine energy, respectively, and believe that a balance of the two brings harmony. We can use this tension of opposites in holding our dreams: Does your dream balance feminine and masculine images? If not, which image/energy predominates? In your dream, does tension resolve when feminine and masculine images come into balance? Which aspect do you think predominates in your daily life?

TRADITIONAL ASSIGNMENT OF TRAITS
TO MALE OR FEMALE

THE ANCIENT CHINESE YIN/YANG SYMBOL shows it so well. Each side is very different, black and white. But, each side has an eye of the opposite color. The black feminine has a white eye, the masculine within, the Animus. The white masculine has a black eye, the feminine within, the Anima. The line between them is not stark and straight; it is gently flowing, like spoons in a drawer or a man and woman together in sleep. These are not competitive opposites but complementary opposites.

PHYSICAL TRAITS	
MALE	FEMALE
cause	effect
dynamic	static
movement	rest
active	passive
dominant	submissive
aggressive	non-aggressive
war	peace
adventurous	cautious
strong	weak
firm	yielding
hard	soft
thrusting	receiving
competitive	non-competitive
output	input
right	left
light	dark
hero	mother
positive	negative
plug	socket
bolt	nut
pen	paper

EMOTIONAL TRAITS	
MALE	FEMALE
unemotional	emotional
not easily hurt	easily hurt
detachment	attachment
objective	subjective
insensitive to others	sensitive to others
rational	irrational
rigid	adaptable
calm	excitable
independent	dependent
power	love
justice	mercy
conflict	harmony
will	understanding

MENTAL/PSYCHOLOGICAL	
MALE	FEMALE
logic/reason	feelings/values
facts	intuitions
rational	irrational
thinking	emotions
analyze differences	compare similarities
linear	global
detailed	holistic
organization	ceremony
differentiating	interweaving
knowledge	inspiration
science	philosophy
plan	work
insights	judgments
discrimination	acceptance
conscious	subconscious
active	passive
clear	diffuse
lead	follow

SPIRITUAL/CREATIVE	
MALE	FEMALE
idea	form
cause	effect
spirit	matter/nature
duration in time	extension in space
will	wisdom
power	love
inner mind	outer body
positive	negative
plan/design	build

SYMBOLIC	
MALE	FEMALE
sun-radiating	moon-reflecting
gold	silver
heaven	earth
dog	cat
dragon	horse
elongated	hollow/round
key	lock

Remember, the goal is balance, the ability to do or be either, depending on the situation. The androgynous being has both male and female traits.

As a man or woman becomes more ideally balanced, their ideal mate will be more balanced. The figures of history and classic literature present us with personifications of different levels of male and female.

MALE	FEMALE
physical/power-Tarzan	physical/playgirl-Eve
adventure-Columbus	romantic/aesthetic-Helen of Troy
intellect/science-Plato	wisdom-Athena
spiritual-Jesus	spiritual-Virgin Mary

Janice Hinshaw Baylis, *Sex, Symbols and Dreams* (Seal Beach, CA: Sun, Man, Moon, Inc., 1997), pp. 225-227.

WRITERS, CREATIVITY, AND DREAMING

In their writings, literary artists express an intuitive understanding of the role of dreams in our lives. Many have done so. Homer, William Blake, and John Steinbeck, among others, here address themes common to all parts of this book and to each other.

Homer

THE ODYSSEY

While there is scholarly debate about the facts, it is generally believed that Greek author Homer wrote The Iliad and The Odyssey in about the 9th century BCE. In his time, dreams were considered autonomous, coming as a message from the outside to the dreamer. Thus, Homeric dreamers spoke of seeing a dream instead of having a dream.

In this selection, Ulysses has just returned home from his decade of wandering after the Trojan War. Not recognizing him beneath beggar's clothes, his wife, Penelope, asks his advice.

AND THUS THE SAGE PENELOPE BEGAN: —
"Stranger, but little longer will I yet
Inquire; the hour of grateful rest is near
For those who, though unhappy, can receive
The balm of slumber. Yet for me some god
Appoints immeasurable grief. All day
In sorrows and in sighs, my solace is
To oversee my maidens at their tasks
Here in the palace; but when evening comes,
And all betake themselves to rest, I lie
Upon my couch, and sorrows thick and sharp
Awake new misery in my heart. As when,
In the fresh spring, the swarthy Nightingale,
Daughter of Pandarus, among thick leaves
Sings sweetly to the woods, and, changing oft
The strain, pours forth her voice of many notes,
Lamenting the beloved Itylus,
Her son by royal Zethos, whom she smote
Unwittingly, and slew; with such quick change
My mind is tossed from thought to thought. I muse
Whether to keep my place beside my son,
And hold what here is mine, my dower, my maids

And high-roofed halls, as one who still reveres
Her husband's bed, and heeds the public voice,
Or follow one of the Achaian chiefs,
The noblest of the wooers, and the one
Who offers marriage presents without stint.
My son's green years, while he was yet a boy,
Unripe in mind, allowed me not to wed,
And leave his father's home; but he is grown,
And on the verge of manhood. He desires
That I should leave the palace, for his wrath
Is great against the men who waste his wealth.
Hear, and interpret now a dream of mine:
Within these courts are twenty geese that eat
Corn from the water, and I look on them
Pleased and amused. From off a mountain came
A hook-beaked eagle, broke their necks, and left
Their bodies strewn about the palace dead,
And soared again into the air of heaven.
I wept and moaned, although it was a dream;
And round me came the fair-haired Grecian maids,
Lamenting wildly that the bird of prey
Had slain my geese. Then came the eagle back,
And took his perch upon the jutting roof,
And thus bespake me in a human voice:— "

   "'O daughter of Icarius, the renowned!
Let not thy heart be troubled; this is not
A dream, but a true vision, and will be
Fulfilled. The geese denote the suitor-train,
And I, who was an eagle once, am come,
Thy husband, now to end them utterly.'"

   "He spake; my slumbers left me, and I looked,
And saw the geese that in the palace still
Were at their trough, and feeding as before."

And thus Ulysses, the sagacious, said:
"Lady, the dream that visited thy sleep
Cannot be wrested to another sense.
Ulysses has himself revealed to thee
The way of its fulfillment. Death is near
The suitors, and not one escapes his doom."
Then spake the sage Penelope again:
"Of dreams, O stranger, some are meaningless
And idle, and can never be fulfilled.
Two portals are there for their shadowy shapes,
Of ivory one, and one of horn. The dreams
That come through the carved ivory deceive
With promises that never are made good;
But those which pass the doors of polished horn,
And are beheld of men, are ever true.
And yet I cannot hope that my strange dream
Came through them, though my son and I would both
Rejoice if it were so. This let me say,
And heed me well. Tomorrow brings to us
The hateful morn which takes me from my home,
The palace of Ulysses. I shall now
Propose a contest. In the palace court
Ulysses in a row set up twelve stakes,
Like props that hold a galley up; each stake
Had its own ring; he stood afar, and sent
An arrow through them all. I shall propose
This contest to the suitors. He who bends
The bow with easy mastery, and sends
Through the twelve rings an arrow, I will take
To follow from the palace where I passed
My youthful married life,—a beautiful home,
And stored with wealth; a home which I shall long
Remember, even in my nightly dreams."

Ulysses, the sagacious, answered thus:
"O gracious consort of Laertes' son!
Let not this contest be delayed; the man
Of ready wiles, Ulysses, will be here
Ere, tampering with the hero's polished bow,
The suitors shall prevail to stretch the cord,
And send an arrow through the rings of steel."
    And thus the sage Penelope rejoined:
"Stranger, if, sitting in the palace here,
Thou still wouldst entertain me as thou dost,
Sleep would not fall upon my lids; and yet
Sleepless the race of mortals cannot be,
So have the gods ordained, who measure out
His lot to man upon the nourishing earth.
I to the upper rooms withdraw, to take
My place upon the couch which has become
To me a place of sorrow and of tears
Since my Ulysses went away to Troy,
That fatal town which should be named no more.
And I will lay me down; but thou remain
Within these walls, and make the floor thy bed,
Or let these maidens spread a couch for thee."
    Penelope, thus having spoken, went
Up to her royal bower, but not alone;
Her maids went with her. When they were within
She wept for her dear husband, till at length
The blue-eyed Pallas graciously distilled
Upon her closing lids the balm of sleep.

Homer, *Odyssey of Homer*, trans. William Cullen Bryant (Boston: Houghton, Mifflin and Company, 1871), Book XIX, pp. 155-159.

Lewis Carroll

ALICE'S DREAM OF WONDERLAND

Lewis Carroll (the pen name for Charles Lutwidge Dodgson) was an English writer, photographer and mathematics teacher. This charming story of Alice is imbued with many familiar ideas about dreams.

"LET THE JURY CONSIDER THEIR VERDICT," the King said, for about the twentieth time that day.

"No, no!" said the Queen. "Sentence first—verdict afterwards."

"Stuff and nonsense!" said Alice loudly. "The idea of having the sentence first!"

"Hold your tongue!" said the Queen, turning purple.

"I won't!" said Alice.

"Off with her head!" the Queen shouted at the top of her voice. Nobody moved.

"Who cares for you?" said Alice, (she had grown to her full size by this time.) "You're nothing but a pack of cards!"

At this the whole pack rose up into the air, and came flying down upon her; she gave a little scream, half of fright and half of anger, and tried to beat them off, and found herself lying on the bank, with her head in the lap of her sister, who was gently brushing away some dead leaves that had fluttered down from the trees upon her face.

"Wake up, Alice dear!" said her sister; "Why, what a long sleep you've had!"

"Oh, I've had such a curious dream!" said Alice. And she told her sister, as well as she could remember them, all these strange Adventures of hers that you have just been reading about; and when she had finished, her sister kissed her, and said, "It *was* a curious dream, dear, certainly; but now run in to your tea: it's getting late." So Alice got up and ran off, thinking while she ran, as well she might, what a wonderful dream it had been.

But her sister sat still just as she left her, leaning her head on her hand, watching the setting sun, and thinking of little Alice and all her wonderful Adventures, till she too began dreaming after a fashion, and this was her dream:—

First, she dreamed about little Alice herself: once again the tiny hands were clasped upon her knee, and the bright eager eyes were looking up into hers—she could hear the very tones of her voice, and see that queer little toss of her head to keep back the wandering hair that *would* always get into her eyes—and still as she listened, or seemed to listen, the whole place around her became alive with the strange creatures of her little sister's dream. . . .

So she sat on, with closed eyes, and half believed herself in Wonderland, though she knew she had but to open them again, and all would change to dull reality—the grass would be only rustling in the wind, and the pool rippling to the waving of the reeds—the rattling teacups would change to tinkling sheep-bells, and the Queen's shrill cries to the voice of the shepherd-boy—and the sneeze of the baby, the shriek of the Gryphon, and all the other queer noises, would change (she knew) to the confused clamor of the busy farm-yard—while the lowing of the cattle in the distance would take the place of the Mock Turtle's heavy sobs.

Lastly, she pictured to herself how this same little sister of hers would, in the after-time, be herself a grown woman; and how she would keep, through all her riper years, the simple and loving heart of her childhood; and how she would gather about her other little children, and make *their* eyes bright and eager with many a strange tale, perhaps even with the dream of Wonderland of long ago; and how she would feel with all their simple sorrows, and find a pleasure in all their simple joys, remembering her own child-life, and the happy summer days.

When sentenced to death, Alice stands up to the queen, grows physically larger, and is therefore no longer vulnerable. What a perfect image to bring to our own nightmares! We can turn and face the fearful image just as Alice and Pema Chödrön's friend (p. 232) have done. Even if we are unable to respond so courageously during the dream, we can blunt the terror after waking by rewriting the dream's end as suggested in the excerpt on post-traumatic stress disorder treatment (p. 60).

When Alice's sister foresees that Alice will maintain her child-like heart even when she's grown up, she is showing us how cultivating our dreams can help us integrate our instinctive self with the adult mind.

Lewis Carroll, *Alice's Adventures in Wonderland and Through the Looking Glass*, (Chicago: Rand McNally & Company, 1865), pp. 111-113.

Charles Dickens

THE REALITY OF DREAMS BEYOND WORDS

In this essay, Charles Dickens, the 19th-century English novelist, bemoans the limitations of words (and even thoughts) when one wants to express the true intensity of an experience.

THE LABOURING OF THE SHIP in the troubled sea on this night I shall never forget. "Will it ever be worse than this?" was a question I had often heard asked, when everything was sliding and bumping about, and when it certainly did seem difficult to comprehend the possibility of anything afloat being more disturbed, without toppling over and going down. But what the agitation of a steam-vessel is, on a bad winter's night, in the wild Atlantic, it is impossible for the most vivid imagination to conceive. To say that she is flung down on her side in the waves, with her masts dipping into them, and that, springing up again, she rolls over on the other side, until a heavy sea strikes her with the noise of a hundred great guns, and hurls her back — that she stops, and staggers, and shivers, as though stunned, and then, with a violent throbbing at her heart, darts onward like a monster goaded into madness, to be beaten down, and battered, and crushed, and leaped on by the angry sea—that thunder, lightning, hail, and rain, and wind, are all in fierce contention for the mastery—that every plank has its groan, every nail its shriek, and every drop of water in the great ocean its howling voice—is nothing. To say that all is grand, and all appalling and horrible in the last degree, is nothing. Words cannot express it. Thoughts cannot convey it. Only a dream can call it up again, in all its fury, rage, and passion.

Charles Dickens, *Pictures from Italy and American Notes* (New York: Belford Clark & Co., 1885), Chapter 2, p. 208.

Mark Twain

THE BEAR BITE HURTS!

Mark Twain wrote the classic American novels Tom Sawyer *and* Huckleberry Finn.

. . . WHILE YOU ARE IN A DREAM it *isn't* a dream—it is reality, and the bear-bite hurts; hurts in a perfectly real way.

Mark Twain, *Which Was the Dream?* (Berkeley: University of California Press, 1967), pp. 46-47.

Kahlil Gibran

TRUST THE DREAMS

Poet, artist and philosopher Kahlil Gibran, was born in Lebanon in 1883. He emigrated to the U.S. and in 1923 published his most famous work, The Prophet, *in English.*

. . . IN THE DEPTH OF YOUR HOPES AND DESIRES lies your silent
    knowledge of the beyond;
And like seeds dreaming beneath the snow your heart dreams of spring.
Trust the dreams, for in them is the hidden gate to eternity.

Kahlil Gibran, *The Prophet* (New York: Alfred A. Knopf, 2005), p. 80.

John Steinbeck

COMMITTEE OF SLEEP

John Steinbeck was the Pulitzer-Prize-winning American author of
Grapes of Wrath.

IT IS A COMMON EXPERIENCE that a problem difficult at night is resolved
in the morning after the *committee of sleep* has worked on it.

Deirdre Barrett, *The Committee of Sleep: How Artists, Scientists and Athletes Use Dreams for
Creative Problem-Solving* (New York: Crown Publishers, 2001), p. ix.

Anaïs Nin

DREAMS ARE NECESSARY TO LIFE

Anaïs Nin was born in France to her Spanish father and Danish
mother. She studied psychoanalysis with Otto Rank (a protégé of
Freud), but is best known for her published journals.

LETTER TO MY MOTHER:

I was in Notre-Dame yesterday afternoon and I heard Vespers, and I
wept and found my old soul again, I don't know where it was. I had found
it once at the Hospital, remember? . . . I stood there in the Church and
cried and today I am happy, it is all so good . . . . I hope Alida liked my
book, you will like it too someday, I don't know when, when you realize
la vida es sueño [life is a dream], and that dreams are necessary to life; and
you know not all our dreams are holy, are they, you had some which were
not so holy, our dreams are not holy but that does not hurt or change
the fundamental soul, maybe some day you will believe so firmly in my

fundamental soul you won't mind my fantasies, you won't frown, you will just listen and smile as I imagine you smiling and listening when you are so far away . . . .

Anaïs Nin, *The Diary of Anaïs Nin, Volume 2* (Orlando, Florida: Harcourt Brace & Company, 1967), pp. 88-89.

Robert Bly

SHADOW: OUR HIDDEN PERSONALITY TRAITS

The American poet Robert Bly doesn't address dreams or dreaming here, but rather the need to integrate the dark and light sides of our personalities, which is also one of the key applications of dream interpretation.

WE NOTICE THAT WHEN SUNLIGHT HITS THE BODY, the body turns bright, but it throws a shadow, which is dark. The brighter the light, the darker the shadow. Each of us has some part of our personality that is hidden from us. Parents, and teachers in general, urge us to develop the light side of the personality—move into well-lit subjects such as mathematics and geometry—and to become successful. The dark part then becomes starved. What do we do then? We send out a crow.

The dove returns: it found no resting place;
It was in flight all night above the shaken seas;
Beneath dark eaves
The dove shall magnify the tiger's bed;
Give the dove peace.
The split-tailed swallow leaves the sill at dawn;
At dusk, blue swallows shall return.
On the third day the crow shall fly,

The crow, the crow, the spider-colored crow,
The crow shall find new mud to walk upon.

The poem refers to the Noah story, though I drew the images from an earlier version composed by the Babylonians, in which three birds took part. The poem came two or three years after college, and it seems to say that if any help was going to arrive to lift me out of my misery, it would come from the dark side of my personality.

Robert Bly, "Problems in the Ark," *The Little Book of the Human Shadow* (San Francisco: Harper & Row, 1988), pp. 7-8.

Kilton Stewart

American anthropologist Kilton Stewart wrote a compelling story about the dream work of an indigenous group he knew from first-hand experience. Yet anthropology colleagues who lived with the Senoi of Malaysia convincingly disputed Stewart's most fundamental claims about the Senoi culture in general and their dream work in particular. Nevertheless, the excerpts here took on a life of their own and some persist still in the lore of dream workers. Even if Stewart's report of Senoi dream work is erroneous (perhaps he was misled), its popularity indicates it touched a chord in our culture. Because of their valuable insights, I've chosen to include them in the "Writers, Creativity and Dreams" section.

THE SENOI:
ASK NIGHTMARE SPIRITS FOR HELP

THE SIMPLEST ANXIETY OR TERROR DREAM I found among the Senoi was the falling dream. When the Senoi child reports a falling dream, the adult answers with enthusiasm, "That is a wonderful dream, one of the best dreams a man can have. Where did you fall to, and what did you discover?" He makes the same comment when the child reports a climbing, traveling, flying, or soaring dream. The child at first answers, as he would in our society, that it did not seem so wonderful, and that he was so frightened that he awoke before he had fallen anywhere.

... "Everything you do in a dream has a purpose, beyond your understanding while you are asleep. You must relax and enjoy yourself when you fall in a dream. Falling is the quickest way to get in contact with the powers of the spirit world, the powers laid open to you through your dreams. Soon, when you have a falling dream, you will remember what I am saying, and as you do, you will feel that you are travelling to the source of the power which has caused you to fall."

"The falling spirits love you. They are attracting you to their land, and you have but to relax and remain asleep in order to come to grips with them. When you meet them, you may be frightened of their terrific power, but go on. When you think you are dying in a dream, you are only receiving the powers of the other world, your own spiritual power which has been turned against you, and which now wishes to become one with you if you will accept it."

The astonishing thing is that over a period of time, with this type of social interaction, praise, or criticism, imperatives, and advice, the dream which starts out with fear of falling changes into the joy of flying. This happens to everyone in the Senoi society. That which was an indwelling fear or anxiety, becomes an indwelling joy or act of will; that which was ill esteem toward the forces which caused the child to fall in his dream, becomes good will towards the denizens of the dream world, because he relaxes in his dream and finds pleasurable adventures, rather than waking up with a clammy skin and a crawling scalp.

> Stewart shows us how even that which frightens us can be transformed
> into a benevolent force. A Buddhist sutra (teaching) makes the same
> point: ... "particularly with someone who becomes a sworn enemy,
> and persecutes us with abusive language. That very abuse conveys
> the Buddha's boundless loving-kindness. It is a compassionate device

to liberate us entirely from the mean-spirited delusions we have built up with our wrongful conduct from the beginningless past." Christian tradition has a similar teaching. Of course when we are hurt, frightened, or upset, it is difficult or impossible to be open to learning, but Stewart's description can help us keep a receptive attitude while we examine even the most threatening dreams.

THE SENOI: RESOLUTION OF SOCIAL TENSION

As Stewart describes it, the communal culture of the Senoi is so strong that even dream work is a task for the entire group. Children are instructed in how to use the tension that arises in their dreams as a basis for improving relationships with others. Because Stewart's Senoi have a shared appreciation of the importance of dream events and use them in their community life, they have an advantage over us. How would you approach those with whom you have dream conflicts in order to bring peace to the relationship?

A CHILD DREAMS that he is attacked by a friend and, on awakening, is advised by his father to inform his friend of this fact. The friend's father tells his child that it is possible that he has offended the dreamer without wishing to do so, and allowed a malignant character to use his image as a disguise in the dream. Therefore, he should give a present to the dreamer and go out of his way to be friendly toward him, to prevent such an occurrence in the future.

The aggression building up around the image of the friend in the dreamer's mind thereby becomes the basis of a friendly exchange. The dreamer is also told to fight back in future dreams, and to conquer any dream character using the friend's image as a disguise.

Another example of what is probably a less direct tension state in the dreamer toward another person is dealt with in an equally skillful manner. The dreamer reports seeing a tiger attack another boy of the long house.

Again, he is advised to tell the boy about the dream, to describe the place where the attack occurred and, if possible, to show it to him so that he can be on his guard, and in future dreams kill the tiger before it has a chance to attack him. The parents of the boy in the dream again tell the child to give the dreamer a present, and to consider him a special friend. . . .

My data on the dream life of the various Senoi age groups would indicate that dreaming can and does become the deepest type of creative thought. Observing the lives of the Senoi it occurred to me that modern civilization may be sick because people have sloughed off, or failed to develop, half their power to think. Perhaps the most important half. Certainly, the Senoi suffer little by intellectual comparison with ourselves. They have equal power for logical thinking while awake, considering their environmental data, whereas our capacity to solve problems in dreams is infantile compared to theirs. . . .

The Senoi does not exhaust the power to think while asleep with these simple social and environmental situations. The bearers who carried out our equipment under very trying conditions became dissatisfied and were ready to desert. Their leader, a Senoi shaman, had a dream in which he was visited by the spirit of the empty boxes. The song and music this dream character gave him so inspired the bearers, and the dance he directed so relaxed and rested them, that they claimed the boxes had lost their weight and finished the expedition in the best of spirits.

Even this solution of a difficult social situation, involving people who were not all members of the dreamer's group, is trivial compared with the dream solutions which occur now that the Senoi territory has been opened up to alien culture contacts.

Datu Bintung at Jelong had a dream which succeeded in breaking down the major social barriers in clothing and food habits between his group and the surrounding Chinesk and Mohammedan colonies. This was accomplished chiefly through a dance which his dream prescribed. Only those who did his dance were required to change their food habits and wear the new clothing, but the dance was so good that nearly all the Senoi along the border chose to do it. In this way, the dream created social change in a democratic manner.

Another feature of Datu Bintung's dream involved the ceremonial status of women, making them more nearly the equals of the men, although equality is not a feature of either Chinese or Mohammedan societies. So far as could be determined this was a pure creative action which introduced greater equality in the culture, just as reflective thought has produced more equality in our society.

In the West the thinking we do while asleep usually remains on a muddled, childish, or psychotic level because we do not respond to dreams as socially important and include dreaming in the educative process. This social neglect of the side of man's reflective thinking, when the creative process is most free, seems poor education.

Kilton Stewart, "Dream Theory In Malaya," *Complex*, 1951.

NEGRITO GOOD DREAMS AND NIGHTMARES

Stewart published a report of his field work with the Negritos of Malaysia in 1954 in which he said the Negritos had little exposure to technology and Westerners. Here Stewart asks a Negrito man, Pana, to tell his worst dream and his best dream.

"FOR MY RECORD I must also have his dreams," I said to Juan [*the translator*]. "Ask him what is the worst dream he can remember."

"A black cloud chasing me" ... [*Pana*] answered. "I've had it many times. Sometimes I was alone, sometimes with the group. The black cloud growled and muttered with the voice of thunder. Always I woke up expecting the lightning to strike me." Pana remembered other dreams ... of black things pursuing him.

His best dream was of a man. The body looked like his father, but he had the head of a horse, light in color, with the mane hanging down in front of his face. He had seen the Filipinos riding horses along the borders of the Negrito territory. This dream character, which he called a "dwindi," had picked him up in his dream and soared through the air with him, showing him strange places where game could be found. Later it had visited him when he was awake, and he had gone off with it alone into the jungle on some very successful hunts. His wife had seen the dwindi one night when it called for him. To break the spell, she had rubbed her naked buttocks all over her husband's body. After that the dwindi had come no more. Pana had beaten his wife for using this magic to scare it away, but his spirit friend had never returned.

"I remember what Pana was like when I was a child," said Juan. "He used to beat his wife and his children. The Negritos think this is very bad. They say a father should never beat his children. Sometimes he would get mad at everyone and challenge other men to duels. This is a great trouble among the Negritos because both men must always die if a duel begins. That's why nobody would fight with him. They called him Thunder Voice when he got mad."

I wondered if the Negritos saw a difference between the dream thunder which had attacked Pana, and the thunder which all of them could hear while awake. Juan had told me that the thunder was the angry voice of Tolandian.

"When Pana was dreaming of the thundercloud chasing him and the group, was Tolandian angry at him and the other Negritos?" I inquired.

"Oh yes," answered Juan. "Someone had probably done something to make Tolandian angry."

"But how could Pana and all the rest of them be running from Tolandian's rage at the same time that they were all sleeping?" I asked.

Juan was a little puzzled about this and inquired of the old men. "They say that your spirit can run away from the thunder even when you are asleep," Juan answered. "But often you can't remember what your spirit does at night."

According to Stewart, The Negrito's worldview is so focused on the interrelatedness of self and world that they don't consider that the thunder in Pana's dream may be something personal, as I am inclined to believe it was. Still, I hesitate to definitively interpret the dream of a man whom I don't know from a different culture a world away. I wonder, too, if we aren't culturally biased to view our dream images as simply personal rather than as manifestations of our interrelatedness to others and the world. What might your dreams mean if they were not just your own, but a record of the events of your place in the world, just as you are, in your waking life?

Kilton Stewart, *Pygmies and Dream Giants* (New York: W.W. Norton & Company, Inc., 1954), pp. 44-45.

Joseph Campbell

DREAM DESIGN

In this selection Joseph Campbell tells of the centrality of dreams and visions in the East, just as in earlier selections we've seen their centrality to the indigenous cultures of the West (p. 144). (Campbell's other selections are on pp. 184 and 235.)

... [ASIAN] INDIAN ART is a yoga and its master a kind of yogi. Having performed through years the assignments of an obedient apprenticeship, and having gained at last recognition as a master, commissioned to erect, say, a temple or to fashion a sacred image, the artist first will meditate, to bring before his inner eye a vision of the symbolic building to be planned, or of the deity to be rendered. Indeed, there are legends even of entire cities envisioned in this way: of some saintly monarch who will have had a dream in which he will have seen, as in a revelation, the whole form of the temple or city to be built. And I wonder if that may not be the reason why, in certain Oriental cities one can feel, even today, that one is moving in a dream: the city is dreamlike because in its inception it was actually suggested by a dream, which then was rendered in stone.

Joseph Campbell, *Myths to Live By* (New York: Bantam Books, 1972), p. 109.

Patricia Reilly Giff

ART LIKE A DREAM

Like dreams, artistic works can give us a window into the deepest parts of ourselves. I had a client who was a sculptor. She didn't believe in dreams, she told me one day. But when she described a sculpture to me, we were able to work with its imagery as if it were a dream and this she believed in; the symbols were as rich and the meaning as deep in her soul.

In this selection from a novel for young adults by the American writer and teacher Patricia Reilly Giff, we are invited into the thoughts of Hollis, a tough 12-year-old girl, as she discovers that the images in her own drawings express her previously hidden understanding. Hollis first thought her presence fractured the love between her foster parents (Izzy and the Old Man) and their son, Steven, so she ran away from them. By looking at her drawings she finds that they were full of love for each other after all. The way she "sees" the meaning, without clouding it with too much thought, is a wonderful model that we can bring to our dream work.

As we join the story, Hollis is with a new foster mother, Josie, who is so senile that Hollis cannot cope with her and considers calling Josie's friend Beatrice for help.

I SAT THERE FOR A LONG TIME, my head against the headboard, knowing what I had to do. I rubbed my hands, still icy cold. It was four miles to the telephone outside the grocery store, a long walk, but I could do it. I'd call Beatrice . . . ask her, beg her.

We'd go home, Josie and I, Josie to Beatrice, me to another place. I looked at a half-finished picture of Izzy at the cemetery with a vase of daisies in her hand. What had she said that day? *"I wanted children for every corner of the house."* And what else? There was something more she had said, something about Steven and the Old Man. *"It's worse this summer."*

I'd have to stop thinking about Izzy, put all of them out of my mind. Before I left I'd get rid of all the pictures of them, burn the drawings in the fireplace. I'd forget about Izzy and the Old Man, forget about Steven.

I stared down at the drawing of Izzy backing out of the door with my WELCOME TO THE FAMILY cake and saw something I hadn't remembered: the Old Man's hand on Steven's shoulder.

Me, catching my first fish. Steven in front of me with the net, the Old Man smiling. But he is looking at Steven, not at me. Looking and smiling.

And another: Steven hanging into the engine of a car, just the back of him visible, with mismatched socks, and the Old Man with his hands on his hips, but his eyes are soft.

Beatrice was in my head again. What had she said to me one time? *"Sometimes we learn from our own drawings; things are there that we thought we didn't know."*

My lips were suddenly dry.

I stood up, walked around to the other side of the bed. There they were in the boat. Steven laughing at something the Old Man had said.

How had I drawn all that and not seen it?

Of course the Old Man loved Steven. He was going to love him whether I was there or not. Had I given them up for nothing, the whole family?

Patricia Reilly Giff, *Pictures of Hollis Woods* (New York: Wendy Lamb Books, 2002), pp. 149-151.

William Blake

COMFORT FOR A CHILD

William Blake (1757-1827), English poet, artist and visionary, here writes of his attempt to comfort a boy for his dreams of his deceased mother. In the boy's dreams she's alive; when he wakes, she's not. It seems simplistic and dismissive to wave off such dreams as "wish fulfillment." Do such dreams indicate that part of us knows where to find the peace we felt in the dream? Or that a lost loved one has not totally left us?

THE LAND OF DREAMS

Awake, awake my little Boy!
Thou wast thy Mother's only joy:
Why dost thou weep in thy gentle sleep?
Awake! thy Father does thee keep.

"O, what land is the Land of Dreams?
What are its mountains, and what are its streams?
O Father, I saw my Mother there,
Among the lilies by waters fair.

Among the lambs clothed in white
She walked with her Thomas in sweet delight.
I wept for joy, like a dove I mourn—
O when shall I return again?"

Dear child, I also by pleasant streams
Have wandered all night in the Land of Dreams;
But though calm and warm the waters wide,
I could not get to the other side.

"Father, O Father, what do we here,
In this land of unbelief and fear?
The Land of Dreams is better far
Above the light of the Morning Star."

William Blake, *The Poems of William Blake* (London: Pickering and Co., 1874), pp. 139-140.

Samuel Taylor Coleridge

Born in 18th century England, Samuel Taylor Coleridge was a poet, critic, and co-founder of the Romantic Movement.

NIGHTMARE'S ANGUISH

THE PAINS OF SLEEP

Ere on my bed my limbs I lay,
It hath not been my use to pray
With moving lips or bended knees;
But silently, by slow degrees,
My spirit I to Love compose,
In humble trust mine eye-lids close,
With reverential resignation,
No wish conceived, no thought exprest,
Only a sense of supplication;
A sense o'er all my soul imprest
That I am weak, yet not unblest,
Since in me, round me, every where
Eternal Strength and Wisdom are.

But yester-night I pray'd aloud
In anguish and in agony,
Up-starting from the fiendish crowd
Of shapes and thoughts that tortured me:
A lurid light, a trampling throng,
Sense of intolerable wrong,
And whom I scorned, those only strong!
Thirst of revenge, the powerless will
Still baffled, and yet burning still!

Desire with loathing strangely mixed
On wild or hateful objects fixed.
Fantastic passions! maddening brawl!
And shame and terror over all!
Deeds to be hid which were not hid,
Which all confused I could not know
Whether I suffered, or I did:
For all seem'd guilt, remorse or woe,
My own or others still the same
Life-stifling fear, soul-stifling shame!

So two nights passed : the night's dismay
Saddened and stunned the coming day.
Sleep, the wide blessing, seemed to me
Distemper's worst calamity.
The third night, when my own loud scream
Had waked me from the fiendish dream,
O'ercome with sufferings strange and wild,
I wept as I had been a child;
And having thus by tears subdued
My anguish to a milder mood,
Such punishments, I said, were due
To natures deepliest stained with sin:
For aye entempesting anew
The unfathomable hell within
The horror of their deeds to view,
To know and loathe, yet wish and do!
Such griefs with such men well agree,
But wherefore, wherefore fall on me?
To be beloved is all I need,
And whom I love, I love indeed.

Samuel Taylor Coleridge, *The Poetical Works of Samuel Taylor Coleridge*, ed. James Dykes Campbell (New York: MacMillan and Co., 1901), pp. 170-171.

REMEMBERING DREAMS

There are lucky people who have no trouble remembering their dreams, but that is not the norm. Here are some ideas I have synthesized from my reading over the years and from what seems to work for me and my clients. See what works for you. Just bringing the intent to remember dreams seems to help many people. (For another approach, see an earlier selection called, "Problem solving," on page 110.)

SLEEP RESEARCHERS HAVE SHOWN CONCLUSIVELY that we all dream every night. You can be confident that you are dreaming; the challenge then is just to recall the dreams.

1. Prepare for your dream by putting a dream journal (or paper) and pen by your bed before going to sleep. If you sleep with another, keep a flashlight by your bed as well. You will be more inclined to write a dream if it doesn't lead to war with a partner.

2. Plant the suggestion before going to sleep. As you lay back, spend some time holding the idea of remembering a dream. A surprising number of my clients who never remembered dreams were able to recall some by just thinking about it at bedtime. See what works for you: ask for a dream about a specific topic, or bring willful intent with a thought such as "tonight I will remember a dream", or find another approach fitting to you.

3. Start writing down dreams as soon as you wake. For some of us, dreams flee the waking mind almost immediately.

4. Write down any image, no matter how small. Sometimes even a fragment can be meaningful. Also, the act of paying attention and starting to explore the details of a single image can initiate recollection of other images.

5. Don't worry about the order as you write. Write as it comes to you so you don't lose it, and then make notes as to the order later, if you can.

6. Beginning to attend to our dreams gives the psyche the message that we care about dreams, and helps to increase our attention in coming nights.

7. Find a ritual that works for you. For some people, setting their alarm 40 minutes before their usual wake time helps them capture their dreams and gives them some leisure time to write before they need to think about the day. For others, having time to lounge in bed, waking and dozing, enables them more easily to recall dreams. For still others, setting the alarm for some time in the middle of the night is most effective.

8. Be creative. Salvador Dali went to sleep holding a spoon in his hand, extended away from the bed, and over a hard floor. When he fell asleep, he would drop the spoon. The sound of the dropped spoon woke him. Rather than writing down his dreams, he drew them on the sketchpad by his bed. What might be your way to foster dream recollection?

9. Get enough sleep. It takes some energy to recall dreams and turn on the light and start writing, all of which can be too burdensome if what you need most is sleep.

10. Watch for the effect of lifestyle factors. Alcohol before bed can result in sleep that isn't restful, and therefore robs one of the energy needed to focus on dreams. Many report that pot smoking inhibits dream recollection. Are there diet factors (i.e., eating before bed) that affect your rest or ability to remember dreams?

11. Don't worry about it if after these suggestions you still don't recall dreams. Sometimes our psyches need to attend to concerns of the waking mind where there is practical and immediate need. If you think this might be the case, consider what needs attention in your waking life, then return to work on recalling dreams in the weeks or months to come.

12. Practice. If you persist patiently and creatively, it will come.

WHAT TO WRITE DOWN ABOUT YOUR DREAM

- Start with whatever you recall, and work from there. Some people have dreams with so much detail they have to be selective about what they write in order to have enough time to go about their day.
- Write down what stands out most – the most vivid images, the ones that raise your curiosity, those images related to the strongest emotions. Let the strength of your reactions be your guide.
- Pick any section of this book for inspiration. If after reading "The three stages of a dream" (p. 25) you are you interested in the drama of the dream, then write about the plot and transitions. Or, if after reading "Biases" (p. 72), you are curious about your automatic responses, write down images that evoke immediate emotional reactions.
- After recording a dream, note the date and make a couple of notes about what you did the day and night before having the dream. Often a dream may relate to or be influenced by recent events.

BIBLIOGRAPHY

Achterberg, Jeanne, *Imagery in Healing: Shamanism and Modern Medicine* (Boston: Shambhala, 1985).

Adler, Alfred, *The Science of Living* (Garden City, NY: Garden City Publishing, 1929).

Adler, Gerhard, *Studies in Analytical Psychology*, (New York: W. W. Norton & Company, Inc., 1948).

Algan, Refik, "The Dream of the Sleeper—Dream Interpretation and Meaning in Sufism," *Gnosis* #22 (Winter 1992).

Andrews, Terri, "Living by the Dream: Native American Interpretation of Night's Visions," *The World and I*, article no. 17616, (November, 1998), http://www.worldandi.com.

Aquinas, Thomas, trans. by Fathers of the English Dominican Province, *Summa Theologica* (New York: Benziger Brothers, 1947).

Barasch, Marc Ian, *Healing Dreams; Experiencing the Dreams that Can Transform Your Life* (New York: Riverhead Books, 2000).

Barrett, Deirdre, *The Committee of Sleep: How Artists, Scientists and Athletes Use Dreams for Creative Problem-Solving* (New York: Crown Publishers, 2001).

Benfey, O. Theodore, "August Kekulé and the Birth of the Structural Theory of Organic Chemistry in 1858," *Journal of Chemical Education*, vol. 35, no. 1, (1958), pp. 21-23.

The Bible, Matthew, 1:18-1:25, King James Version.

Blake, William, *The Poems of William Blake* (London: Pickering and Co., 1874).

Bly, Robert, "Problems in the Ark," *The Little Book of the Human Shadow* (San Francisco: Harper & Row, 1988).

Boa, Fraser, *The Way of the Dream: Conversations on Jungian Dream Interpretation with Marie-Louise von Franz* (Boston: Shambhala, 1994).

Bodian, Stephan, "Field of Dreams: An Interview with Arnold Mindell," *Yoga Journal* (March/April 1990).

Bonime, Walter, *The Clinical Use of Dreams* (New York: Basic Books, Inc., 1962).

Bulfinch, Thomas, *The Age of Fable or Stories of Gods and Heroes* (New York: Thomas Y. Crowell Company Publishers, 1913).

Bulkeley, Kelly, "Reflections on the Dream Traditions of Islam," *Sleep and Hypnosis*, 4:1 (2002).

Campbell, Joseph, *The Power of Myth* (New York: Doubleday, 1988).

Campbell, Joseph, *Myths to Live By* (New York: Bantam Books, 1972), pp. 112-114.

Carroll, Lewis, *Alice's Adventures in Wonderland and Through the Looking Glass*, (Chicago: Rand McNally & Company, 1865).

Carpenter, Siri, "Freud's dream theory gets boost from imaging work: Meaning in dreams may be less disguised than commonly believed," *American Psychological Association Monitor*, volume 30, number 7 (July/August, 1999).

Chödrön, Pema, *When Things Fall Apart* (Boston: Shambhala Publications, Inc., 1997), pp. 28-30.

Chow, Kai-wing, "Identity and Cultural Pluralism: Confucius in Early Narratives" (Association for Asian Studies, Annual Meeting, 1998).

Chuang Tsu, *Chuang Tsu: Inner Chapters*, trans. Gia-Fu Feng and Jane English (New York: Vintage Books, 1974).

Coleridge, Samuel Taylor, *The Poetical Works of Samuel Taylor Coleridge*, ed. James Dykes Campbell (New York: MacMillan and Co., 1901).

Dement, William C., *Sleepwatchers* (Stanford, CA: The Portable Stanford Book Series, 1992).

Dickens, Charles, *Pictures from Italy and American Notes* (New York: Belford Clark & Co., 1885).

Erdoes, Richard, *Crying for a Dream; the World Through Native American Eyes* (Santa Fe, NM: Bear & Company Publishing, 1990).

Estes, Clarissa Pinkola, *Women Who Run With the Wolves* (New York: Ballantine Books, 1992).

Foulkes, David, "Understanding Our Dreams," *The World and I*, article no. 15471, (1989), http://www.worldandi.com.

Frankl, Viktor, *Man's Search for Meaning* (New York: Pocket Books, 1985).

Frazer, James George, "The Perils of the Soul," *The Golden Bough; a Study of Magic and Religion*, 3rd ed., Part II, *Taboo and the Perils of the Soul* (New York: St. Martin's Press, 1976).

Freedman, Jill and Combs, Gene, *Narrative Therapy: The Social Construction of Preferred Realities* (New York: W.W. Norton Company, Inc., 1996).

Freud, Sigmund, *The Interpretation of Dreams*, trans. A. A. Brill (New York: Gramercy Books, a division of Random House Value Publishing, Inc., 1996).

Gendlin, Eugene, *Let Your Body Interpret Your Dreams*, (Wilmette, IL: Chiron Publications, 1986) pp. 9-17, pp. 73-75.

George, Mimi, "In a Pig's Eye: Learning from Tattoos and Dreams Among the Barok," *The World and I*, article no. 13757, (1995), http://www.worldandi.com.

Gibran, Kahlil, *The Prophet* (New York: Alfred A. Knopf, 2005).

Giff, Patricia Reilly, *Pictures of Hollis Woods* (New York: Wendy Lamb Books, 2002).

Grimm, Jacob and Wilhelm, *Fairy Tales of the Brothers Grimm (Household Tales)*, trans. Margaret Hunt, (1884).

HaKohain, Yakov Leib, ed. J. Marvin Spiegelman, "Kabbalah and the Interpretation of Dreams," in *Modern Jew in Search of a Soul* (Tempe, AZ: New Falcon Press, 1986). Updated version at http://www.donmeh-west.com/intrpdrms.shtml.

Heaton, Kristin J., "Working with Nightmares," *Dream Work in Psychotherapy*, ed. Clara E. Hill (Washington D.C.: American Psychological Association, 2004).

Hill, Clara E., *Working with Dreams Psychotherapy* (New York: Guilford Publications, Inc., 1996).

Hill, Clara E., *Dream Work in Psychotherapy*, ed. Clara E. Hill (Washington D.C.: American Psychological Association, 2004).

Hillman, James, *Archetypal Psychology: A Brief Account* (Dallas: Spring Publications, Inc., 1983).

Hillman, James, *The Dream and the Underworld* (New York: Harper & Row, Publishers, 1979).

Hinshaw Baylis, Janice, *Sex, Symbols and Dreams* (Seal Beach, CA: Sun, Man, Moon, Inc., 1997).

Hippocrates, *Hippocratic Writings*, ed. G.E.R. Lloyd, trans. J. Chadwick and W. N. Mann (London: Penguin Books, 1978).

The Holy Scriptures (Hebrew Bible), (Philadelphia: The Jewish Publication Society of America, 1960).

Homer, *Odyssey of Homer*, trans. William Cullen Bryant (Boston: Houghton, Mifflin and Company, 1871).

Ingold, Tim, "A Circumpolar Night's Dream," *Figured Worlds; Ontological Obstacles in Intercultural Relations*, ed. John Clammer, Sylvie Poirier, and Eric Schwimmer (Toronto: University of Toronto Press, 2004).

Irwin, Lee, The Dream Seekers: Native American Visionary Traditions of the Great Plains (Norman, OK: University of Oklahoma Press, 1994).

Jung, C. G., "The Meaning of Psychology for Modern Man," in *Civilization in Transition*, trans. R. F. C. Hull (New York: Bollingen Foundation, 1964).

Jung, C. G., *Dreams*, ed. Gerhard Adler, trans. R. F. C. Hull (Princeton, New Jersey: Princeton University Press, 1974).

Jung, C. G., *Psyche and Symbol*, ed. Violet S. de Laszlo, trans. R. F. C. Hull (Princeton, New Jersey: Princeton University Press, 1991).

Jung, C. G., *The Archetypes and the Collective Unconscious*, ed. Herbert Read, Michael Fordham, Gerhard Adler, & William McGuire, trans. R. F. C. Hull (Princeton, New Jersey: Princeton University Press, 1975).

Kierkegaard, Søren, *The Journals of Søren Kierkegaard*, ed. and trans. by Alexander Dru (New York: Oxford University Press, 1959).

Krakow, Barry, et al., "Imagery Rehearsal Therapy for Chronic Nightmares in Sexual Assault Survivors With Posttraumatic Stress Disorder," *Journal of the American Medical Association*, 2001; 286:537-545.

Krippner, Stanley, Bogzaran, Fariba, and De Carvalho, Andre Percia, *Extraordinary Dreams and How to Work with Them*, (New York: State University of New York Press, 2002).

Kutz, Ilan, *The Dreamland Companion: A Bedside Diary and Guide to Dream Interpretation* (New York: Hyperion, 1993).

Linderman, Frank, *Plenty-Coups, Chief of the Crows* (Lincoln, NE: University of Nebraska Press, 1962).

Marcus, Yosef, "Dreams and Circles" (KabbalaOnline.org: 2003). Adapted from discourses of Rabbi Dovber Shneerson, "Maamorei Admur Haemtzai, Miketz and Vayigash 5670 (Genesis 41:1-44:17)." http://www.kabbalaonline.org/WeeklyTorah/ChabadDiscourses/Dreams_and_Circles.asp.

Momaday, N. Scott, "The Gourd Dancer," *Carriers of the Dream Wheel; Contemporary Native American Poetry,* ed. Duane Niatum (New York: Harper and Row, Publishers, 1975).

Masson, Jeffrey Moussaieff and McCarthy, Susan, *When Elephants Weep,* (New York: A Delta Book, 1995).

Mindell, Arnold, *Dreambody: The Body's Role in Revealing the Self* (Boston: Sigo Press, 1982). www.aamindell.net & www.processwork.org.

Mitchell, Stephen A. and Black, Margaret J., *Freud and Beyond,* (New York: Basic Books, 1995).

Newsweek, "Perchance to Dream," (November 30, 1959), p. 104.

Nietzsche, Friedrich, "The Birth of Tragedy," trans. Ian C. Johnston (Nanaimo, British Columbia: Malaspina University-College, 1871). http://www.mala.bc.ca/~Johnstoi/Nietzsche/tragedy_all.htm.

Nietzsche, Friedrich, *The Complete Works of Friedrich Nietzsche,* ed. Oscar Levy, trans. J. M. Kennedy (New York: Gordon Press, 1974).

Niiniluoto, Ilkka, "Dream and Reality," 11th European Congress on Sleep Research, Helsinki, July 6, 1992.

Nin, Anaïs, *The Diary of Anaïs Nin, Volume 2* (Orlando, Florida: Harcourt Brace & Company, 1967).

Porier, Sylvie, "Ontology, Ancestral Order, and Agencies among the Kukatija of the Australian Western Desert," *Figured Worlds; Ontological Obstacles in Intercultural Relations,* ed. John Clammer, Sylvie Poirier, and Eric Schwimmer (Toronto: University of Toronto Press, 2004).

Radin, Paul, *The Story of the American Indian* (New York: Liveright Publishing Corporation, 1944).

Rock, Andrea, *The Mind at Night,* (Cambridge: Basic Books, 2004).

Stewart, Kilton, "Dream Theory in Malaya," *Complex,* 1951.

Stewart, Kilton, *Pygmies and Dream Giants* (New York: W.W. Norton & Company, Inc., 1954).

Talmud (Babylonian): Seder Zera'im, ed. Isodore Epstein, trans. Maurice Simon (London: Soncino Press, 1948), Berakoth 55a-55b, 56a, 57a-57b.

Tucker, Gary, "Controlling Nightmares with Image Rehearsal Therapy," *Journal Watch Psychiatry,* no. 7 (September 5, 2001): p. 77.

Twain, Mark, *Which Was the Dream?* (Berkeley: University of California Press, 1967).

Varela, Francisco (ed.), *Sleeping, Dreaming, and Dying: An Exploration of Consciousness with the Dalai Lama* (Boston: Wisdom Publications, 1997).

Virkler, Mark and Patti, "Principles of Christian Dream Interpretation," (New York: Communion with God Ministries, 2004), http://www.cwgministries.org/books/Christian-Dream-Interpretation.pdf.

Walker, Karen, review of *The Way of the Dream: Conversations on Jungian Dream Interpretation with Marie-Louise von Franz* (Boston: Shambhala, 1994), Electric Dreams 5, no. 1 (January 1998), www.Dreamgate.com.

Wasilewska, Ewa, "The Destruction of Mankind: Creation Myths of the Middle East: Part Four," *The World and I,* article no. 12274, (1994), http://www.worldandi.com.

Waters, Frank, *The Book of The Hopi* (New York: Penguin Books, 1963).

White, Sarah, "Dreamwork as Etymology," *Dreaming,* Volume 9, No. 1, (1999).

Wilder, G.D. and Ingram, J.H., *Analysis of Chinese Characters,* (New York: Dover Publications, Inc., 1974)

Winnicott, D. W., *Playing and Reality* (London: Routledge, 1971).

Woodman, Marion, *Addiction to Perfection: The Still Unravished Bride* (Toronto: Inner City Books, 1982).

INDEX

Note:
+ Bold page numbers indicate text selections.
+ Page numbers followed by *n* or *+n* indicate footnotes or footnotes in addition to text.

A

Abraham (prophet of Islam): dream of sacrificing his own son, 217–219

abuse: taking as loving-kindness, 256–257

Achterberg, Jeanne: on dream therapy in ancient Greece, 9, **93–95**

acting out dreams, 156–157
foolishly, 157–158

action in dreams, 64–65

action stage of dream work, 54, 58–60

activation-synthesis hypothesis of dreaming, 114–115

Adler, Alfred:
on dream interpretation, **20–21**
on dreams, **17–22**

Adler, Gerhard: dream interpretation by, **30–36**

aesthetic dreams, 15

African dream worker on understanding dreams, **173**

aggression in dreams, 105

"Aha!" experiences in dream interpretation, 57–58, 89, 214

Ahab (king of Israel): as a character in dreams, 206

Algan, Refik: on Sufi teachings on dreams and dreaming, **225–228**

Alice's dream of Wonderland, 249–251

all things as illusory (Nietzsche), 127

all things as sought after (Rumi), 228

amplification of dream images, 31–32, 34–36

ancestral order: communication in dreams with, 174

Andrews, Terri: on living by the dream, **160–162**

anguish in dreams, 265–266

animals dreaming, 112

animals in dreams, 34–36, 105

the animus (archetype), 28

anxiety (restlessness): as neurosis, 27–28

Aquinas, Thomas: on the causes of dreams, **212–213**

archetypal psychology, 40

archetypes in dreams, 31–32
the animus, 28
the demon lover, 38–39
the Self, 27, 28
See also the shadow

Aristotle:
on dreams, 132
on imagery and health, 94

art as imagery, 262–263

artistic design: dreams and, 261

Asclepia: dream therapy in, 93–94

Asclepius, 93

asking dreams what's wanted, 173
See also dream work questions

associations (mental): dreaming and, 113–114

associations to dreams:
gathering, 55–56
questions regarding, 66–67

AUM: the four elements, 235–237

awakening:
from dreaming, 228
dreaming and, 125, 126
kinds, 233
See also waking (wakefulness)

COPYRIGHT PERMISSIONS

Science, Sleep, and Dreaming

"August Kekulé and the Birth of the Structural Theory of Organic Chemistry in 1858," by O. Theodore Benfey, Division of Chemical Education, Inc., Vol. 35, No. 1, 1958, pp. 21-23.

The Committee of Sleep: How Artists, Scientists and Athletes Use Dreams for Creative Problem-Solving, Copyright © 2001 by Deirdre Barrett, Ph.D. Reprinted by permission of the Stuart Krichevsky Literary Agency, Inc.

The World and I Archive, http://www.worldandi.com. "Understanding Our Dreams," by David Foulkes, article no. 15471, 1989. "Living by the Dream: Native American Interpretation of Night's Visions," by Terri Andrews. Article 17616, November, 1998. "In a Pig's Eye: Learning from Tattoos and Dreams Among the Barok," by Mimi George, Article 13757, November, 1995. "The Destruction of Mankind: Creation Myths of the Middle East: Part Four," by Ewa Wasilewska, article no. 12274, 1994. WorldandIJournal.com

Philosophy, Philosophers, and Dreaming

Chuang Tsu: Inner Chapters, copyright 1974, Chuang Tsu, translated by Gia-Fu Feng and Jane English, Vintage Books, a division of Random House, Inc. Used by permission of the author.

The Journals of Søren Kierkegaard, Copyright 1938, 1951, 1959, edited and translated by Alexander Dru, Oxford University Press (New York, Toronto). Reprinted by permission.

"Dream and Reality," by Ilkka Niiniluoto, 11th European Congress on Sleep Research, Helsinki, July 6, 1992. Used by permission of the author.

Indigenous Peoples, Visions, and Dreams

The Dream Seekers: Native American Visionary Traditions of the Great Plains, Copyright © 1994 by Lee Irwin. Published by the University of Oklahoma Press, Norman, Publishing Division of the University.

Crying for a Dream: The World Through Native American Eyes, by Richard Erdoes, Copyright © 1990 by Richard Erdoes, Bear & Company Publishing.

[Plenty-Coups, Chief of the Crows,] Copyright © 1930 by Frank B. Linderman. Copyright (c) renewed 1957 by Norma Linderman Waller, Verne Linderman and Wilda Linderman. Reprinted by permission of HarperCollins Publishers.

The Story of the American Indian by Paul Radin. Copyright 1927 by Boni & Liveright, Inc., renewed 1954 by Liveright Publishing Corporation. Revised edition copyright 1934 and renewed (c) 1961 by Liveright Publishing Corporation. Used by permission of Liveright Publishing Corporation.

"The Road of Life," from Book of the Hopi by Frank Waters, copyright (c) 1963 by Frank Waters. Used by permission of Viking Penguin, a division of Penguin Group (USA) Inc. Illustration used by permission of the estate of Oswald White Bear Fredricks.

Writers, Creativity, and Dreaming

LELAND SHIELDS holds a Master's degree in clinical psychology, and practices psychotherapy in Seattle. He has worked with dreams for more than twenty-five years, drawing inspiration from the approaches of C. G. Jung, Jung's followers, and from the wisdom about the psyche offered by a variety of cultural traditions. His publications in psychology have focused on dreams, myths, cult survivors, and meditation. Prior to working as a psychotherapist, he was an engineering consultant and researcher in failure analysis, with many publications on vehicle fire safety. This background adds depth, worldly experience, and creativity to his psychology practice. Family life and regular meditation balance the joys and demands of a rich professional life. He brings to his counseling practice an open-minded curiosity, an understanding that our questions lead to new insight and choices, and a respect for the individuals he counsels as being the experts of their own lives.

Printed in Great Britain
by Amazon